HOUGHTON
★ MIFFLIN ★
HISTORY PROGRAM

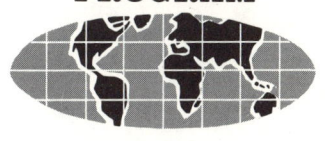

★ ★ ★

■ *Life in America Series*

General Editor: **Richard C. Wade**
Editorial Adviser: **Howard D. Mehlinger**

HOUGHTON MIFFLIN COMPANY / Boston

EDUCATION IN AMERICAN LIFE

Selected Readings

W. RICHARD STEPHENS
Greenville College

WILLIAM VAN TIL
Indiana State University

Atlanta / Dallas / Geneva, Ill. / Hopewell, N.J. / Palo Alto

■ *About the Editors*

W. RICHARD STEPHENS

Dr. Stephens was recently Professor of History and Philosophy of Education at Indiana University. He is author of Social Reform and the Origins of Vocational Guidance, 1890–1925. Currently he is Vice President for Academic Affairs, Greenville College, Illinois.

WILLIAM VAN TIL

Dr. Van Til is author of Education: A Beginning and Curriculum: Quest for Relevance. He teaches social foundations and curriculum at Indiana State University where he is Coffman Distinguished Professor in Education.

RICHARD C. WADE

General editor of the LIFE IN AMERICA series, Dr. Wade is Professor of American History, Graduate Center, The City University of New York.

HOWARD D. MEHLINGER

Dr. Mehlinger is adviser for the Houghton Mifflin Social Studies program. He is Associate Professor of History and Education and Director of the Social Studies Development Center, Indiana University.

Copyright © 1972 by Houghton Mifflin Company
All rights reserved. No part of this book may be reproduced or transmitted in any form or by any means, electronic or mechanical, including photocopying and recording, or by any information storage or retrieval system, without permission in writing from the publisher.
Printed in the United States of America
Library of Congress Catalog Card Number: 72–3496
ISBN: 0–395–03143–5

*This book is for our students
who have taught us much.*

■ Contents

- *The Life in America Series*   xi

PART ONE · European Transplants in Colonial America: 1620-1776   2

I. The Sacred Emphasis of Education
1. So That Learning Might Not Perish / *Founders of Harvard College*   10
2. A Father's Advice to His Son / *Thomas Shepard, Jr.*   12
3. The State Requires Education / *Massachusetts Bay General Court*   15
4. A Parent's Responsibility / *Cotton Mather*   17
5. The Puritan Ethic / *New England Primer*   19
   - A. Praise to God for Learning to Read   20
   - B. The Shorter Catechism   21

II. The Conduct of Education
1. To Instruct with All Diligence / *Hopkins Grammar School Trustees*   23
2. The Ideal of Student Learning / *Ebenezer Turell*   25
3. The Reality of Student Learning / *John Barnard*   27
4. The Apprenticeship Agreement / *Thomas Stoughton and Nathan Day*   31

III. Education in the South
1. The Tutorial System / *Philip Fithian*   34
2. Creation of an Orphanage / *George Whitefield*   36
3. An Argument for the Instruction of Slaves / *Thomas Bacon*   38

PART TWO · The Search for the New America: 1776-1900   42

IV. Defining a New American Education
1. From Puritan to Yankee / *Benjamin Franklin*   48
2. Education for Nationalism / *Noah Webster*   55
3. Towards an Enlightened Community / *Thomas Jefferson*   57
4. Common Schools for a Secular Republic / *Horace Mann*   60

V. Educational Provisions for the New America

1. A Sunday School Proposal / *William Thurston* — 64
2. Constitutional Provisions for State Education / *Constitution of Indiana, 1816* — 65
3. High School for Adolescent Boys / *Boston School Committee* — 67
4. A Plan for Improving Female Education / *Emma Willard* — 71
5. A School for Delinquent Youth / *Society for the Reformation of Juvenile Delinquents* — 74
6. Political Pressure for Common Schools / *Working Men of Pennsylvania* — 77

VI. Christianizing the Common School

1. The Schoolchild's "Bible" / *William Holmes McGuffey* — 82
   A. All Must Work — 82
   B. The Bible — 83
   C. Respect for the Sabbath Rewarded — 84
2. Religious Exercises Challenged — 85
   A. The Common School May Continue Bible Reading / *Minor v. Board of Education of Cincinnati* — 86
   B. The Common School Must Promote National Unity / *Rev. Henry Ward Beecher* — 88

VII. Character and Conduct of the Common School

1. Teacher Training / *Michigan Teachers' Institute* — 90
2. The Teacher at Work / *D. S. Domer* — 94
3. The Curriculum / *Marshall Barber* — 97

VIII. Beginning of Black Education

1. Slavery and Education Incompatible / *Frederick Douglass* — 101
2. Constitutional Provisions for Racial Segregation — 106
3. A Yankee Teacher in the South / *Elizabeth Rice* — 109
4. Hostility Towards White Teachers of Negroes / *Cornelius McBride* — 112
5. Accommodation with White Power / *Booker T. Washington* — 115

Contents **IX**

PART THREE · Urbanization of American Education: 1900-Present   120

IX. Inadequate Schooling
1. Traditional High School Curriculum   124
2. Mindless Rote Learning / *Joseph Rice*   125
3. The Deadening Classroom Routine / *Randolph Bourne*   129
4. The Obstacle of Child Labor / *Jacob Riis*   131
5. Americanization of the Immigrant / *A. R. Dugmore*   133
6. Civilizing the American Indian / *Polingaysi Qoyawayma*   136

X. Educational Reform
1. My Pedagogic Creed / *John Dewey*   141
2. Schools to Conserve Agrarianism / *William Starr Myers*   145
3. Vocational Education and Vocational Guidance / *William Redfield*   148
4. Secondary Education Redefined / *National Education Association*   151
5. Bureaucratizing American Schools   154
    A. The School As Factory / *Ellwood Cubberley*   155
    B. Manufacturing Citizenship / *Ellwood Cubberley*   157
    C. The School Board As Management / *Ellwood Cubberley*   159
    D. Education Measured by the Dollar / *F. E. Spaulding*   160
6. Should Teachers Affiliate with Organized Labor? / *Harry Overstreet and David Snedden*   162

XI. Debate over the Curriculum
1. Schools Must Reconstruct America / *George Counts*   168
2. Schools Must Adapt to Change / *Harold Benjamin*   173
3. Schools Must Foster National Survival / *Hyman Rickover*   179
4. Schools Must Prepare for the Future / *Jerome Bruner*   185

XII. Striving for Equal Opportunity
1. Perpetuating the Inequity   188
    A. Limited Aspirations / *William Bulkley*   189
    B. Separation in Effect / *E. George Payne*   190
2. Rejecting the Doctrine of Innate Inferiority / *Charles Thompson*   192

    3. Outlawing the Inequity / *Brown v. Board of Education*   194
    4. The Battle of Little Rock / *Daisy Bates*   197
    5. Neighborhoods and Schools / *Peggy Streit*   200

XIII. Separation of Church and State
    1. The Legality of Private Schools / *Pierce v. Society of Sisters*   202
    2. Compulsory Prayer Illegal / *Engel v. Vitale*   204
    3. Compulsory Bible Reading Illegal / *Abington v. Schempp*   207
    4. Financial Aid and the Parochial School / *Lemon v. Kurtzman*   210

XIV. Continuing Criticism
    1. The Grim Reality of Ghetto Schools / *Jonathan Kozol*   215
    2. Revolt Reaches the High School / *Michael Marqusee*   220
    3. The Generation Gap   223
        A. It's Time to Stop Apologizing / *K. Ross Toole*   223
        B. Democracy and Communication / *College Students*   225

The Student's Paperback Library   229

Questions for Study and Discussion   230

Acknowledgments   235

Index   236

■ *Life in America Series*

Almost a half century ago the philosopher George Santayana, writing about his fellow Americans in *Character and Opinion in the United States,* had this to say:

> ... if there are immense differences between individual Americans ... yet there is a great uniformity in their environment, customs, temper, and thoughts. They have all been uprooted from their several soils and ancestries and plunged together into one vortex, whirling irresistibly in a space otherwise quite empty. To be an American is of itself a moral condition, an education, and a career....

One might express this idea another way by saying that there is indeed broad diversity in American life and yet enough similarity in the American experience to enable us profitably to explore that experience in its various facets — whether we are speaking of its rich cultural heritage or of the development of its political and social institutions. For "this soil is propitious to every seed," wrote Santayana. And it will be the purpose of the LIFE IN AMERICA series — of which the present volume is one — to trace the planting and the growth of those many seeds that go to make up American civilization as we know it today.

Coming originally from different — often disparate — national and social backgrounds, speaking a multiplicity of languages, our colonial forebears found on this broad continent the room and the freedom they sought. Here they shaped a new society while yet preserving much of their older heritage. From this interaction between the old and new, between the land and the people, a distinctively American civilization emerged.

For nearly two hundred years the mainstream of American life has remained sufficiently broad and open to contain a great variety of views and experience while continuing to add to — and thereby to enrich — our total cultural heritage.

This series examines what has come to be known as the American way of life by looking into the separate aspects of the American experience. It emphasizes not only the crises in the American past but traces the continuities as well. It discovers meaning in the life of ordinary people as well as in the achievements of their leaders. It illumines the great movements of history by viewing them first hand through the eyes of contemporaries. Most of all, it puts the student on the stage of history, making him a companion of the generations and the groups that have gone before.

Each volume in the LIFE IN AMERICA series relates the experience of a single group. One group will be distinguished by its common background; others by religion, race, or occupation. In each, the story will begin by examining the way in which the given group has become a part of the American story. Other selections will trace their development, chronicle their troubles and achievements and, finally, suggest present problems and prospects.

In this way the student will receive a balanced picture of the growth of his country. Instead of seeing American history as a series of crises and conflicts only, he will perceive also the continuing, if sometimes uneven, development of a free society. Instead of trying to find in Washington all the keys to understanding the American achievement, he will be encouraged to seek them as well in the many other sections of the country. And in searching for the significance of events, he will focus his attention not only on the prominent figures of history but on the experiences of ordinary citizens as well. He will be invited to participate vicariously, as he reads, in their struggles, hopes, aspirations, failures, and successes.

The present volume deals with the American experience as a distinctive approach to education developed in this country. Part I describes how European transplants took root in colonial America and were heavily influenced by the environment in which they grew. Part II describes the search for the new America as the idea of the public common school gained widespread acceptance. Part III deals with the quest, during the twentieth century, for an approach to education appropriate to an urbanized civilization. The readings have been reproduced as they appeared in the original sources, save that in certain instances spelling and punctuation have been modernized and obscure words defined in order to facilitate comprehension.

The creators of this volume particularly thank Ronald M. Leathers and R. Joseph Dixon, graduate students at Indiana State University, and Thomas J. Loyal, graduate student at Indiana University, for their faithful research and checking. Thanks too to Gail Rudd, Donna Fisher, Sandy Sievers, and Marilyn Reinhard for secretarial assistance.

Part One

Introduction
I. The Sacred Emphasis of Education
II. The Conduct of Education
III. Education in the South

European Transplants in Colonial America: 1620-1776

Part One: Introduction

Education in colonial America, as might be expected, involved the transplanting of European ideas, culture, and social institutions. But in the New World the early colonists modified the European tradition. The gradual evolution of a distinctly American education took place.

Nearly all of the earliest white settlers of America came from Western Europe. Though representing many nationalities, they had in common a set of general religious beliefs which are central to understanding the political, intellectual, and educational legacies they left to the nation. Whether in New England, the Middle Colonies, or the South, and whatever their social class, all but a very few shared a Christian outlook on man and his world. The colonial interpretation of Christianity was one among several views supported by Christians throughout the centuries. Consequently, the outlook which most colonists accepted in the seventeenth and eighteenth centuries is not necessarily the same as that held by many twentieth century Christians today. But it was the way the colonists, especially the large majority who were of Protestant denominations, perceived and interpreted Christianity in their times.

The Church and Home as Educators

The church, the home, and the community were the main influences shaping the personality and life style of a child in the American colonies. To make the child a worthy Christian and to prepare him for life after death was the overriding concern of most adults in colonial America. This concern led them to develop both informal and formal means of education.

The task of education was formidable, given the view of life that children were, in Jonathan Edwards' classical phrase, "young vipers and infinitely more hateful than vipers." Being naturally depraved, the child needed to be educated to seek a religious conversion which would bring him into the fold of God's elect and make him an acceptable member of colonial society. Since the "plan of salvation" was recorded in Scripture, the paramount goal of education was to teach children to read the Bible. When the church, as the central social institution of colonial society (especially in New England), recognized the need for making such education compulsory, it passed resolutions and saw to it that colonial legislatures passed the necessary laws.

The Bible and the Curriculum

Predominantly Protestants, the colonists transplanted the Bible in the New World as the chief source of knowledge of God's plan. In the homes, in the churches, and in the seats of government of colonial America, the Bible was regarded as the infallible and inerrant guide for individual and collective life on earth. It was also the only sure source of knowledge of the way to salvation and everlasting life in heaven. Therefore, the Bible and related theological literature written by learned ministers became the most essential subject matter to be studied by young and old alike.

Though Biblical and theological literature dominated both the formal and informal education of the young, many classical Greek, Latin, and Hebrew authors were also studied, especially in the academies and colleges which soon emerged. Knowledge of the classics and the civil laws was regarded as the mark of an educated man. But the chief reason for studying classical authors was to develop the ability to read in Latin, Greek, and Hebrew so that the young scholars could study the Bible in these original languages. Being at odds politically with King James I of England, and inclined not to trust his English translation of the Bible, New England Puritans were determined to create a group of theologians and ministers who could do their own translation of the Bible.

The Emergence of Colleges

Within a decade of their coming to the New World the Puritans of Massachusetts Bay Colony appropriated funds for a college. Fearing that when the first generation of ministers died there might be no one to take their place, the colonists founded Harvard College. Harvard's major role was to prepare young men, thirteen to eighteen years of age, in Biblical and classical studies. The hope of the colonists was that these students, in time, would assume positions of leadership in the church and in the Commonwealth. Similar reasons led to the establishment of colleges in other colonies. By 1770 nine "temples of piety and intellect," as one historian has called them, had been founded. In addition to Harvard, there were Yale, William and Mary, New Jersey, King's, Philadelphia, Rhode Island, Queen's, and Dartmouth. Even so it has been estimated that by 1775 only one colonist per thousand had been a college student at one time or another. The largest graduating class of any college during the eighteenth century was the 1771 class of Harvard which numbered sixty-three. Most of these graduates went into the ministry.

Though colonial society needed college-educated youth, the institutions did not attract many students from the ranks of the common people. The following statement by a devotee of Anne Hutchinson reflects a common sentiment among many colonists towards the college-educated: "I had rather hear such a one that speaks from the mere motion of the spirit, without any study at all, than any of your learned Scollers, although they may be fuller of Scripture. . . ." However, colleges did produce such social and religious leaders as Jonathan Edwards and Cotton Mather. But it was through self-education and apprenticeship that men such as Benjamin Franklin and Patrick Henry emerged from the lower classes to share positions of prominence with the college-educated.

Colleges were the highest level of schooling developed in colonial America. Upon successful completion of the Biblical, theological, and classical curriculum, called the arts, the young bachelor would have conferred upon him by the Board of Overseers the degree "Bachelor of Arts." He was then ready to become an apprentice to the minister of a church or, in some cases, to become an apprentice to a physician or a lawyer.

Education Laws and Schools

However, an increasing number of "unregenerate" youth troubled colonial society. In the Massachusetts Bay Colony, colonial leaders felt that parental failure was slowing progress toward the achievement of a Christian society, often referred to as the "New Jerusalem." The colony valued conformity and strict obedience, and considered toleration of diversity in thought or life style to be unchristian. Concerned about what it considered poorly educated youth, the General Court in 1642, "taking into consideration the great neglect of many parents and masters in training up their children," passed a law requiring parents and masters to see that children were prepared for some gainful employment and acquired the "ability to read and understand the principles of religion and the capital laws of this country." The law did not provide for "schools" but established a principle which governs American education even today: <u>No parent has the legal right to refuse to have his child educated in the values deemed necessary by the state for its own well-being.</u>

Because the Act of 1642 was difficult if not impossible to enforce, it provided no solution for the "evil" of uneducated and unregenerate youth. Consequently the General Court in 1647 passed a law requiring towns of fifty families to provide a school for instruction in reading, writing, and religion, and towns of one hundred families to employ a teacher of Latin and Greek to prepare boys for admission to Harvard. This Act established the principle of state regulation of education to be carried on in schools provided by the local residents of a community.

Clearly these schools were conceived to be a means of furthering social reform as well as individual development. The utilitarian motive underlying early education laws greatly influenced the future course of American education. <u>Colonial America did not consider the school an institution where teachers and pupils acquired knowledge for its own sake.</u> Such an outlook evolved later in the aristocratic colonial colleges.

Laws to Eradicate Evil

Sandwiched between the education laws of 1642 and 1647 was the law of 1646 which gave the General Court ultimate power of life and death over any youth "of sufficient years of understanding" (age 16), who was "rebellious" and would not "obey the voice of his father or the voice of his mother." Parents were authorized to bring such a youth before the legal authorities. Presented with "sufficient evidence that this their son is stubborn" and "rebellious," the magistrates could order that "such a son will be put to death." Apparently society considered it better to put an unpromising youth to death than to permit him to grow up to become a "curse" to himself and society.

This harsh law attests to the belief in the reality of satanic power and the obligation to oppose it uncompromisingly. The Puritans held that all men have a spiritual calling to advance the kingdom of God on earth through their vocational calling. Hence, work was given a religious justification. Children were seen as important instruments of God. All children and youth, whatever their social class, had to be educated with great care for both callings, whatever the cost. Some youth met these adult expectations; more did not. Of course many were given no opportunity to fulfill these expectations because adults of the community often failed to establish tuition-free schools or to enforce regular attendance.

Early Colonial Schooling

Reading material in colonial America was meagre, and much of it was transplanted from England. Given the scarcity of printed matter, the role of teacher was necessarily that of an authoritative conveyer of information. The role of the pupil was that of obedient listener and memorizer. Recitation was the main teaching method: the teacher cited God's Truth and heard pupils recite it.

As important as *how* sacred values were taught was *what* would be taught. Colonial leaders believed that God "spoke" truths to them in words as well as in mighty acts. They believed that God's "word" was inerrantly recorded in the Bible. It logically followed, therefore, that if the schools were to help children and youth develop the proper relationship both to God and neighbor, the curriculum must be based on the literature of sacred traditions. Instructional materials were carefully censored and the loyalty of teachers checked, especially as new ideas began to find their way to colonial America. The theory that instruction should be focused on subject matter to be learned, rather than on the desires and felt needs of the students, is deeply rooted in the colonial tradition.

"Dame" schools were classes in reading and ciphering taught to a few of the town's boys and girls by a woman in her home as she went about her daily chores. These schools, common in New England, were the forerunners of elementary reading and writing schools. "Grammar" schools were the first colonial public schools to be supported by taxes and tuition. They had as their chief goal to provide young males, seven to thirteen years old, with sufficient knowledge of Latin and Greek to gain admission to a colonial college. A dozen such "grammar" schools were found in the Bay Colony by 1700, the best known being the "Free Grammar School" of Boston. For 38 years one of its teachers was Ezekiel Cheever, the famous schoolmaster who "held the rod for 70 years" in New England.

Discrimination Against the Black Child

Though laws were passed and schools were established to make white children literate Christian citizens, emerging customs and laws kept black children out of school to make them slaves. The custom of equating black with evil and with God's punishment, together with the need for cheap labor, seemed to the white man a justification of the enslavement of the African Negro. Discriminatory customs and laws against the education of blacks emerged early in colonial America. In time these practices helped to create a socially and racially segregated America. In 1740, two years after George Whitefield, the famous evangelist, established an orphanage in Georgia to care for the homeless youth of poor whites, the legislature of South Carolina passed a law making it a crime punishable by a stiff fine to "teach, or cause any slave or slaves to be taught to write." ■

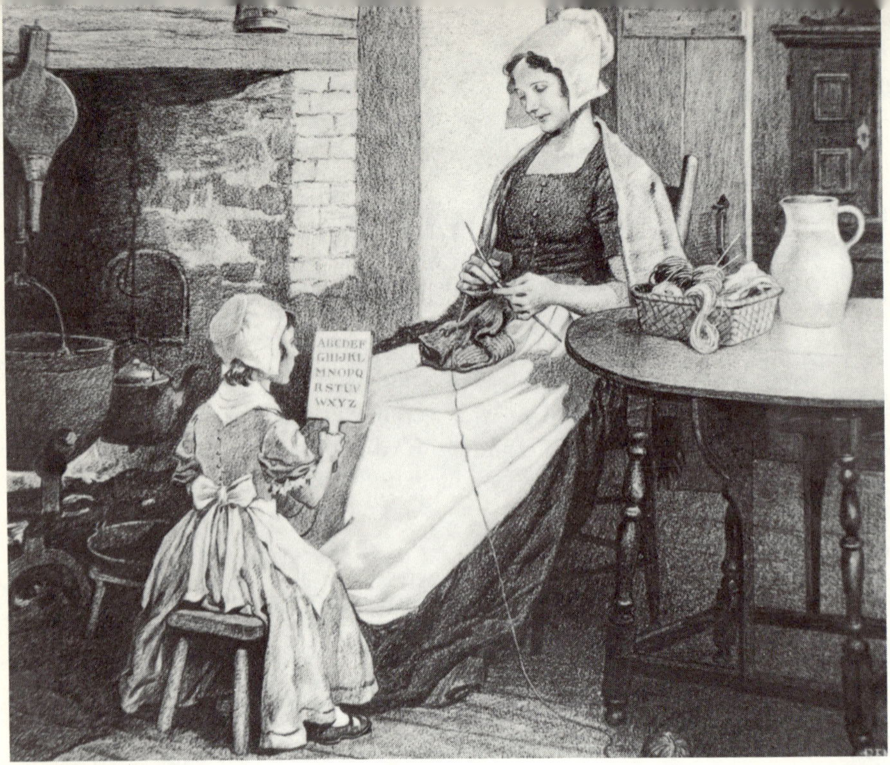
ABCDEF
GHIJKL
MNOPQ
RSTUV
WXYZ

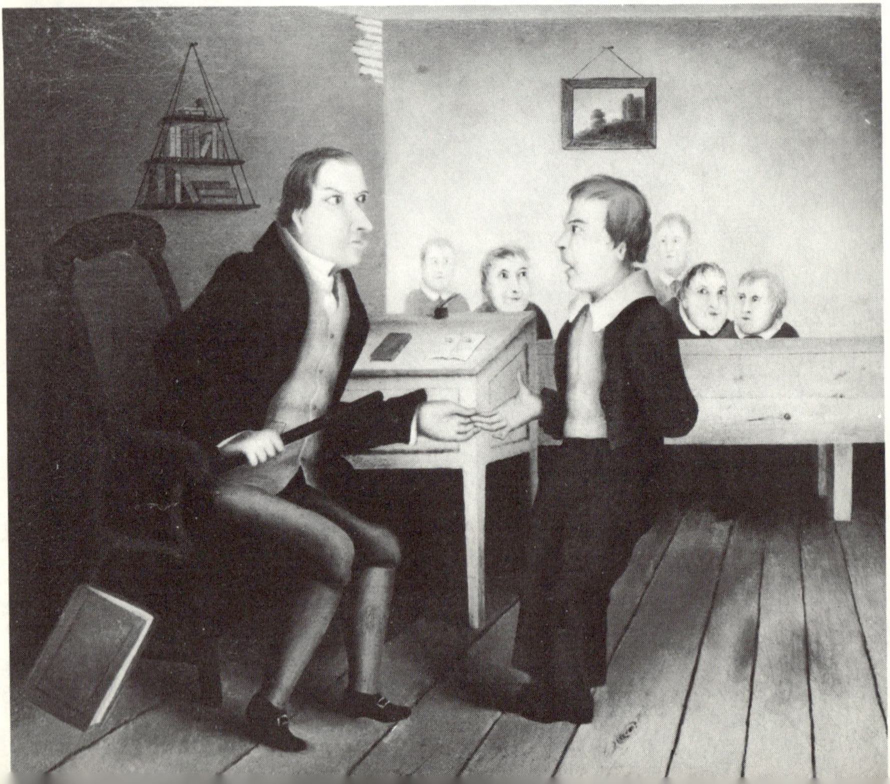

A		In *Adam's* Fall We Sinned all.
B		Thy Life to Mend This *Book* Attend.
C		The *Cat* doth play And after slay.
D		A *Dog* will bite A Thief at night.
E		An *Eagles* flight Is out of sight.
F		The Idle *Fool* Is whipt at School.
G		As runs the *Glafs* Mans life doth pafs.
H		My *Book* and *Heart* Shall never part.
J		*Job* feels the Rod Yet blefses GOD.
K		Our *KING* the good No man of blood.
L		The *Lion* bold The *Lamb* doth hold.
M		The *Moon* gives light In time of night.
N		*Nightingales* fing In Time of Spring.
O		The *Royal Oak* it was the Tree That fav'd His Royal Majeftie.
P		*Peter* denies His Lord and cries.
Q		Queen *Efther* comes in Royal State To Save the JEWS from difmal Fate.
R		*Rachel* doth mourn For her firft born.
S		*Samuel* anoints Whom God appoints.

COLONIAL BEGINNINGS: The most influential of forces operating on colonial education was the religious. Puritan children learned their letters along with a strong dose of theology, as shown in the illustrated alphabet (*left*) from a 1727 version of the New England Primer. Before formal schools became widespread, much of a child's learning took place at home (*opposite page, top*). Sometimes young children learned to read in "dame schools." These were informal sessions conducted by a woman in the neighborhood who, for a small fee, taught children the rudiments of education as she went about her daily household chores.

Probably the first teaching aid in colonial America was the hornbook, a flat piece of wood with a handle. On the face was fastened a piece of paper with the letters of the alphabet and usually the Lord's Prayer. The handle was often pierced with a hole through which a string was attached, enabling the child to carry his hornbook around his neck.

Though rewards for merit were used to encourage the colonial scholar (as shown below), a more common incentive to diligence is illustrated in the drawing on the opposite page (below).

Remember now thy Creator in the days of thy youth.

THIS MAY CERTIFY, That *Mary Bruce* for good conduct, and close attention to studies, has merited the approbation of *her* instructor.

I. The Sacred Emphasis of Education

The church and the state in the American colonies were separate institutions. Yet each in its own way perpetuated the values of a Christian society. In many colonies one had to be a member of the legally-established church in order to hold a position in the government or to vote in elections. Some colonial governments levied taxes to support the official church. If the church was the institution where the elect heard God's will spelled out, it was through the civil government that they exercised the power to foster Christian values on society. The establishment of colleges and the enactment of education laws were two ways several colonial governments sought to further this goal. ■

1. So That Learning Might Not Perish[1]
✤ Founders of Harvard College

No other colonists in the Western world provided for higher education so soon after their arrival as those in Massachusetts Bay. In 1636, six years after the founding of the colony, the General Court voted money towards the establishment of a college. Given the vocational skills needed to transform the wilderness into a livable society, one might expect that the first schools would have emphasized the learning of a trade. The following narrative explains why Harvard did not adopt this pattern. It also provides an insight into the Puritan educational ideal. ■

After God had carried us safe to New England, and we had builded our houses, provided necessaries for our livelihood, reared convenient places for God's worship, and settled the civil government: one of the next things we longed for, and looked after, was to advance learning

[1] Adapted from "New Englands First Fruits; In Respect . . . of the Progress of Learning in the College at Cambridge in Massachusetts Bay," pp. 12, 13–14, 16. London, 1643.

and perpetuate it to posterity; dreading to leave an illiterate ministry to the churches, when our present ministers shall lie in the dust. And as we were thinking and consulting how to effect this great work, it pleased God to stir up the heart of one Mr. Harvard (a godly gentleman, and a lover of learning, there living amongst us) to give the one half of his estate (it being in all about 1700 pounds) towards the erecting of a college, and all his library; after him another gave 300 pounds, others after them cast in more, and the public hand of the state added the rest: the college was, by common consent, appointed to be at Cambridge, (a place very pleasant and accommodate) and is called (according to the name of the first founder) Harvard College. . . .

Rules and Precepts

1. When any scholar is able to understand Tully, or such like classical Latin author [extemporaneously], and make and speak true Latin in verse and prose, . . . and decline perfectly the [inflectional forms] of nouns and verbs in the Greek tongue: let him then and not before be capable of admission into the college.

2. Let every student be plainly instructed, and earnestly pressed to consider well, [what] the main end of his life and studies is, to know God and Jesus Christ which is eternal life, John 17:3, and therefore to [consider] Christ . . . as the only foundation of all sound knowledge and learning. . . .

3. Every one shall so exercise himself in reading the Scriptures twice a day, that he shall be ready to give such an account of his proficiency therein . . . as his tutor shall require, according to his ability. . . .

5. That they studiously redeem the time; observe the general hours appointed for all the students, and the special hours for their own classes: and then diligently attend the lectures, without any disturbance by word or gesture. And if in anything they doubt, they shall enquire, as of their fellows, so, (in case of non satisfaction) modestly of their tutors.

6. None shall under any pretence whatsoever, frequent the company and society of such men as lead an unfit and [immoral] life.

Nor shall any without his tutor's leave, or (in his absence) the call of parents or guardians, go abroad to other towns.

7. Every scholar shall be present in his tutor's chamber at the 7th hour in the morning, immediately after the sound of the bell, at his

opening the Scripture and prayer, so also at the 5th hour at night, and then give account of his own private reading, as aforesaid . . . and constantly attend lectures in the hall at the hours appointed. But if any (without necessary impediment) shall absent himself from prayer or lectures, he shall be liable to admonition, if he offend above once a week. . . .

Graduation Requirements

Every scholar, that on proof is found able to read the originals of the Old and New Testament into the Latin tongue, and to resolve them logically; withal being of godly life and [behavior]; and at any public act hath the approbation of the overseers and master of the college, is fit to be dignified with his first degree.

Every scholar that giveth up in writing a system, or synopsis, or sum of logic, natural and moral philosophy, arithmetic, geometry and astronomy, and is ready to defend his theses or positions, withal skilled in the originals as abovesaid, and of godly life and [behavior], and so approved by the overseers and master of the college, at any public act, is fit to be dignified with his second degree.

2. A Father's Advice to His Son[1]
✣ *Thomas Shepard, Jr.*

The goals that Harvard set for its students were rooted in the beliefs and values of Bay Colony parents as well as its political and religious leaders. Well-to-do parents expected the college to educate their sons to "make their calling and election sure." Upon successful completion of the Biblical, theological, and classical curriculum, the young student would be awarded the degree of Bachelor of Arts. He was then ready to become an apprentice to a minister or, in some cases, to a physician or lawyer. The following letter, written in the 1670's, reflects a parent's deep concern that education would help his son overcome the power of Satan. ■

---

[1] "A Letter from the Reverend Mr. Thomas Shepard to His Son at His Admission into the College," reprinted in *Publications of the Colonial Society of Massachusetts*, XIV (1913), pp. 192–198.

A Father's Advice to His Son

DEAR SON, I think meet (partly from the advice of your renowned grandfather to myself at my admission into the college, and partly from some other observations I have had respecting studies in that society) to leave the remembrances and advice following with you, in this great change of your life, rather in writing, than [by word of mouth] only; that so they may be the better considered and improved by you, and may abide upon your heart when I shall be (and that may be sooner than you are aware) taken from thee, and speak no more: requiring you frequently to read over, and seriously to ponder, and digest, as also conscientiously to put in practice the same through the Lord's assistance....

II. Remember the end of this turn of your life, [namely] your coming into the college, it is to fit you for the most glorious work, which God can call you to, [that is] the Holy Ministry; that you may declare the name of God to the conversion and salvation of souls....

III. Remember therefore that God looks for and calls for much holiness from you. I had rather see you buried in your grave, than grow light, loose, wanton, or profane. God's secrets in the Holy Scriptures, which are left to instruct ministers, are never made known to common and profane spirits: and therefore be sure you begin, and end every day wherein you study with earnest prayer to God, lamenting after the favor of God; reading some part of the Scriptures daily; and setting apart some time every day (though but one quarter of an hour) for meditation of the things of God. *Children are not as worthy as adults.*

IV. Remember therefore, that though you have spent your time in the vanity of childhood, sports and mirth, little minding better things, yet that now, when come to this ripeness of admission to the college, that now God and man expects you should put away childish things; now is the time come, wherein you are to be serious, and to learn sobriety, and wisdom in all your ways which concern God and man.

V. Remember that these are times and days of much light and knowledge and that therefore you had as good be no scholar as not excel in knowledge and learning. Abhor therefore one hour of idleness as you would be ashamed of one hour of drunkenness. Look that you lose not your precious time by falling in with idle companions, or by growing weary of your studies, or by love of any filthy lust; or by discouragement of heart that you shall never attain to any excellency of knowledge, or by thinking too well of yourself.... And therefore though I would not have you neglect seasons of recreation a little before and after meals (and although I would not have you study late in the night usually, yet look that you rise early and lose not your morning thoughts, when your mind is most fresh, and fit for study), but be no wicked example all the day to any of your fellows in spending your time idly: and do not content yourself to do as much as your tutor sets you about, but know that you will never excel in learning, unless you do somewhat else in private hours. . . .

VI. Remember that in ordering your studies you make them as pleasant as may be, and as fruitful as possibly you are able, that so you may not be weary in the work God sets you about: and for this end remember these rules, [namely]:

Rules for a Diligent Scholar

1. Single out two or three scholars most godly, learned and studious, and whom you can most love, and who love you best, to be helps to you in your studies; get therefore into the acquaintance of some of your equals, to spend some time with them often in discoursing and disputing about the things you hear and read and learn; [and] also grow acquainted with some that are your superiors, of whom you may often ask questions and from whom you may learn more than by your equals only. . . .

3. Let your studies be so ordered as to have variety of studies before you, that when you are weary of one book, you may take pleasure (through this variety) in another: and for this end read some histories often, which (they say) make men wise, as poets make witty; both which are pleasant things in the midst of more difficult studies. . . .

6. Come to your studies with an appetite, and weary not your body, mind, or eyes with long poring on your book, but break off and meditate on what you have read, and then to it again; or (if it be in fit season) recreate yourself a little, and so to your work afresh; let your recreation be such as may stir the body chiefly, yet not violent. . . .

8. Choose rather to confess your ignorance in any matter of learning, that you may [be] instructed by your tutor, or another, as there may be occasion for it, than to pass from it, and so continue in your ignorance thereof, or in any error about it. . . .

12. Be sparing in your diet, as to meat and drink, that so after any repast your body may be a servant to your mind, and not a clog and burden. . . .

VIII. Remember to be grave (not childish) and amiable and loving toward all the scholars, that you may win their hearts and honor.

IX. Remember now to be watchful against the two great sins of many scholars; the first is youthful lusts, speculative wantonness, and secret filthiness, which God sees in the dark, and for which God hardens and blinds young men's hearts, his Holy Spirit departing from such, unclean [swine]. The second is malignancy and secret distaste of holiness and the power of godliness, and the professors of it, both these sins you will quickly fall into, unto your own perdition, if you be not careful of your company; for there are and will be such in every scholastic society for the most part, as will teach you how to be filthy and how to jest and scorn at godliness, and the professors thereof, whose company I charge you to fly from as from the Devil, and abhor; and that you may be kept from these, read often that Scripture, Prov. 2: 10, 11, 12, 16.

X. Remember to intreat God with tears before you come to hear any sermon, that thereby God would powerfully speak to your heart, and make His truth precious to you. . . .

XI. Remember that whenever you read, hear or conceive of any divine truth, you study to affect your heart with it and the goodness of it. Take heed of receiving truth into your head without the love of it in your heart, lest God give you up to strong delusions to believe lies, and that in the conclusion all your learning shall make you more fit to deceive yourself and others. . . .

Prov. 23:15. My Son, if thine heart be wise, my heart shall rejoice, even mine.

Pater tuus,[2]
T. Shepard

[2] **Pater tuus:** Latin, for "your father."

3. The State Requires Education[1]
✣ Massachusetts Bay General Court

Colonial leaders soon recognized that additional educational opportunities were needed besides that of Harvard College. The General Court of Massachusetts — troubled by a growing number of poorly educated and "unregenerate" youth — passed the following education laws in the 1640's. The law of 1642, the nation's first compulsory education act, sought to guarantee at

[1] Laws of 1642 and 1647 reprinted in *Records of the Governor and Company of the Massachusetts Bay* (Boston: William White, 1853), Vol. II, pp. 6–7, 203.

least a minimum level of education for all children. The 1647 law sought to establish compulsory schools. Often referred to as "The Old Deluder Satan Act," it suggests the great importance of the Bible in the education of the young. The colonists believed that in the past Satan had kept men from knowledge of God's will by keeping the Bible in Latin, Greek, and Hebrew, "an unknown tongue." They thought that even in their own times Satan was still at work "by persuading from the use of tongues," through the English translation of the Bible authorized by King James I of England. Therefore, education of the colonists' youth for literacy both in English and the classical languages was thought to be imperative. These two early laws established the principle that when some parents either cannot or will not educate their young, the state can assume that responsibility. ■

A. LAW OF 1642

This court, taking into consideration the great neglect of many parents and masters in training up their children in learning, and labor, and other employments which may be profitable to the Commonwealth, do hereupon order and decree, that in every town the chosen men appointed for managing the prudential affairs of the same shall henceforth stand charged with the care of the redress of this evil, so as they shall be sufficiently punished by fines for the neglect thereof, upon presentment of the grand jury, or other information or complaint in any court within this jurisdiction; and for this end they . . . shall have power to take account from time to time of all parents and masters, and of their children, concerning their calling and employment of their children, especially of their ability to read and understand the principles of religion and the capital laws of this country, and to impose fines upon such as shall refuse to render such accounts to them when they shall be required; and they shall have power, with consent of any court or the magistrate, to put forth apprentices the children of such as they shall [find] not to be able and fit to employ and bring them up . . . and they are to take care of such as are set to keep cattle [or] be set to some other employment . . . , as spinning . . . , knitting, weaving tape, etc., and that boys and girls be not suffered to converse together, so as may occasion any wanton, dishonest, or immodest behavior; and for their better performance of this trust committed to them, they may divide the town amongst them, appointing to every of the said townsmen a certain number of families to have special oversight of....

B. LAW OF 1647

It being one chief project of that old deluder, Satan, to keep men from the knowledge of the Scriptures, as in former times by keeping them in an unknown tongue, so in these latter times by persuading from the use of tongues, that so at least the true sense and meaning of the original might be clouded by false glosses of saint seeming deceivers, that learning might not be buried in the grave of our fathers in the church and Commonwealth, the Lord assisting our endeavors —

It is therefore ordered, that every township in this jurisdiction, after the Lord hath increased them to the number of 50 householders, shall then forthwith appoint one within their town to teach all such children as shall resort to him to write and read, whose wages shall be paid either by the parents or masters of such children, or by the inhabitants in general, by way of supply, as the major part of those that order the prudentials of the town shall appoint; provided, those that send their children be not oppressed by paying much more than they [who] can have them taught for in other towns; and it is further ordered, that where any town shall increase to the number of 100 families or householders, they shall set up a grammar school, the master thereof being able to instruct youth so far as they may be fitted for the university, provided, that if any town neglect the performance hereof above one year, that every such town shall pay five pounds to the next school till they shall perform this order.

4. A Parent's Responsibility[1]
✤ Cotton Mather

Much of a child's education, despite early attempts to establish formal schools, was acquired in the home. Cotton Mather, grandson of two founders of the Massachusetts Bay Colony and

[1] Cotton Mather, *Bonifacius: An Essay upon the Good, that is to be Devised and Designed, by those Who Desire to Answer the Great End of Life, and to Do Good While they Live* (Boston, 1710), pp. 55–61, 63–64.

prominent Puritan minister, wrote the following advice to parents in 1710. The author stresses the generally accepted practices of teaching in the home and emphasizes the role parents are expected to play in the religious inculcation of their offspring. Parents are admonished to be on their guard against the wiles of Satan — lest children read evil books and fall in with evil companions. Balanced against Mather's strictness, however, is his warning against sadistic punishment for minor offenses. ■

I would betimes entertain the children with delightful stories out of the Bible. In the talk of the table, I would go through the Bible.... But I would always conclude the stories with some lessons of piety, to be inferred from them.

I would single out some Scriptural sentences, of the greatest importance; and some also that have special antidotes in them against the common errors and vices of children. They shall quickly get those Golden Sayings by heart, and be rewarded with silver or gold, or some good thing, when they do it....

I would betimes cause my children to learn the Catechism. In catechising of them, I would break the answer into many lesser and proper questions; and by their answer to them, observe and quicken their understandings. I would bring every truth into some duty and practice, and expect them to confess it, and consent to it, and resolve upon it. As we go on in our catechising, they shall, when they are able, turn to the proofs, and read them, and say to me what they prove and how. Then I will take my times, to put nicer and harder questions to them; and improve the times of conversation with my family, which every man ordinarily has or may have, conferences on matters of religion....

I would be solicitous to have my children expert, not only at reading handsomely, but also at writing a fair hand. I will then assign them such books to read, as I may judge most agreeable and profitable; obliging them to give me some account of what they read; but keep a strict eye upon them, that they don't stumble on the Devil's library, and poison themselves with foolish romances, or novels, or plays, or songs, or jests that are not convenient....

Learning Out of Respect, Not Fear

I wish that my children may, as soon as may be, feel the principles of reason and honor working in them, and that I may carry on their education very much upon those principles. Therefore, first, I will wholly avoid that harsh, fierce, crabbed usage [with] the children that would make them tremble, and abhor to come into my presence. I will so use them, that they shall fear to offend me, and yet mightily love to see me, and be glad of my coming home, if I have been abroad at any time. . . . I will never dispense a blow, except it be for an atrocious crime, or for a lesser fault obstinately persisted in; either for an enormity, or for an obstinacy. I would ever proportion chastisements unto miscarriages; not smite bitterly for a very small piece of childishness, and only frown a little for some real wickedness. Nor shall my chastisements ever be dispensed in a passion, and a fury; but with them, I will first show them the command of God, by transgressing whereof they have displeased me. The slavish raving, fighting way of education too commonly used, I look upon it, as a considerable article in the wrath and curse of God, upon a miserable world. . . .

I would be very watchful and cautious about the companions of my children. I will be very inquisitive what company they keep. If they are in hazard of being ensnared by any vicious company, I will earnestly pull them out of it, as brands out of the burning. I will find out, and procure, laudable companions for them. . . .

I incline, that among all the points of a polite education which I would endeavor for my children, they may each of them, the daughters as well as the sons, have so much insight into some skill, which lies in the way of gain, . . . that they may be able to subsist themselves, and get something of a livelihood, in case the Providence of God should bring them into necessities. . . .

5. The Puritan Ethic[1]
♣ New England Primer

The following pieces are representative of the kind of material colonial youth studied after they had "learned their letters." Strongly reflecting the values of Protestant Christianity, these readings were dedicated to the maintenance of strict moral and religious beliefs and contributed to social control. In England such selections were part of primers, or books of private devo-

[1] *The New England Primer* (Boston: Ginn and Company, Twentieth Century Reprint; Boston: Draper, 1785–1790).

tions. In America colonial leaders combined them with other writings into The New England Primer. *This book, which sold more than three million copies, as well as the family Bible were found in most New England homes. For one hundred years the Primer served as the schoolbook of that region. Much of its moralistic tone and many of its grave sayings found their way into later schoolbooks.* ■

A. PRAISE TO GOD FOR LEARNING TO READ

The Praises of my Tongue
    I offer to the Lord,
That I was taught and learnt so young
    To read his Holy Word.

That I was brought to know
    The Danger I was in,
By Nature and by Practice too
    A wretched slave to Sin.

That I was led to see
    I can do nothing well;
And whither shall a Sinner flee
    To save himself from Hell.

Dear Lord this Book of thine,
    Informs me where to go
For Grace to pardon all my Sin,
    And make me holy too.

Here I can read and learn
    How Christ the Son of God
Has undertook our great concern,
    Our Ransom cost his Blood.

And now he reigns above,
    He sends his Spirit down
To show the wonders of his Love,
    And make his Gospel known.

O may that Spirit teach,
    And make my heart receive
Those Truths which all thy Servants preach,
    And all thy Saints believe!

>   Then shall I praise the Lord
>   In a more cheerful Strain,
>   That I was taught to read his Word,
>   And have not learnt in vain.

B. THE SHORTER CATECHISM

Q. What is the chief end of man?
A. Man's chief end is to glorify God and enjoy him forever.
Q. What rule hath God given to direct us how we may glorify and enjoy him?
A. The Word of God which is contained in the Scriptures of the Old and New Testaments is the only rule to direct us how we may glorify and enjoy Him.
Q. What do the Scriptures principally teach?
A. The Scriptures principally teach what man is to believe concerning God, and what duty God requires of man.
Q. What is God?
A. God is a Spirit, Infinite, Eternal and Unchangeable in his Being, Wisdom, Power, Holiness, Justice, Goodness, and Truth.
Q. Are there more Gods than one?
A. There is but ONE only, the living and true God.
Q. How many Persons are there in the Godhead?
A. There are three Persons in the Godhead, the Father, the Son, and the Holy Ghost, and these three are one GOD, the same in Substance, equal in Power and Glory. . . .
Q. What is the work of creation?
A. The work of creation is God's making all things of nothing, by the Word of His Power, in the space of six days, and all very good.
Q. How did God create man?
A. God created man male and female after his own image, in knowledge, righteousness and holiness, with dominion over the creatures. . . .
Q. What special act of providence did God exercise towards man in the estate wherein he was created?
A. When God had created man he entered into a covenant of life with him upon condition of perfect obedience, forbidding him to eat of the Tree of Knowledge of Good and Evil, upon pain of death.

Q. Did our first parents continue in the estate wherein they were created?
A. Our first parents being left to the freedom of their own will fell from the estate wherein they were created, by sinning against God.
Q. What is Sin?
A. Sin is any want of conformity unto, or transgression of the Law of God.
Q. What was the sin whereby our first parents fell from the estate wherein they were created?
A. The sin whereby our first parents fell from the estate wherein they were created, was their eating the forbidden fruit.
Q. Did all mankind fall in Adam's first transgression?
A. The Covenant being made with Adam, not only for himself but for his posterity, all mankind descending from him by ordinary generation, sinned in him, and fell with him in his first transgression.
Q. Into what estate did the fall bring mankind?
A. The fall brought mankind into a state of sin and misery....
Q. What is the misery of that estate whereinto man fell?
A. All mankind by the fall, lost communion with God, are under his wrath and curse, and so made liable to all miseries in this life, to death itself and to the pains of hell forever.
Q. Did God have all mankind to perish in the state of sin and misery?
A. God having out of his mere good pleasure, from all eternity, elected some to everlasting life, did enter into a Covenant of Grace, to deliver them out of a state of sin and misery, and to bring them into a state of salvation by a Redeemer....

II. The Conduct of Education

For the parent, the minister, and the teacher, common sense and tradition suggested the methods to be used in teaching the young. To learn to read children were first taught to recognize letters, then sounds in various combinations, and finally words. Religion and commerce provided the vocabulary the young colonist was expected to master, which led one colonial father to conclude that the standard diet of education consisted of the "Bible and figgers." Recitation and catechizing were the two main methods of teaching. In recitation the teacher would first say (cite) the letter or word and then the pupil would repeat it (re-cite). In catechizing the teacher would ask a prepared question to which the student would respond with a pat answer. Both methods involved a great deal of repetition, necessitated extensive memorization, and allowed for no variation in acceptable responses. Fear — of failure, of the teacher, and of losing one's soul — pervaded the colonial classroom. ∎

1. To Instruct with All Diligence[1]
✣ Hopkins Grammar School Trustees

Three years after Massachusetts passed the Act of 1647, Connecticut enacted similar legislation. Public grammar schools were soon established in several towns throughout the colony. The following rules were drawn up for the New Haven Hopkins Grammar School. Rigorous discipline was considered essential to ensure that graduates were Christians and scholars, well qualified to serve their church and state. ∎

Orders of the Committee of Trustees for the Grammar School at Newhaven to be observed and attended in the said school, made, agreed upon and published in the said school in the year 1684:

[1] "Code of Regulations" reprinted in *The American Journal of Education*, IV, No. XII (March, 1858), p. 710.

1. The erection of the said school being principally for the instruction of hopeful youth in the Latin tongue, and other learned languages so far as to prepare such youths for the college and public service of the country in church, and Commonwealth. The chief work of the schoolmaster is to instruct all such youth as are or may be by their parents or friends sent, or committed unto him to that end with all diligence, faithfulness, and constancy out of any of the towns of this county of Newhaven. . . . And if any boys are sent to the master of the said school from any other part of the colony, or country, each such boy or youth to pay ten shillings to the master at or upon his entrance into the said school.

2. That no boys be admitted into the said school for the learning of English books, but such as have been before taught to spell the letters well and begin to read, thereby to perfect their right spelling and reading, or to learn to write and cipher for numeration, and addition, and no further; and that all others either too young and not instructed in letters and spelling, ==and all girls be excluded as improper and inconsistent with such a grammar school as the law injoins==, as is the design of this settlement. And that no boys be admitted from other towns for the learning of English, without liberty and special license from the Committee.

3. That the master and scholars duly attend the school hours, [namely], from six in the morning to eleven o'clock in the forenoon, and from one o'clock in the afternoon to five o'clock in the afternoon in summer and four in winter.

4. That the master shall make a list or catalogue of his scholars' names and appoint a monitor in his turn for one week or longer time as the master shall see cause, who shall every morning and noon at least once a day at the set time call . . . the names of the scholars and note down the latecomers, or absent, and in fit season call such to an [account] that the faulty and truants may be corrected or reproved, as their fault shall deserve.

5. That the scholars being called together the master shall every morning begin his work with a short prayer for a blessing on his labors and their learning.

6. That [the] prayer being ended ==the master shall assign to every of his scholars their places of sitting according to their degrees of learning==. And that (having their parts, or lessons appointed them) they keep their seats, and stir not out of doors, with [out] leave of the master, and not above two at one time, and so successively: unless in cases of necessity.

7. That the scholars behave themselves at all times, especially in school time with due reverence to their master, and with sobriety and quietness among themselves, without fighting, quarrelling or calling one another . . . bad names, or using bad words in cursing, taking the name of God in vain, or other profane, obscene, or corrupt speeches; which if any do, that the master forthwith give them due correction. And if any prove incorrigible in such bad manners and wicked corrupting language and speeches, notwithstanding former warnings, admonitions and correction that such be expelled [from] the school as [destructive] and dangerous examples to the rest.

8. That if any of the school boys be observed to play, sleep, or behave themselves rudely, or irreverently, or be any way disorderly at meeting on the Sabbath days or any other times of the public worships of God . . . the master shall give them due corrections to the degree of the offence. And that all corrections be with moderation.

9. That no Latin boys be allowed upon any pretence (sickness and disability excepted) to withdraw, or absent themselves from the school, without liberty granted by the master, and that no such liberty be granted but upon ticket from the parents or friends, and on grounds sufficient as in cases extraordinary or [of] absolute necessity.

10. That all the Latin scholars, and all other of the boys of competent age and capacity give the master an [account] of one passage or sentence at least of the sermons the foregoing Sabbath on the second morning. And that from one to three in the afternoon of every last day of the week be improved by the master in catechizing of his scholars that are capable.

2. The Ideal of Student Learning[1]

♣ *Ebenezer Turell*

When evaluating the effects on students of the education received in colonial times, one must note the difference between the ideal and the real. Whether or not Jane Turell, as described below, actually achieved everything her biographer claimed, her life gives us insight into the colonists' beliefs regarding the ideal

---

[1] Ebenezer Turell, "Memoirs of the Life and Death of the Pious and Ingenious Mrs. Jane Turell," published with *Two Sermons Preached at Medford*, April 6, 1735, by Benjamin Colman (Boston: Kneeland and Green, 1735), pp. 60–61, 78–79.

accomplishments of a child. The selection was written by Jane Turell's husband, a minister for more than 50 years at Medford, Massachusetts. ■

Her father the Reverend Dr. Benjamin Colman (through the gracious favor of God) is still living among us, one universally acknowledged to be even from his younger times (at home and abroad) a bright ornament and honor to his country, and an instrument in God's hand of bringing much good to it.

Her mother, Mrs. Jane Colman, was a truly gracious woman, daughter of Mr. Thomas Clark, gentleman.

Mrs. Turell was their third child, graciously given them after they had mourned the loss of the two former; and for seven years their only one. Her constitution from her early infancy was wonderful weak and tender, yet the organs of her body so formed as not to obstruct the free operations of the active and capacious spirit within. The buddings of reason and religion appeared [in] her sooner than usual. — Before her second year was completed she could speak distinctly, knew her letters, and could relate many stories out of the Scriptures to the satisfaction and pleasure of the most judicious. I have heard that Governor Dudley, with other wise and polite gentlemen, have placed her on a table and setting round it owned themselves diverted with her stories. — Before she was four years old (so strong and tenacious was her memory) she could say the greater part of the Assembly's Catechism, many of the Psalms, some hundred lines of the best poetry, read distinctly, and make pertinent remarks on many things she read. —

She grew in knowledge (the most useful) day by day, and had the fear of God before her eyes. . . .

Even at the age of four, five, and six she asked many astonishing questions about divine mysteries, and carefully laid up and hid the answers she received to them, in her heart. . . .

Before she had seen eighteen, she had read, and (in some measure) digested all the English poetry, and polite pieces in prose, printed and manuscripts in her father's well furnished library, and much she borrowed of her friends and acquaintance. She had indeed such a thirst after knowledge that the leisure of the day did not suffice, but she spent whole nights in reading.

I find she was sometimes fired with a laudable ambition of raising the honor of her sex, who are therefore under obligations to her; and all will be ready to own she had a fine genius, and is to be placed among those who have excelled.

When I was first inclined (by the motions of God's Providence and Spirit) to seek her acquaintance (which was about the time she entered her nineteenth year) I was surprised and charmed to find her so accomplished. I found her in a good measure mistress of the politest writers and their works; could point out the beauties in them, and had made many of their best thoughts her own: and as she went into more free conversation, she discoursed how admirably on many subjects!

3. The Reality of Student Learning[1]
✤ John Barnard

A more typical colonial education is found in the autobiography of John Barnard. Born in Boston in 1681, Barnard was educated at the Free Grammar School under the famous schoolmaster, Ezekiel Cheever. Grammar schools — designed only for boys — were devoted to the study of the classics. To enter, a student had to be at least seven years old and already able to read. Beginning students were drilled in the basics of Latin grammar; by the fourth year they were mastering Greek. Although most boys did not enter Harvard as Barnard did, many colonial children had similar grammar school experiences. ■

I, John Barnard was born at Boston, the sixth of November, 1681; descended from reputable parents, [namely], John and Esther Barnard, remarkable for their piety and benevolence, who devoted me to the service of God, in the work of the ministry, from my very conception and birth; and accordingly took special care to instruct me themselves in the principles of the Christian religion, and kept me close at school to furnish my young mind with the knowledge of letters. By [the] time I had a little passed my sixth year, I had left my reading school, in the latter part of which my mistress made me a sort of [assistant], appointing me to teach some children that were older than myself, as well as smaller ones; and in which time I had read my

[1] Extracted from "The Autobiography of The Reverend John Barnard" in *Collections of the Massachusetts Historical Society*, Vol. V of the Third Series (Boston, 1836), pp. 178–180. *** indicates illegible words in the original manuscript.

Bible through thrice. My parents thought me to be weakly, because of my thin [physical appearance], and therefore sent me into the country, where I spent my seventh summer, and by the change of air and diet and exercise I grew more fleshy and hardy; and that I might not lose my reading, was put to a schoolmistress, and returned home in the fall.

In the spring of my eighth year I was sent to the grammar school[2] under the tuition of the aged, venerable, and justly famous Mr. Ezekiel Cheever. But after a few weeks, an odd accident drove me from the school. There was an older lad entered the school the same week with me; we strove who should outdo; and he beat me by the help of a brother in the upper class, who stood behind master with the [grammar book] open for him to read out of; by which means he could recite his *** three and four times in a forenoon, and the same in the afternoon; but I who had no such help, and was obliged to commit all to memory, could not keep pace with him; so that he would be always one lesson before me. My ambition could not bear to be outdone, and in such a fraudulent manner, and therefore I left the school. About this time arrived a dissenting minister[3] from England, who opened a private school for reading, writing, and Latin. My good father put me under his tuition, with whom I spent a year and a half. The gentleman receiving but little encouragement, [gave] up his school, and returned me to my father, and again I was sent to my aged Mr. Cheever, who placed me in the lowest class; but finding I soon read through my *** in a few weeks he advanced me to the ***, and the next year made me the head of it. . . .

Though my master advanced me . . . yet I was a very naughty boy, much given to play, insomuch that he at length openly declared, "You Barnard, I know you can do well enough if you will; but you are so full of play that you hinder your classmates from getting their lessons; and therefore, if any of them cannot perform their duty, I shall correct you for it." One unlucky day, one of my classmates did not look into his book, and therefore could not say his lesson, though I called upon him once and again to mind his book; upon which our master beat me. . . . The boy was pleased with my being corrected, and persisted in his neglect, for which I was still corrected, and that for several days. I thought, in justice, I ought to correct the boy, and

---

[2] The Free Grammar School, better known as the Boston Latin School, is one of the country's oldest secondary schools. It first opened in 1635.
[3] **dissenting minister:** not of the Church of England.

compel him to a better temper; and therefore, after school was done, I went up to him, and told him I had been beaten several times for his neglect; and since master would not correct him I would, and I should do so often as I was corrected for him; and then drubbed him heartily. The boy never came to school any more, and so that unhappy affair ended.

Though I was often beaten for my play, and my little roguish tricks, yet I don't remember that I was ever beaten for my book more than once or twice. . . .

I remember once, in making a piece of Latin, my master found fault with the syntax of one word, which was not so used by me heedlessly, but designedly, and therefore I told him there was a plain grammar rule for it. He angrily replied there was no such rule. I took the grammar and showed the rule to him. Then he smilingly said, "Thou art a brave boy; I had forgot it." And no wonder, for he was then above eighty years old.

*   *   *   *   *

College Days

From the grammar school I was admitted into the college in Cambridge, in New England, in July, 1696. . . .

Upon my entering into college, I became chamber-mate, the first year, to a senior and junior [student], which might have been greatly to my advantage, had they been of a studious disposition, and made any considerable progress in literature. But, alas! they were an idle pack, who knew but little, and took no pains to increase their knowledge. When therefore, according to my disposition, which was ambitious to excel, I applied myself close to books, and began to look forward into the next year's exercises, this unhappy pair greatly discouraged me, and beat me off from my studies, so that by their persuasions I foolishly threw by my books, and soon became as idle as they were. Oh! how baneful is it to be linked with bad company! and what a vile heart had I to hearken to their wretched persuasions! I never, after this, recovered a good studious disposition, while I was at college. Having a ready, quick memory, which rendered the common exercises of the college easy to me, and being an active youth, I was hurried almost continually into one diversion or another, and gave myself to no particular studies, and therefore made no great proficiency in any part of solid learning. . . .

In the last year of my being at college, it pleased God, in righteous judgment, so far to deliver me up to the corrupt workings of my own heart, that I fell into a scandalous sin, in which some of my classmates were concerned. This roused me more seriously to bethink myself of the wickedness of my heart and life; and though I had kept up some little show of religion, yet now I saw what a terrible punishment it was to be left of God, and exposed to His wrath and vengeance, and set myself upon seeking an interest in the favor of God, through the blessed Mediator; and resolved, through the grace of God assisting of me, to lead a sober, a righteous, and a godly life, and improve my time and talents in the service of my Maker and Redeemer, and applied myself more closely to my studies: but I found I could not recover what I had lost by my negligence.

In July, 1700, I took my first degree, Dr. Increase Mather being President, after which I returned to my honored father's house, where I betook myself to close studying, and humbling myself before God with fasting and prayer, imploring the pardon of all my sins, through the mediation of Christ; begging the divine Spirit to sanctify me throughout, in spirit, soul, and body, and fit me for, and use me in the service of the sanctuary, and direct and bless all my studies to that end. I joined to the North Church in Boston, under the pastoral care of the two Mathers.[4] . . .

The pulpit being my great design, and divinity my chief study, I read all sorts of authors, and as I read, compared their sentiments with the sacred writings, and formed my judgment of the doctrines of Christianity by that only and infallible standard of truth; which led me insensibly into what is called the Calvinistical scheme, (though I never to this day have read Calvin's Works, and cannot call him master,) which sentiments, by the most plausible arguments to the contrary, that have fallen in my way, (and I have read the most of them,) I have never yet seen cause to depart from.

. . . By August, 1702, I became almost a constant preacher, both on week days, and on the Lord's day. . . . This constant preaching took me off from all other studies. About two months before I took my second degree, the reverend and deservedly famous Mr. Samuel Willard, then Vice-President, called upon me, (though I lived in Boston), to give a lecture in the college hall; which I did, endeavoring to prove the divine inspiration and authority of the Holy Scriptures. . . .

[4] **the two Mathers:** Increase and Cotton Mather.

4. The Apprenticeship Agreement[1]
✤ Thomas Stoughton and Nathan Day

The following apprentice contract is typical of those used throughout the colonies. It states clearly the duties of the apprentice and the responsibilities of the master craftsman. Serving in an apprenticeship was often a grueling experience. Many apprentices who hoped to learn a trade or profession often found that they were made to work more than they were permitted to learn. Nevertheless, the apprenticeship did provide many colonial youths, especially those from poor families, with at least the rudiments of education. ■

This indenture witnesseth that Jonathan Stoughton, son of Thomas Stoughton of Windsor in the county of Hartford and colony of Connecticut in New England, with his father's consent hath put himself an apprentice to Nathan Day of the above said Windsor county and colony: blacksmith and whitesmith[2] to learn his art, trade or mystery after the manner of an apprentice to serve him until the said Jonathan Stoughton attains the age of twenty-one years, during all which time the said apprentice his master faithfully shall serve, his secrets keep, his lawful commands gladly obey. He shall not do any damage to his said master nor see it done by others without giving notice thereof to his said master. He shall not waste his said master's goods or lend them unlawfully to any. He shall not commit fornication nor contract matrimony within the said term; at cards, dice, or any other unlawful game he shall not play whereby his said master may suffer damage. He shall not absent himself day nor night from his master's service without his leave, nor haunt ale houses, taverns, or playhouses but in all things behave himself as a faithful apprentice ought to do during the said term, and the said master shall do his utmost to teach and instruct the said apprentice in the above mentioned blacksmith and whitesmith's trade and mystery, and to teach or cause the said apprentice to be taught the art of arithmetic to such

---

[1] Stiles, Henry R., *The History and Genealogies of Ancient Windsor, Connecticut, 1635–1891.* Vol. I, p. 442.

[2] **whitesmith:** A whitesmith was sometimes distinguished from a blacksmith as the worker who finished or polished the work.

a degree that he may be able to keep a book well, and provide for him meat, drink, apparel, washing and lodging, and [medicine] in sickness and health suitable for such apprentice during the said term; and at the end of said term the said master shall furnish the said apprentice with two good new suits of apparel, both wooling and lining for all parts of his body suitable for such an apprentice, besides that apparel he carries with him and for the performance of all . . . covenants and agreement either of the said parties bind themselves unto the other, by these present in witness whereof they have interchangeably put their hands and seals this first day of September in the year of our Lord God, 1727.

III. Education in the South

While the Northern colonists aspired to create a new England in the harsh Massachusetts wilderness, the Southern colonists sought to transplant old England intact in the congenial climate of the tidelands of the Carolinas and Virginia. Though most of the colonists came from Protestant backgrounds, differences in church affiliations and social class led to the development of different life styles. The middle-class, hard working, thrifty, intolerant-of-evil ideal of the New England Puritan stands in sharp contrast to the upper-class, managerial, well-mannered ideal of the Southern Anglican. Concern for social position, wealth, and political power shaped the Southerner's concept of education: to prepare the gentleman to play his social role. Formal education, therefore, was of less importance than the influence of family and social peers.

Custom required white youth to strive for accepted ideals, whether in the schools of New England or under the tutorial system of the South. But in both regions black children were barred from such educational opportunities. A few Negroes, to be sure, did learn to read, but far fewer were permitted to become genuinely well educated. Talented blacks such as the poet Phillis Wheatley were sometimes educated. Some schooled blacks occasionally served as tutors for white children. George Washington, for example, had a black tutor. Generally, however, three dominant patterns of education developed in the colonial South: 1) a tutorial system that prepared white boys and girls of wealthy families to become genteel mannerly slaveowners; 2) apprenticeships and orphanages that trained indigent white children for occupations not open to the slave but not suitable for the upper-class slaveowner; and 3) a slave system that taught black children to work as field hands and household servants on the plantation. ■

1. The Tutorial System[1]

✣ Philip Fithian

Formal schools in the Southern colonies were rare during the colonial period. Children were widely scattered on the plantations. Consequently, it was difficult for children to travel to schools. Tutors were hired to live in the home of a planter and to instruct his children. The following description is taken from the diary of Philip Fithian, a young Princeton divinity student who served as a tutor on a Virginia plantation in the 1700's. As the selection illustrates, sometimes the task of teacher extended beyond that of formal instructor in the classics. ■

Monday, November 1st, 1773

We began school — The school consists of eight — Two of Mr. Carter's sons — One nephew — And five daughters — The eldest son is reading Sallust[2]; grammatical exercises, and Latin grammar — The second son is reading English grammar . . . ; writing and ciphering in subtraction — The nephew is reading and writing as above; and ciphering in reduction — The eldest daughter is reading the Spectator[3]; writing; and beginning to cipher — The second is reading next out of the spelling-book, and beginning to write — The next is reading in the spelling-book — The fourth is spelling in the beginning of the spelling-book — And the last is beginning her letters. . . .

Friday, December 17, 1773

I dismissed the children this morning 'til Monday on account of Mr. Christian's Dance, which, as it goes through his scholars in rotation, happens to be here today — and I myself also am unwell, so as not to go out. . . . Towards evening I grew better, and walked down, with a number of young fellows to the river; after our return I was

---

[1] Adapted from the *Journal and Letters of Philip Vickers Fithian, 1773–1774: A Plantation Tutor of the Old Dominion*, edited by Hunter Dickenson Farish, Rev. Ed. (Williamsburg, Virginia: Colonial Williamsburg, Inc., 1957), pp. 20, 32–33, 49–50. Reprinted by permission of The University Press of Virginia.

[2] **Sallust:** Roman historian and politician (86–34 B.C.).

[3] **Spectator:** the famous British periodical (1711–1712), largely composed of essays by Joseph Addison and Sir Richard Steele.

strongly solicited by the young gentlemen to go in and dance. I declined it, however, and went to my room, not without wishes that it had been a part of my education to learn what I think is an innocent and an ornamental, and most certainly, in this province is a necessary qualification for a person to appear even decent in company! —

Mrs. Carter in the evening, sent me for supper, a bowl of hot green tea, and several tarts. I expected that they would have danced 'til late in the night, but entirely contrary to my expectation, the company were separated to their respective apartments before half after nine o'clock....

Wednesday, January 5, 1774

Rose at seven. The morning very stormy. Bob and Nancy before breakfast had a quarrel — Bob called Nancy a liar; Nancy upbraided Bob, on the other hand, with being often flogged by their Pappa; ... that he had stolen rum, and had got drunk; and that he used to run away — These reproaches when they were set off with Miss Nancy's truly feminine address, so violently exasperated Bob that he struck her in his rage — I was at the time in my chamber; when I entered the room each began with loud and heavy complaints; I put them off however with sharp admonitions for better behavior.

The morning was so extremely stormy that I declined going to breakfast — All the others went; my breakfast was sent over — Immediately after breakfast Ben came over with a message from Mr. Carter, that he desired me to correct Bob severely immediately — Bob, when I went into [the] school sat quiet in the corner, and looked sullen, and penitent; I gave some orders to the children, and went to my room. — I sent for Bob — He came crying — I told him his father's message; he confessed himself guilty — I sent him to call up Harry — He came — I talked with them both a long time. Recommended diligence, and good behavior, but concluded by observing that I was obliged to comply with Mr. Carter's request; I sent Harry therefore for some whips. — Bob and poor I remained trembling in the chamber (for Bob was not more uneasy than I, it being the first attempt of the kind I have ever made) — The whips came! — I ordered Bob to strip! — He desired me to whip him in his hand in tears — I told him no — He then patiently, and with great deliberation took off his coat and laid it by — I took him by the hand and gave him four or five smart twigs; he cringed, and bawled and promised — I repeated then about eight more, and demanded and got immediately his solemn promise for peace among the children, and good behavior in general — I then sent him down — He conducts himself through this day with great humility, and unusual diligence; it will be fine if it continues. . . .

2. Creation of an Orphanage[1]
✢ George Whitefield

When poor white children, often homeless, were not put out as apprentices by court order, charity organizations commonly provided for their care and education. One such organization was the Bethesda Orphan House, founded in 1738 near Savannah, Georgia, by George Whitefield. While on one of his several trips to the American colonies, the famous English evangelist raised money to build and operate the orphanage. In this report to the contributors in 1741, Whitefield tells of efforts to combine vocational training and elementary education as well as to Christianize the orphans. ■

I think, with a full assurance of faith, I may affirm the Lord put it into my heart to build that house. It has prospered beyond expectation. It has already, and I hope will yet more and more answer its name (Bethesda) and be a House of Mercy to the souls and bodies of many people, both old and young.

When I left England, I proposed to take in only twenty children. But when I arrived at Georgia, I found so many objects of charity, besides the orphans among the poor people's children, that I resolved in this, as well as in all other respects, to . . . make a provision for their maintenance also.

Practical Training

Two of the orphan boys were put out [as] apprentices, just before I left Savannah; one to a bricklayer, another bound to a carpenter; a

---

[1] George Whitefield, "An Account of Money Received and Disbursed For the Orphan House in Georgia," reprinted in Grace Abbott, ed., *The Child and the State*, Vol. II (Chicago: The University of Chicago Press, 1938), pp. 25–26, 28, 29. Reprinted by permission of the American Public Health Association.

Creation of an Orphanage 37

third is to be bound to the surgeon belonging to the orphan house; one weaves in a loom at home; two I put to a tailor I brought over, and the rest are now fitting themselves to be useful to the Commonwealth. Whoever among them appear to be sanctified, and have a good natural capacity, those, under God, I intend for the ministry.

None of the girls are put out as yet, but are taught such things as may make them serviceable whenever they go abroad. Two or three of them spin very well. Some of them knit, wash, and clean the house and get up the linen, and are taught housewifery. All capable are taught to sew. And the little girls, as well as the boys, are employed in picking cotton. I think I have no less than 382 yards of cloth already in the house, and as much yarn spun as will make near the same quantity, "A thing not known before in Georgia...."

A Spiritual Emphasis

The account which I find Mr. Seward has given of our economy, has in a great measure prevented my doing it as I intended. Let it suffice to inform our benefactors, that though the children are taught to labor for the meat which perisheth, yet they are continually reminded to seek *first* the Kingdom of God and his Righteousness, and then to depend upon God's blessing on their honest endeavors for having food and raiment added unto them....

I have left behind me, as my assistants, who have no other gratuity than food and raiment, two schoolmasters and their wives who are school-mistresses; one young man . . . at the orphan house, as superintendent, and chief manager of the outward things; the surgeon and his wife; a shoemaker and spinstress; besides laborers and monthly hired servants. I think, in all, I have upwards of 80. The Lord, I am persuaded, is able and willing to provide for them.

I think we have near 200 hogs, and 100 head of cattle....

As for manuring more land than the hired servants and great boys can manage, I think it is impracticable without a few Negroes. It will in no wise answer the expense.

I am now several hundred pounds in debt, on the orphan house account. Some particular friends have been pleased to assist me. I doubt not but our Lord will enable me to pay them, and also raise up fresh supplies for the maintenance of my large family.

I much rejoice in the institution. It has been very beneficial not only to the bodies, but also to the souls of the laborers. One woman received Christ very lately at Bethesda; and I have great reason to believe that three or four strangers, that came to see us, have been effectually brought home to God. My journal must be referred to for particulars.

[Slanderous remarks] have been spread abroad concerning our management of the children. People shoot out their bitter arrows in America, as well as in England. One poor man was filled with such resentment at the reports he had heard of our cruelty to the children, that he came one day out of South Carolina, to take away two of his boys, which, out of compassion, I had taken into the orphan house. But, when he came and saw the manner in which they were educated, he was so far from taking his children away that he desired to come and live at the orphan house himself.

I speak not this by way of boasting, or to wipe off reproach; for I know, let me do what I will, I shall never please natural men. I thought proper to give this short account, for the satisfaction of those who have already contributed, or shall be stirred up by our good God to contribute hereafter towards carrying on this good design.

3. An Argument for the Instruction of Slaves[1]
✣ Thomas Bacon

Formal education for blacks — slave or free — before the Revolutionary War was almost nonexistent. Some states, such as South Carolina in 1740, passed laws which prohibited the teaching of slaves. The following extracts from a sermon by an Anglican clergyman in Maryland criticize the common attitude that Negroes were "unteachable." Despite Thomas Bacon's strong appeal to the slavemaster's sense of Christian duty, there is little evidence that his views were widely accepted. ■

Next to our children and brethren by blood, our servants, and especially our slaves, are certainly in the nearest relation to us. They are

[1] Thomas Bacon, "Extracts from the Sermons of Reverend Thomas Bacon Addressed to Masters and Servants About 1750," reprinted in Carter G. Woodson, *The Education of the Negro Prior to 1861* (New York: G. P. Putnam's Sons, 1915), pp. 346–351. Reprinted by permission of G. P. Putnam's Sons.

an immediate and necessary part of our households, by whose labors and assistance we are enabled to enjoy the gifts of Providence in ease and plenty; and surely we owe them a return of what is just and equal for the drudgery and hardships they go through in our service. . . .

It is objected, they are so ignorant and unteachable, they cannot be brought to any knowledge in these matters.

Answer. This objection seems to have little or no truth in it, with respect to the bulk of them. Their ignorance, indeed, about matters of religion, is not to be disputed; they are sunk in it to a sad and lamentable degree, which has been shown to be chiefly owing to the negligence of their owners. But that they are so stupid and unteachable, as that they cannot be brought to any competent knowledge in these matters, is false, and contrary to fact and experience. In regard to their work, they learn it, and grow dexterous enough in a short time. Many of them have learned trades and manufactures, which they perform well, and with sufficient ingenuity: whence it is plain they are not unteachable. . . . Most masters and mistresses will complain of their art and cunning in contriving to deceive them. Is it reasonable to deny then they can learn what is good, when it is owned at the same time they can be so artful in what is bad? Their ignorance, therefore, if born in the country, must absolutely be the fault of their owners: and such as are brought here from Africa may, surely, be taught something of advantage to their own future state, as well as to work for their masters' present gain. The difference plainly consists in this; that a good deal of pains is taken to show them how to labor, and they are punished if they neglect it. This sort of instruction their owners take care to give them every day, and look well to it that it be duly followed. But no such pains are taken in the other case. They are generally left to themselves, whether they will serve God, or worship Devils — whether they become Christians, or remain heathens as long as they live: as if either their souls were not worth the saving, or as if we were under no obligation of giving them any instruction: which is the true reason why so many of them who are grown up, and lived many years among us, are as entirely ignorant of the principles of religion, as if they had never come into a Christian country: at least, as to any good or practical purposes. . . .

Our Christian Duty

We ought to make this reading and studying the Holy Scriptures, and the reading and explaining them to our children and slaves, and the catechizing or instructing them in the principles of the Christian religion, a stated duty.

We ought in a particular manner to take care of the children, and instill early principles of piety and religion into their minds . . .

To you of the female sex, (whom I have had occasion more than once to take notice of with honor in this congregation) I would address a few words on this head. You, who by your stations are more confined at home, and have the care of the younger sort more particularly under your management, may do a great deal of good in this way. I know not when I have been more affected, or my heart touched with stronger and more pleasing emotions, than at the sight and conversation of a little Negro boy, not above seven years old, who read to me in the New Testament, and perfectly repeated his catechism throughout, and all from the instruction of his careful, pious mistress. . . . This example I would recommend to your serious imitation, and to enforce it shall only remark, that a shining part of the character of Solomon's excellent daughter is, that she looketh well to the ways of her household.

Part Two

    Introduction
- IV. Defining a New American Education
- V. Educational Provisions for the New America
- VI. Christianizing the Common School
- VII. Character and Conduct of the Common School
- VIII. Beginning of Black Education

The Search for the New America: 1776-1900

Part Two: Introduction

Although there are no reliable statistics on the proportion of Americans who were literate in 1790, many historians believe that the United States had the highest literacy rate (ability to read and write) of any country in the world. The educational efforts of Calvinists and Quakers in colonial times had contributed to much of this widespread literacy.

The Conflict of Doctrines

Many colonial leaders had hoped through education to create a Protestant Christian America. However, despite the success of such religious proponents as Jonathan Edwards and George Whitefield, by 1776 only about 5 per cent of the national population were church members. During the latter part of the 1700's the westward expansion, the War for Independence, and the establishment of a new government claimed the energies of colonists more than did religious matters. "The continuing fragmentation of Protestantism and the influence of new scientific and humanistic voices thwarted the growth of a unified Protestant Christian society in America." "From education for eternal salvation to education for political and personal self-determination — this suggests the dimension of change which occurred during the National Period." In the new America, public schools were to teach American youth new beliefs that would undergird life in the new nation. Among them were beliefs in man's perfectibility through knowledge, the right of each person to "life, liberty, and the pursuit of happiness," government by the consent of the governed, and that all of these beliefs were self-evident truths. Yet it would be inaccurate to imply that democratic values and humanistic purposes were fully achieved in the public schools or national government in the early nineteenth century. Indians and Negroes were excluded both from the political freedoms and from the education envisioned by revolutionary ideology. When common schools eventually were developed in cities from Boston to Cincinnati, and later on the frontier, the local culture of Protestant republicanism often provided the values stressed in these schools.

Failure of Revolutionary Ideology

Both white and black colonial children had been indoctrinated in the belief that blacks were descendants of Ham, upon whom had fallen Noah's curse of blackness and slavery. Yet there was reason to hope that the revolutionary ideas of liberty and equality might bring education and political freedom to blacks. After all, hundreds of Negroes had joined white patriots to fight the British. Indeed many blacks had been promised their freedom if they served in the Continental Army for three years.

In some colonies abolition gained a measure of acceptance among whites. For example, whites in New York in 1785 formed the Society for Promoting the Manumission of Slaves and Such of Them As Have Been and May Be Liberated. John Jay became the Society's first president and Alexander Hamilton its secretary. Since 1750 the Quakers had distributed anti-slavery literature throughout the colonies, arguing that the slave system was both unchristian and immoral. The Friends also developed a number of schools for the education of Negroes. A prominent Quaker, John Woolman, argued eloquently that the black man's abject condition was due to a lack of equal educational, political, and economic opportunity — not to an innate mental and moral inferiority. Most whites, however, disagreed with Woolman. Serious doubts were expressed about the educability of the Negro. Even Thomas Jefferson, although he opposed slavery, propagated the majority view of white superiority.

A white superiority view dominated the thinking of American society for the next 150 years. It was used to justify racially segregated schools wherever Negroes were permitted to have schools. It robbed the black child of his self-respect and freedom of self-determination. And it created in the white child a distorted view both of himself and his black peer.

The Common School

There were other sources of strain in American society. Conflicts were frequent between farmers and city-dwellers, between immigrants and the native born, between workingmen and industrialists. "The more homogeneous our citizens can be made" in their "principles, opinions, and manners," said George Washington, "the greater will be our prospect of permanent union." Many political leaders and social reformers believed that neither private academies nor the extensive parochial schools of the Presbyterians, Congregationalists, Episcopalians, and Lutherans were the best instrument for creating "a more perfect union." Since the child's education in the home, church, and community tended to perpetuate diversity, the idea of a public common school as a homogenizing institution began to gain acceptance. In theory, the common school was to be a free, tax-supported, and non-sectarian institution of eight grades controlled by the states. Its purpose was to teach children a common language of words and numbers, a common reverence for American patriots, places and wars, and a common commitment to libertarian principles. In fact, however, the common school was painfully slow in coming into being and received meager financial support.

Because the most populated section of the new nation first encountered the problems growing out of industrialization, immigration, and urbanization, the first common schools were established in the East. There they were viewed both as instruments of social reform and as a means of creating the new American. In the Northwest Ordinance of 1787 Americans recognized that common schools would also be needed along the frontier. By setting aside the sixteenth section of each township in the Northwest Territory for schools, the federal government gave support to education. Protestant evangelists and circuit-riding preachers were among the best educated in the new western lands. Often they combined teaching in the new common schools with their religious responsibilities. Gradually state systems of public education were built upon these early beginnings.

Such educational statesmen as Horace Mann of Massachusetts, Henry Barnard of Connecticut, Caleb Mills of Indiana, and Thaddeus Stevens of Pennsylvania were tireless in their efforts to persuade members of state legislatures to enact educational laws favoring the common school. Nevertheless, the actual development of such schools was slow and spotty, and well-to-do citizens, often for reasons of economic advantage, tended to discount the views of reformers. When public schools were provided by the states, they were by no means well attended. For example, in Ohio in 1836, less than 30 per cent of the white children between the ages of six and twenty-one attended school of some sort.

Introduction to Part Two   **45**

During the next 25 years school attendance increased — because of population growth and growing support for the common school. In 1870 approximately 60 per cent of the youth between five and nineteen years were enrolled in school. The average length of the school year, however, was only 78 days. Of the total number enrolled, 10 per cent were black students. By 1880 the figure for black students had jumped to 33 per cent, a reflection of the impact of Reconstruction governments in the South. But relatively few youth — black or white — attended high school or college.

Missionary and government efforts at Indian education during the mid-nineteenth century were minimal and unsuccessful. The Indian Removal Act of 1830 colonized Indians on reservations. Reservation education typically destroyed Indian culture and taught the white man's ways. Where schools were founded for Indians, such as the Carlisle Industrial School in 1879, they were segregated in patterns similar to that for black students. The few Indian schools offered vocational training only; it was not expected that the "savage heathen" would occupy positions of leadership in white society.

Many of the students attended the common school only when not planting or harvesting crops; often they found schooling lacked any kind of intellectual stimulation. An Ohio legislator described with satiric exaggeration what schooling was like in these times:

> The children begin at a-b, ab and get over as far (in the *Speller*) as b-oo-b-y, when school gives out and they take up their spring work on the farm. The next winter, when school takes up, if it takes up so soon again, having forgotten all they had been taught previously . . . they begin again at a-b, ab, but year after year never get any farther than b-oo-b-y, booby.

The pattern of schooling was distressingly similar to that of colonial times despite the revolutionary ideas of the new nation.

Whereas sketchy schooling produced minimal intellectual results, it did confirm the religious, economic, and middle-class values of the local community. Despite its shortcomings, schooling also helped to reduce illiteracy. Between 1870 and 1900 public school enrollments increased from 60 to 72 per cent of the eligible youth. In 1870, 20 per cent of the forty million Americans above age ten were illiterate; by 1900, only 10 per cent of seventy-five million were illiterate. Daily newspapers, which multiplied rapidly during this period, also contributed to increased literacy.

Though the common school was slow in developing, was handicapped by meager teaching materials, and was taught by poorly educated "schoolmarms," the public school idea had caught fire. In 1852 Massachusetts passed the first compulsory school attendance law and by 1890 twenty-seven states and territories had followed suit. By the twentieth century, the public school had far outdistanced the private school in popularity and student enrollment and had become the chief socializing institution for American youth. More than 15 million children between five and seventen years of age were enrolled in public schools; slightly more than one million were in private schools. The average length of the school year had increased to 144 days. And some people were beginning to fear that the public school would soon replace the family as the main source of values. ■

1776 → 1900

Common school
 to proved social reform ⎫ p 44
 to build a new nation ⎭
 due to a short school year,
 low attendance and discrimination
 the schools were not very successful
 in raising the literate rate. -p 45

Many leaders of the young Republic saw the public school as the "great equalizer" of society. Despite such optimism it was not until the 1860's that elementary education received widespread support. The majority of states by the Civil War had established a public school system, and one-half of the nation's children were receiving at least some formal education. The McGuffey readers (right) played a major role in this educational process.

With the rising feminist movement of the early 1800's, equal education for girls became a lively public issue. A milestone was reached in 1837 when Mary Lyon founded Mount Holyoke — today considered the oldest women's college. By the end of the century, higher education for many women had become a reality.

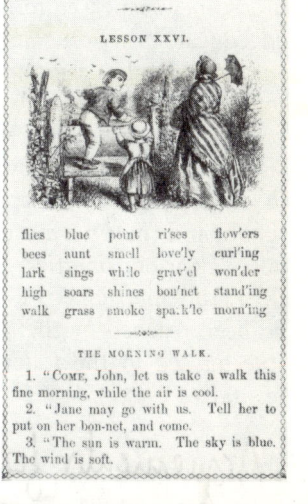

IV. Defining a New American Education

During the summer of 1787, when the Constitution of the new nation was being forged at Philadelphia, a question was emerging which to this day has concerned the common man, the statesman, and the educator. "What then is this American, this new man?" asked the French settler, Hector Crèvecoeur, in his Letters from an American Farmer.

Answers arose from all segments of American society — the church pulpits, newspaper editorials, political rallies, legislative assemblies, and educators. Numerous proposals envisioned the creation of the common school as a means of teaching patriotism and acceptance of the ideals expressed in the Constitution. Said Horace Bushnell, reflecting this sentiment, "We cannot have Puritan common schools — these are gone already — we cannot have Protestant common schools or those which are distinctly so; but we can have common schools, and these we must agree to have and maintain, till the last or latest day of our liberties. These are American, as our liberties themselves are American. . . ." National support for Bushnell's position had been reached by the time of the Civil War. Arguments such as those quoted in the following selections helped to create this consensus. ■

Arguments for support of Common Schools

1. From Puritan to Yankee[1]

✜ Benjamin Franklin

Ben Franklin — scientist, diplomat, and educator — was in his lifetime one of the first American "success stories." Young Franklin was raised in Boston by his father, a poor candlemaker, to be a sincere Presbyterian. But by the age of fifteen, Franklin declared himself to be a "thorough deist." Nevertheless, he retained the life-style embodied in the Protestant Ethic.

[1] John Bigelow, ed., *Autobiography of Benjamin Franklin* (Philadelphia: J. B. Lippincott & Co., 1868), pp. 85–86, 91–93, 94–96, 213, 214–217, 219–221.

Acting on humanistic and libertarian ideas, Franklin developed a plan for personal self-improvement without dependence upon religion. He also founded a school in Philadelphia in which students were taught the usefulness of scientific theories as well as the Protestant Ethic of thrift, hard work, and frugality. For Franklin the goal of education was to produce intellectual and practical skills and moral improvement, not religious conversion to Christianity. People who were morally sound, had scientific habits of mind, and were useful to society — thought Franklin — could build a new and enduring American nation. In the first portion from his autobiography quoted below, Franklin describes his early apprenticeship training. The selection ends with his plan for moral improvement devised when he was twenty-seven. ■

My elder brothers were all put [as] apprentices to different trades. I was put to the grammar-school at eight years of age, my father intending to devote me, as the tithe[2] of his sons, to the service of the Church. My early readiness in learning to read (which must have been very early, as I do not remember when I could not read), and the opinion of all his friends, that I should certainly make a good scholar, encouraged him in this purpose of his. My uncle Benjamin, too, approved of it, and proposed to give me all his shorthand volumes of sermons, I suppose as a stock to set up with, if I would learn his character. I continued, however, at the grammar-school not quite one year, though in that time I had risen gradually from the middle of the class of that year to be the head of it, and farther was removed into the next class above it, in order to go with that into the third at the end of the year. But my father, in the meantime, from a view of the expense of a college education, which having so large a family he could not well afford, and the [meager] living many so educated were afterwards able to obtain — reasons that he gave to his friends in my hearing — altered his first intention, took me from the grammar-school, and sent me to a school for writing and arithmetic, kept by a then famous man, Mr. George Brownell, very successful in his profession generally, and that by mild, encouraging methods. Under him I acquired fair writing pretty soon, but I failed in the arithmetic, and made no progress in it. At ten years old I was taken home to assist

---

[2] **tithe:** the tenth part of something paid as a voluntary contribution to the Church.

my father in his business, which was that of a tallow-chandler[3] and soap-boiler. . . .[4] Accordingly I was employed in cutting wick for the candles, filling the dipping mold and the molds for cast candles, attending the shop, going [on] errands, etc.

I disliked the trade, and had a strong inclination for the sea, but my father declared against it. . . .

An Unquenchable Thirst for Books

From a child I was fond of reading, and all the little money that came into my hands was ever laid out in books. . . . My father's little library consisted chiefly of books in [theological doctrine], most of which I read, and have since often regretted that, at a time when I had such a thirst for knowledge, more proper books had not fallen in my way, since it was now resolved I should not be a clergyman. . . .

This bookish inclination at length determined my father to make me a printer, though he had already one son (James) of that profession. In 1717 my brother James returned from England with a press and letters to set up his business in Boston. I liked it much better than that of my father, but still had a hankering for the sea. To prevent the apprehended effect of such an inclination, my father was impatient to have me bound to my brother. I stood out some time, but at last was persuaded, and signed the indentures when I was yet but twelve years old. I was to serve as an apprentice till I was twenty-one years of age, only I was to be allowed journeyman's wages[5] during the last year. In a little time I made great proficiency in the business, and became a useful hand to my brother. I now had access to better books. An acquaintance with the apprentices of booksellers enabled me sometimes to borrow a small one, which I was careful to return soon and clean. Often I sat up in my room reading the greatest part of the night, when the book was borrowed in the evening and to be returned early in the morning, lest it should be missed or wanted.

And after some time an ingenious tradesman, Mr. Matthew Adams, who had a pretty collection of books, and who frequented our printing-house, took notice of me, invited me to his library, and very kindly lent me such books as I chose to read. . . .

---

[3] **tallow-chandler:** candlemaker.
[4] **soap-boiler:** soap maker.
[5] **journeyman's wages:** A journeyman was one who had fully served his apprenticeship and was, hence, paid more for his work.

Debating the Value of Female Education

There was another bookish lad in the town, John Collins by name, with whom I was intimately acquainted. We sometimes disputed, and very fond we were of argument, and very desirous of [proving one another wrong]. . . .

A question was once, somehow or other, started between Collins and me, of the propriety of educating the female sex in learning, and their abilities for study. He was of opinion that it was improper, and that they were naturally unequal to it. I took the contrary side, perhaps a little for dispute's sake. He was naturally more eloquent, had a ready plenty of words; and sometimes, as I thought, bore me down more by his fluency than by the strength of his reasons. As we parted without settling the point, and were not to see one another again for some time, I sat down to put my arguments in writing, which I copied fair and sent to him. He answered, and I replied. Three or four letters of a side had passed, when my father happened to find my papers and read them. Without entering into the discussion, he took occasion to talk to me about the manner of my writing; observed that, though I had the advantage of my antagonist in correct spelling and [punctuation] (which I owed to the printing-house), I fell far short in elegance of expression, in method, and in [clarity], of which he convinced me by several instances. I saw the justice of his remark, and thence grew more attentive to the manner in writing, and determined to endeavor at improvement.

Striving for Self-Improvement

About this time I met with an odd volume of the *Spectator*. It was the third. I had never before seen any of them. I bought it, read it over and over, and was much delighted with it. I thought the writing excellent, and wished, if possible, to imitate it. With this view I took some of the papers, and, making short hints of the sentiment in each sentence, laid them by a few days, and then, without looking at the book, tried to complete the papers again, by expressing each hinted sentiment at length, and as fully as it had been expressed before, in any suitable words that should come to hand. Then I compared my *Spectator* with the original, discovered some of my faults, and corrected them. . . . By comparing my work afterwards with the original, I discovered many faults and amended them; but I sometimes had the pleasure of fancying that, in certain particulars of small import, I had been lucky enough to improve the method or the language, and this encouraged me to think I might possibly in time come to be a tolerable English writer. . . .

* * * * *

Aiming at Moral Perfection

It was about this time [at the age of 27] I conceived the bold and arduous project of arriving at moral perfection. I wished to live without committing any fault at any time; I would conquer all that either natural inclination, custom, or company might lead me into. As I knew, or thought I knew, what was right and wrong, I did not see why I might not always do the one and avoid the other. . . . For this purpose I therefore contrived the following method. . . .

I proposed to myself . . . thirteen names of virtues all that at that time occurred to me as necessary or desirable, and annexed to each a short precept, which fully expressed the extent I gave to its meaning.

These names of virtues, with their precepts were:

1. TEMPERANCE.

Eat not to dullness; drink not to elevation.

2. SILENCE.

Speak not but what may benefit others or yourself; avoid trifling conversation.

3. ORDER.

Let all your things have their places; let each part of your business have its time.

4. RESOLUTION.

Resolve to perform what you ought; perform without fail what you resolve.

5. FRUGALITY.

Make no expense but to do good to others or yourself; *i.e.*, waste nothing.

6. INDUSTRY.

Lose no time; be always employed in something useful; cut off all unnecessary actions.

7. Sincerity.
Use no hurtful deceit; think innocently and justly; and, if you speak, speak accordingly.

8. Justice.
Wrong none by doing injuries, or omitting the benefits that are your duty.

9. Moderation.
Avoid extremes; forbear resenting injuries so much as you think they deserve.

10. Cleanliness.
Tolerate no uncleanliness in body, clothes, or habitation.

11. Tranquillity.
Be not disturbed at trifles, or at accidents common or unavoidable.

12. Chastity.
Rarely use [sexual activity] but for health or offspring, never to dullness, weakness, or the injury of your own or another's peace or reputation.

13. Humility.
Imitate Jesus and Socrates.

My intention being to acquire the [habit] of all these virtues, I judged it would be well not to distract my attention by attempting the whole at once, but to fix it on one of them at a time; and, when I should be master of that, then to proceed to another, and so on, till I should have gone through the thirteen. . . .

I made a little book, in which I allotted a page for each of the virtues. I ruled each page with red ink, so as to have seven columns, one for each day of the week, marking each column with a letter for the day. I crossed these columns with thirteen red lines, marking the beginning of each line with the first letter of one of the virtues, on which line, and in its proper column, I might mark, by a little black spot, every fault I found upon examination to have been committed respecting that virtue upon that day.

Form of the pages.

	S.	M.	T.	W.	T.	F.	S.
	TEMPERANCE						

			TEMPERANCE				
		EAT NOT TO DULLNESS; DRINK NOT TO ELEVATION.					
	S.	M.	T.	W.	T.	F.	S.
T.							
S.	*	*		*		*	
O.	* *	*	*		*	*	*
R.			*			*	
F.		*			*		
I.			*				
S.							
J.							
M.							
C.							
T.							
C.							
H.							

I determined to give a week's strict attention to each of the virtues successively. Thus, in the first week, my great guard was to avoid [even] the least offence against *Temperance,* leaving the other virtues to their ordinary chance, only marking every evening the faults of the day. Thus, if in the first week I could keep my first line, marked T clear of spots, I supposed the habit of that virtue so much strengthened, and its opposite weakened, that I might venture extending my attention to include the next, and for the following week keep both lines clear of spots. Proceeding thus to the last, I could go through a course complete in thirteen weeks, and four courses in a year. And like him who, having a garden to weed, does not attempt to [get rid of] all the bad herbs at once, which would exceed his reach and his strength, but works on one of the beds at a time, and, having accomplished the first, proceeds to a second, so I should have, I hoped, the encouraging pleasure of seeing on my pages the progress I made in virtue, by clearing successively my lines of their spots, till in the end, by a number of courses, I should be happy in viewing a clean book, after a thirteen weeks' daily examination.

2. Education for Nationalism[1]
✤ Noah Webster

> The guns of the Revolution had hardly subsided when such American patriots as Noah Webster began to advocate a distinctly American education. Webster vigorously condemned the practice of sending American boys to Europe for schooling. To become a strong nation more was required than a new government, declared Webster. America also needed a system of education that would impress upon the minds of all citizens "the principles of virtue and liberty" and an "unviolable attachment to their own country." Believing that the new American nationalism would benefit from the mastery of a common language, Webster helped establish standards for American usage of the English language. His American Spelling Book first appeared in 1783 and sold over twenty million copies. ■

... Before I quit this subject, I beg leave to make some remarks on a practice which appears to be attended with important consequences; I mean that of sending boys to Europe for an education, or sending to Europe for teachers. That this was right before the Revolution will not be disputed, at least so far as national attachments were concerned; but the propriety of it ceased with our political relation to Great Britain.

An Independent Nation Needs Its Own Educational Institutions

In the first place, our honor as an independent nation is concerned in the establishment of literary institutions, adequate to all our own purposes; without sending our youth abroad, or depending on other nations for books and instructors. It is very little to the reputation of America to have it said abroad, that after the heroic achievements of the late war, this independent people are obliged to send to Europe for men and books to teach their children A B C.

But in another point of view, a foreign education is directly opposite to our political interests and ought to be [treated with disfavor], if not prohibited. ...

[1] Noah Webster, *A Collection of Essays and Fugitiy Writings on Moral, Historical, Political and Literary Subjects* (Boston: I. Thomas and E. E. Andrews, 1790), pp. 30–33, 35.

Political and Social Attachments Are Acquired in Youth

The period from twelve to twenty is the most important in life. The impressions made before that period are commonly [forgotten]; those that are made during that period *always* remain for many years, and *generally* through life.

Ninety-nine persons of a hundred, who pass that period in England or France, will prefer the people, their manners, their laws, and their government to those of their native country. Such attachments are injurious, both to the happiness of the men, and to the political interests of their own country. As to private happiness, it is universally known how much pain a man suffers by a change of habits in living. The customs of Europe are and ought to be different from ours; but when a man has been bred in one country, his attachments to its manners make them in a great measure, necessary to his happiness; on changing his residence, he must therefore break his former habits, which is always a painful sacrifice; or the discordance between the manners of his own country and his habits, must give him incessant uneasiness; or he must introduce, into a circle of his friends, the manners in which he was educated. All these consequences may follow at the same time, and the last, which is inevitable, is a public injury. The refinement of manners in every country should keep pace exactly with the increase of its wealth — and perhaps the greatest evil America now feels is, an improvement of taste and manners which its wealth cannot support.

A foreign education is the very source of this evil — it gives young gentlemen of fortune a relish for manners and amusements which are not suited to this country; which, however, when introduced by this class of people, will always become fashionable.

But a corruption of manners is not the sole objection to a foreign education. An attachment to a *foreign* government, or rather a want of attachment to our *own*, is the natural effect of a residence abroad, during the period of youth. . . .

It may be said that foreign universities furnish much better opportunities of improvement in the sciences than the American. This may be true, and yet will not justify the practice of sending young lads from their own country. There are some branches of science which may be studied to much greater advantage in Europe than in America, particularly chemistry. When these are to be acquired, young gentlemen ought to spare no pains to attend the best professors.

It may, therefore, be useful, in some cases, for students to cross the Atlantic to *complete* a course of studies; but it is not necessary for them to go early in life, nor to continue a long time. Such instances need not be frequent even now; and the necessity for them will diminish in proportion to the future advancement of literature in America. . . .

Travel Is for Men, Not Boys

It is therefore of infinite importance that those who direct the councils of a nation, should be educated in that nation. Not that they should restrict their personal acquaintance to their own country, but their first ideas, attachments, and habits should be acquired in the country which they are to govern and defend. When a knowledge of their own country is obtained, and an attachment to its laws and interests deeply fixed in their hearts, then young gentlemen may travel with infinite advantage and perfect safety. I wish not therefore to discourage traveling but, if possible, to render it more useful to individuals and to the community. My meaning is, that *men* should travel, and not *boys*.

But it is time for the Americans to change their usual route, and travel through a country which they never think of, or think beneath their notice — I mean the United States. . . .

3. Towards an Enlightened Community[1]

✤ Thomas Jefferson

"If a nation expects to be ignorant and free, in a state of civilization," declared Thomas Jefferson, "it expects what never was and never will be." Jefferson had undaunted confidence in the power of knowledge to produce American citizens who were intelligent, free, and morally strong. He was unflagging in his pursuit of public schools which would be dedicated to this purpose.

In Jefferson's plan for education in Virginia, the school would replace the church as the central social institution of the culture. Jefferson believed that by enrolling the young in public schools

---

[1] Thomas Jefferson, *Notes on the State of Virginia*, edited by Paul Leicester Ford (Brooklyn, New York: Historical Printing Club, 1894), pp. 185–188.

[Handwritten at top: A democratic government relies on an educated voting public.]

where they could learn the natural laws of the physical world and of human society, they would be rendered intelligent and thereby made free to live in conformity with nature's laws. Jefferson stated: . . . "In the present spirit of extending to the great mass of mankind the blessing of instruction, I see a prospect of great advancement in the happiness of the human race. . . ." Financial responsibility for Jefferson's plan would be placed on the public according to the general tax rate. However, it was this latter idea — that the rich should help pay for the education of the poor — which led to the eventual defeat of the bill which is described below. ■ *[Handwritten: see pp 34, 36]*

Another object of the [educational reform] is to diffuse knowledge more generally through the mass of the people. This bill proposes to lay off every county into small districts of five or six miles square, called hundreds and in each of them to establish a school for teaching, reading, writing, and arithmetic. The tutor to be supported by the hundred, and every person in it entitled to send their children three years gratis, and as much longer as they please, paying for it. These schools to be under a visitor who is annually to choose the boy of best genius in the school, of those whose parents are too poor to give them further education, and to send him forward to one of the grammar schools, of which twenty are proposed to be erected in different parts of the country, for teaching Greek, Latin, Geography, and the higher branches of numerical arithmetic. Of the boys thus sent in any one year, trial is to be made at the grammar schools one or two years, and the best genius of the whole selected, and continued six years, and the residue dismissed. By this means twenty of the best geniuses will be raked from the rubbish annually, and be instructed, at the public expense, so far as the grammar schools go. At the end of six years' instruction, one half are to be discontinued (from among whom the grammar schools will probably be supplied with future masters); and the other half, who are to be chosen for the superiority of their parts and disposition, are to be sent and continued three years in the study of such sciences as they shall choose, at William and Mary College. . . .

The ultimate result of the whole scheme of education would be the teaching all the children of the state reading, writing, and common arithmetic; turning out ten annually, of superior genius, well taught in Greek, Latin, Geography, and the higher branches of arithmetic; turning out ten others annually, of still superior parts, who, to those branches of learning, shall have added such of the sciences as their genius shall have them led to; the furnishing to the wealthier part of the people convenient schools at which their children may be educated at their own expense. — The general objects of this law are to provide an education adapted to the years, to the capacity, and the condition of every one, and directed to their freedom and happiness. . . .

History Instead of the Scriptures   *New Curriculum*

The first stage of this education being the schools of the hundreds, wherein the great mass of the people will receive their instruction, the principal foundations of future order will be laid here. Instead, therefore, of putting the Bible and Testament into the hands of the children at an age when their judgments are not sufficiently matured for religious inquiries, their memories may here be stored with the most useful facts from Grecian, Roman, European, and American history. The first elements of morality too may be instilled into their minds; such as, when further developed as their judgments advance in strength, may teach them how to work out their own greatest happiness, by showing them that it does not depend on the condition of life in which chance has placed them, but is always the result of a good conscience, good health, occupation, and freedom in all just pursuits. — Those whom either the wealth of their parents or the adoption of the state shall destine to higher degrees of learning, will go on to the grammar schools, which constitute the next stage, there to be instructed in the languages. . . .

The Talented Poor As Well As the Rich

As soon as they are of sufficient age, it is supposed they will be sent on from the grammar schools to the university, which constitutes our third and last stage, there to study those sciences which may be adapted to their views. — By that part of our plan which prescribes the selection of the youths of genius from among the classes of the poor, we hope to avail the state of those talents which nature has shown as liberally among the poor as the rich, but which perish without use, if not sought for and cultivated. — But of all the views of this law none is more important, none more legitimate, than that of rendering the people the safe, as they are the ultimate, guardians of their own liberty. For this purpose the reading in the first stage, where they will receive their whole education, is proposed, as has been said, to be chiefly historical. History, by [informing] them of the past, will enable them to judge of the future; it will avail them of the experience of other times and other nations; it will qualify them as judges of the actions and designs of men; it will enable them to know ambition under every disguise it may assume; and knowing it, to defeat its views. In every government . . . is some trace of human weakness, some germ of corruption and degeneracy, which cunning will discover, and wickedness insensibly open, cultivate and improve. Every government degenerates when trusted to the rulers of the people alone. The people themselves therefore are its only safe depositories. And to render even them safe, their minds must be improved.

4. Common Schools for a Secular Republic[1]
✢ Horace Mann

Under the able leadership of Horace Mann, Massachusetts became the first state in the new republic to establish a free, public, tax-supported, common school system. As a state senator, Mann aided in the drive to establish a state board of education, and in 1837 he was appointed secretary of the Massachusetts Board of Education. In this position — which he held for twelve years — he labored diligently for the development of common schools. He expressed his views by publishing annual reports on the status, needs, and character of education required in the new nation.

The moralistic tone of Mann's reports reflects his total dedication to the principle of human improvability. "Be ashamed to die," asserted Mann, "until you have won some victory for humanity." In his tenth report, from which the following excerpt is taken, Mann spells out the secular principles of education which would require that citizens tax themselves to establish common schools. ■

[1] Horace Mann, *The Ground of the Free School System*. From his tenth annual report as secretary of the Massachusetts State Board of Education, 1846 (Old South Leaflets, Vol. V, No. 109, Boston: Published by the Directors of the Old South Work, Old South Meeting-house, 1902), pp. 4, 13, 14, 16.

I believe in the existence of a great, immortal, immutable principle of natural law . . . a principle antecedent to all human institutions, . . . a principle of divine origin, . . . which proves the *absolute right* to an education of every human being that comes into the world, and which, of course, proves the correlative duty of every government to see that the means of that education are provided for all. . . .

Education a Right As Much As Food and Shelter

According to the very constitution of things, each individual must obtain sustenance and succor as soon as his eyes open in quest of light or his lungs gasp for the first breath of air. His wants cannot be delayed until he himself can supply them. If the demands of his nature are ever to be answered, they must be answered years before he can make any personal provision for them, either by the performance of any labor or by any exploits of skill. The infant must be fed before he can earn his bread, he must be clothed before he can prepare garments, he must be protected from the elements before he can erect a dwelling; and it is just as clear that he must be instructed before he can engage or reward a tutor. A course contrary to this would be the destruction of the young, that we might rob them of their rightful inheritance. . . .

But to preserve the animal life of a child only, and there to stop, would be — not the bestowment of a blessing or the performance of a duty — but the infliction of a fearful curse. A child has interests far higher than those of mere physical existence. Better that the wants of the natural life should be disregarded, than that the higher interests of the character should be neglected. If a child has any claim to bread to keep him from perishing, he has a far higher claim to knowledge to preserve him from error. . . . If a child has any claim to shelter to protect him from the destroying elements, he has a far higher claim to be rescued from . . . vice and crime. . . .

In obedience to the laws of God and to the laws of all civilized communities, society is bound to protect the natural life of children; and this natural life cannot be protected without the appropriation and use of a portion of the property which society possesses. We prohibit infanticide under penalty of death. We practice a refinement in this particular. The life of an infant is [sacred], even before he is born; and he who feloniously takes it, even before birth, is as subject to the extreme penalty of the law, as though he had struck down manhood in its vigor, or taken away a mother by violence from the sanctuary of home, where she blesses her offspring. But why preserve the natural life of a child, why preserve unborn embryos of life, if we do not intend to watch over and to protect them, and to expand their subsequent existence into usefulness and happiness? ... We are brought then to this startling but inevitable alternative, — the natural life of an infant should be extinguished as soon as it is born, or the means should be provided to save that life from being a curse to its possessor; and, therefore every state is morally bound to enact a code of laws legalizing and enforcing infanticide, or a code of laws establishing free schools!

Author — *Thesis*

1. Ben Franklin — Education is to produce intellectual and practical ~~schools~~ skills and moral improvement.

2. Noah Webster — young men educated in Europe will not make good patriots. American

3. Horace Mann & Thomas Jefferson — We have a duty to educate children and The masses must be educated to run a government.

V. Educational Provisions for the New America

While national leaders advanced eloquent arguments in behalf of a new education for the new America, men with less national visibility began to plan a variety of local educational institutions. Riding the crest of a revival of Protestant Christianity — a religious awakening that was intended to turn back the forces of deism and atheism — nearly one thousand church-related colleges were established before 1865. The 250 colleges which managed to survive usually combined courses in the classics with theological studies, required daily chapel and attendance at yearly revival meetings. Another educational response to the resurgence of religion was the rise of Sunday schools. Their purpose was to teach children of the lower classes not only the values of Protestant Christianity but also the skills of reading and writing.

Educational innovations also stemmed from secular sources. In some states constitutional conventions made legal provisions for the establishment of public schools at all levels — elementary, secondary, and college. The growing need for practical education prompted citizens' committees to propose new types of secondary schools which would provide job-related instruction, including courses in English for the foreign born. Humanitarians proposed that delinquent youths be given a second chance through educational programs in institutions specially designed for them. Labor organizations in the industrial cities lobbied for public common schools supported at state expense. Congress, under the persistent prodding of Senator Justin Morrill from 1855–1862, capped the common school system with land grant colleges. In these colleges secular, commercial, and scientific interests were available to the sons of the common man. "Democracy's colleges," as these schools have been called, fostered the scientific study of industrial and agricultural production, and broke the monopoly on higher education long held by the "aristocratic" private college. ∎

64   Educational Provisions for the New America

1. A Sunday School Proposal[1]
✣ William Thurston

Before the introduction of the public common schools in the mid-nineteenth century, the children of the poor typically received no more education than that informally provided in the home. To meet the needs of these children, churches and other benevolent organizations in the early nineteenth century organized Sunday schools to teach poor children the three "R's" and Christian morality. The underlying assumption was that this education would make children sound persons politically and morally, and therefore would create better citizens.

By 1824 there were so many Sunday schools and Sunday school teachers that a national organization, The American Sunday School Union (ASSU), was formed. With westward expansion, the ASSU in 1830 set out to establish a Sunday school in "every destitute place" throughout the Mississippi Valley.

The Sunday school doubtless was a factor in arousing the educational consciousness of the nation and, thereby, helped prepare the way for the public common school. As the common school gradually assumed responsibility for general education, the Sunday school became a place where each Protestant church taught its children Christianity, Bible history, and sectarian beliefs. ■

BOSTON,
Mar. 18, 1818

TURNER PHILLIPS, ESQ., CHAIRMAN OF THE HONORABLE BOARD OF SELECTMEN:

SIR: — Since I called on you, I have been to Mr. Webb's school in Mason Street, to know if it would be convenient to have the rooms occupied by the school under his care for a Sunday school; he replied that the writing books, etc., are all locked up, and that no inconvenience would be sustained by the Sunday school, which he believed

[1] "William Thurston to Turner Phillips, March 18, 1818" in Joseph Wightman, *Annals of the Boston Primary School Committee, from Its First Establishment in 1818, to Its Dissolution in 1855* (Boston: Geo. C. Rand & Avery, 1860), p. 13n.

was productive of much good. Permit me, therefore, to request that you would lay our application for a second room in Mason street school-house, if you think it necessary, having already obtained a general consent of it for the use of that school-house last May.

Our objects in attending to Sunday schools, are, to reclaim the vicious, to instruct the ignorant, to secure the observance of the Sabbath, to induce the children to attend public worship, and to raise the standard of morals among the lower classes of society. We are encouraged in obtaining these, by the experience which other places have declared to result from Sunday schools, and upon the little good which we hope has been done by them in this town.

We believe in this way we strike at the foundation of the evils incidental to society, and with greater prospect of success than to reform the hardened offenders, — and yet through the children, not unfrequently the parent is reclaimed.

Respectfully yours,
WILLIAM THURSTON,

In behalf of the Committee of Boston Society for the Moral and Religious Instruction of the Poor.

2. Constitutional Provisions for State Education[1]
✤ Constitution of Indiana, 1816

The Tenth Amendment to the United States Constitution reserves to state governments all duties, privileges, and responsibilities not specifically delegated to the federal government. Since the Constitution does not mention education, state governments by default have assumed responsibility for its provision. Some people thought that the division of power between federal and state governments prohibited the federal government from taking any action with respect to public education. This, however, was not the understanding of the early national leaders. For example, the Northwest Ordinance of 1787 set aside the

---

[1] Excerpted from *The Constitution of the State of Indiana; adopted in convention at Corydon, on the Twenty-ninth Day of June, in the year of our Lord Eighteen Hundred and Sixteen and of the United States, the Fortieth* (Louisville: Butler and Wood, 1816), pp. 18–19.

sixteenth section of each township in the Northwest Territory to provide for "schools and the means of education." President Thomas Jefferson signed into law a bill which allocated money to Catholic nuns for Christianizing and educating Indians. And in 1862 President Lincoln signed the Land Grant College Act which helped states establish agricultural and mechanical colleges. Indeed, co-operating with states in furthering education has traditionally been the policy of the federal government.

The original constitution of Indiana, adopted in 1816, made reference to grants of land from the federal government for the development of public schools in the state. The educational provisions of Indiana's constitution expressed the belief that secular knowledge, disseminated by the public schools, was essential to the development of an informed electorate and a free government. But in Indiana, as in most other states, nothing was done by the General Assembly to implement these lofty Jeffersonian ideals until mid-century. ■

ARTICLE IX. SECTION 1. Knowledge and learning, generally diffused through a community, being essential to the preservation of a free government, and spreading the opportunities and advantages of education through the various parts of the country being highly conducive to this end, it shall be the duty of the General Assembly to provide, by law, for the improvement of such lands as are or hereafter may be granted by the United States to this state for the use of schools, and to apply any funds which may be raised from such lands or from any other quarter to the accomplishment of the grand object for which they are or may be intended. But no lands granted for the use of schools or seminaries of learning shall be sold by authority of this state prior to the year 1820; and the moneys which may be raised out of the sale of any such lands, or otherwise obtained for the purposes aforesaid, shall be and remain a fund for the exclusive purpose of promoting the interest of literature and the sciences, and for the support of seminaries and public schools. The General Assembly shall, from time to time, pass such laws as shall be calculated to encourage intellectual, scientific and agricultural improvements, by allowing rewards and immunities for the promotion and improvement of arts, sciences, commerce, manufacture and natural history; and to countenance and encourage the principles of humanity, honesty, industry, and morality.

SECTION 2. It shall be the duty of the General Assembly, as soon as circumstances will permit, to provide, by law, for a general system of education, ascending in a regular gradation from township schools to a State University, wherein tuition shall be gratis, and equally open to all.

3. High School for Adolescent Boys[1]
✤ Boston School Committee

During the eighteenth and early nineteenth centuries schooling beyond the primary level was provided by private academies. Their exclusive purpose was to prepare boys — girls were not formally educated beyond the elementary level — with enough skill in reading and writing Latin for them to gain admission to a church-related liberal arts college. But with the proliferation of mechanical and business vocations which accompanied industrialization and scientific advances, some cities recognized the need for free public high schools to prepare boys for the new vocations.

The document which follows is an account of the founding of the first American high school. The school opened in Boston in May, 1821, with an enrollment of 176 boys. Two years later, however, 76 pupils had dropped out. The School Committee was alarmed. Some of the teachers already had deviated from the plan in the disposition of the studies and others had even introduced some studies not originally included. The Committee recommended that the school return to its original purpose, with the most useful and practical studies being offered the first year, and that the school's name be changed from the "English Classical School" to the "English High School."

Throughout the nineteenth century, cities and towns which had developed public elementary schools also established public high schools. In time, there were more high schools than private academies. But by 1900 the high school curriculum had become almost wholly college-preparatory in function. ■

---

[1] *Proceedings of the School Committee of the Town of Boston, Respecting an English Classical School.* June 17, 1820, pp. 2–7.

Though the present system of education, and the [generosity] with which it is supported, are highly beneficial and honorable to the town; yet, in the opinion of the Committee, it is susceptible of a greater degree of perfection and usefulness without materially [increasing] the weight of the public burdens. Till recently our system occupied a middle station: it neither commenced with the rudiments of education, nor extended to the higher branches of knowledge. This system was supported by the town at a very great expense, and to be admitted to its advantages, certain preliminary qualifications were required at individual cost, which had the effect of excluding many children of the poor and unfortunate classes of the community from the benefits of a public education. The town saw and felt this inconsistency in the plan, and have removed the defect by providing schools in which the children of the poor can be fitted for admission into the public seminaries.[2]

The Need

The present system, in the opinion of the Committee, requires still farther amendment. The studies that are pursued at the English grammar schools are merely elementary, and more time than is necessary is devoted to their acquisition. A scholar is admitted at seven, and is dismissed at fourteen years of age; thus, seven years are expended in the acquisition of a degree of knowledge, which, with ordinary diligence and a common capacity, may be easily and perfectly acquired in five. If, then, a boy remain the usual term, a large portion of the time will have been idly, or uselessly expended, as he may have learned all that he has been taught long before its expiration. This loss of time occurs at that interesting and critical period of life, when the habits and inclinations are forming by which the future character will be fixed and determined. This evil, therefore, should be removed, by enlarging the present system, not merely that the time now lost may be saved, but that those early habits of industry and application may be acquired, which are so essential in leading to a future life of virtue and usefulness.

Nor are these the only existing evils. The mode of education now adopted, and the branches of knowledge that are taught at our English grammar schools, are not sufficiently extensive, nor otherwise

---

[2] **seminaries**: secondary schools.

calculated to bring the powers of the mind into operation, nor to qualify a youth to fill usefully and respectably many of those stations, both public and private, in which he may be placed. A parent who wishes to give a child an education that shall fit him for active life, and shall serve as a foundation for eminence in his profession, whether mercantile or mechanical, is under the necessity of giving him a different education from any which our public schools can now furnish. Hence many children are separated from their parents and sent to private academies in this vicinity, to acquire that instruction which cannot be obtained at the public seminaries. Thus, many parents, who contribute largely to the support of these institutions, are subjected to heavy expense for the same object, in other towns.

The Organization

The Committee, for these and many other weighty considerations that might be offered, and in order to render the present system of public education more nearly perfect, are of [the] opinion that an additional school is required. They, therefore, recommend the founding of a seminary to be called the English Classical School, and submit the following as a general outline of a plan for its organization and of the course of studies to be pursued.

1st. That the term of time for pursuing the course of studies proposed be three years.
2ndly. That the school be divided into three classes and one year be assigned to the studies of each class.
3dly. That the age of admission be not less than twelve years.
4thly. That the school be for boys exclusively.
5thly. That candidates for admission be proposed on a given day annually; but scholars, with suitable qualifications, may be admitted at any intermediate time to an advanced standing.
6thly. That candidates for admission shall be subject to a strict examination, in such manner as the School Committee may direct, to ascertain their qualifications according to these rules.
7thly. That it be required of every candidate to qualify him for admission, that he be well acquainted with reading, writing, English grammar in all its branches, and arithmetic as far as simple proportion.
8thly. That it be required of the Masters and [assistants], as a

necessary qualification, that they shall have been regularly educated at some university.

The Studies of the first class to be as follows —
    Composition;
    Reading from the most approved authors;
    Exercises in criticism; comprising critical analyses of the language, grammar, and style of the best English authors, their errors and beauties;
    Declamation;
    Geography;
    Arithmetic continued;
    Algebra.

The Studies of the second class —
    Composition;
    Reading;
    Exercises in criticism;   Continued
    Declamation;
    Algebra;
    Ancient and modern history and chronology;
    Logic;
    Geometry;
    Plane Trigonometry and its application to [measuring] of heights and distances;
    Navigation;
    Surveying; . . .
    Forensic Discussions.

The Studies of the third class —
    Composition;
    Exercises in criticism;
    Declamation;
    Mathematics;   Continued
    Logic;
    History; particularly that of the United States;
    Natural Philosophy, including Astronomy;
    Moral and Political Philosophy.

To conduct a seminary of this description, the Committee are of [the] opinion, that one principal master, one sub-master and two [assistants] will be required;

The Principal at a salary of	$1500 per year
Sub-Master	$1200 per year
Two [Assistants], one at $700, one at $600	$1300 per year
	$4000

... The Committee are further of [the] opinion, that the expense which would be incurred by the establishment of such an institution, would be fully justified by its great and manifold advantages. No money can be better expended, than that which is appropriated to the support of public schools. [If anything will preserve tranquillity and order in a community, perpetuate the blessing of society and free government, and promote the happiness and prosperity of a people, it must be the general diffusion of knowledge.] These salutary effects, the Committee conceive, would flow from the institution of this seminary. Its establishment, they think, would [raise the literary and scientific character of the town, would incite our youth to a laudable ambition of distinguishing themselves in the pursuit and acquisition of knowledge, and would give strength and stability to the civil and religious institutions of our country.]

4. A Plan for Improving Female Education[1]
✤ Emma Willard

During the 1700's, a girl's education clearly reflected her family's economic position. Daughters of poor families were taught only the rudiments of reading and writing in the home; wealthier parents either engaged a private tutor or sent their daughters to a dame school or girl's seminary. Thomas Jefferson in 1783 outlined a course of study for his daughter which included music, drawing, dancing, French, English, and letter writing. By the 1790's, private academies began admitting girls; however, girl students were strictly segregated from the boys and were given a less demanding curriculum. With the emergence of the women's-rights movement, and the efforts of such feminist leaders as Emma Willard and Catherine Beecher, equal education for adolescent girls became a lively public issue. The editor

[1] Emma Willard, "A Plan for Improving Female Education," in Anna C. Brackett, ed., *Woman and the Higher Education* (New York: Harper & Brothers, 1893), pp. 12–14, 42–45.

of a Massachusetts newspaper in 1828 still believed that the "most acceptable degree" for a young woman was the "degree of M.R.S."

The following selection is excerpted from a speech by Emma Willard to the New York legislature in 1818 in behalf of public schools for females. Mrs. Willard's Female Seminary, which opened in Troy, New York, in 1821, was one of the first institutions to offer girls an education equal to that for boys. ■

To contemplate the principles which should regulate systems of instruction, and consider how little those principles have been regarded in educating our sex, will show the defects of female education. . . .

Education should seek to bring its subjects to the perfection of their moral, intellectual, and physical nature, in order that they may be of the greatest possible use to themselves and others; or, to use a different expression, that they may be the means of the greatest possible happiness of which they are capable, both as to what they enjoy and what they communicate.

Those youth have the surest chance of enjoying and communicating happiness who are best qualified, both by internal disposition and external habits, to perform with readiness those duties which their future life will most probably give them occasion to practice.

Studies and employments should therefore be selected from one or both of the following considerations: either because they are peculiarly fitted to improve the faculties, or because they are such as the pupil will most probably have occasion to practice in future life.

These are the principles on which systems of male education are founded; but female education has not yet been systematized. Chance and confusion reign here. Not even is youth considered in our sex, as in the other, a season which should be wholly devoted to improvement. Among families so rich as to be entirely above labor, the daughters are hurried through the routine of boarding-school instruction, and at an early period introduced into . . . [society]; and thenceforth their only object is amusement. Mark the different treatment which the sons of these families receive. While their sisters are gliding through the mazes of the midnight dance, they employ the lamp to treasure up for future use the riches of ancient wisdom, or to gather strength and expansion of mind in exploring the wonderful paths of philosophy. When the youth of the two sexes has been spent so differently, is it strange, or is nature in fault, if more mature age has brought such a difference of character that our sex have been considered by the other as the pampered, wayward babies of society, who must have some rattle put into our hands to keep us from doing mischief to ourselves or others? . . .

Proposed Benefits of Girls' Seminaries

1. Females, by having their understandings cultivated, their reasoning powers developed and strengthened, may be expected to act more from the dictates of reason and less from those of fashion and caprice.

2. With minds thus strengthened, they would be taught systems of morality, enforced by the sanctions of religion; and they might be expected to acquire juster and more enlarged views of their duty, and stronger and higher motives to its performance.

3. This plan of education offers all that can be done to preserve female youth from a contempt of useful labor. The pupils would become accustomed to it, in conjunction with the high objects of literature and the elegant pursuits of the fine arts; and it is to be hoped that both from habit and association they might in future life regard it as respectable.

To this it may be added that if housewifery could be raised to a regular art, and taught upon philosophical principles, it would become a higher and more interesting occupation; and ladies of fortune, like wealthy agriculturists, might find that to regulate their business was an agreeable employment.

4. The pupils might be expected to acquire a taste for moral and intellectual pleasures which would buoy them above a passion for show and parade, and which would make them seek to gratify the natural love of superiority by endeavoring to excel others in intrinsic merit rather than in the extrinsic frivolities of dress, furniture, and equipage.

5. By being enlightened in moral philosophy, and in that which teaches the operations of the mind, females would be enabled to perceive the nature and extent of that influence which they possess over their children, and the obligation which this lays them under to watch the formation of their characters with unceasing vigilance, to become their instructors, to devise plans for their improvement, to weed out the vices of their minds, and to implant and foster the virtues. And surely there is that in the maternal bosom which, when its pleadings shall be aided by education, will overcome the seductions

of wealth and fashion, and will lead the mother to seek her happiness in communing with her children, and promoting their welfare. . . .

In calling on my patriotic countrymen to effect so noble an object, the consideration of national glory should not be overlooked. Ages have rolled away; barbarians have trodden the weaker sex beneath their feet; tyrants have robbed us of the present light of heaven, and fain would take its future. Nations calling themselves polite have made us the fancied idols of a ridiculous worship, and we have repaid them with ruin for their folly. But where is that wise and heroic country which has considered that our rights are sacred, though we cannot defend them? that, though a weaker, we are an essential part of the body politic, whose corruption or improvement must affect the whole? and which, having thus considered, has sought to give us by education that rank in the scale of being to which our importance entitles us?

5. A School for Delinquent Youth[1]
✣ *Society for the Reformation of Juvenile Delinquents*

The nineteenth century saw the rise of formal institutions of education as panaceas for America's social ills. The assumption was emerging that the refugee and the orphan could best be aided and the young delinquent could be most effectively reformed by proper education. The House of Refuge, instituted in 1824 by the Society for the Reformation of Juvenile Delinquents in the City of New York, illustrates the growing confidence in formal education. It also represents a national trend in cities to deal with the human casualties the city itself was creating. The following is a report made in 1826 to the state legislature on the New York City House of Refuge and its educational functions. ∎

Every person that frequents the out-streets of this city, must be forcibly struck with the ragged and uncleanly appearance, the vile language, and the idle and miserable habits of great numbers of chil-

[1] Grace Abbott, ed., *The Child and the State*, II (Chicago: The University of Chicago Press, 1938), pp. 347, 348–349, 351–353, 356. Reprinted by permission of the American Public Health Association.

dren, most of whom are of an age suitable for schools, or for some useful employment. The parents of these children, are, in all probability, too poor, or too degenerate, to provide them with clothing fit for them to be seen in at school; and know not where to place them in order that they may find employment, or be better cared for. . . .

The design of the proposed institution is, to furnish, in the first place, an asylum in which boys under a certain age, who become subject to the notice of our police, either as vagrants, or houseless, or charged with petty crimes, may be received, judiciously classed according to their degree of depravity or innocence, put to work at such employments as will tend to encourage industry and ingenuity, taught reading, writing, and arithmetic, and most carefully instructed in the nature of their moral and religious obligations; while at the same time, they are subjected to a course of treatment, that will afford a prompt and energetic corrective of their vicious [tendencies], and hold out every possible inducement to reformation and good conduct. . . .

The following list is extracted from the four hundred and fifty cases of Juvenile Offenses, furnished by the District Attorney, from the Records of the Police Office, for 1822.

> David B. aged 12, brought up by the [night watchman], charged with stealing, vagrant thief; 6 months Penitentiary. . . .
> George D. aged 14, father dead, mother in Baltimore, picks up chips, begs for victuals, and steals, vagrant thief; 6 months Penitentiary.
> Francis J. aged 17, has no money, no clothes, no residence; 4 months Penitentiary.
> Jane Ann S. aged 14, has been twice in Bridewell; 6 months Penitentiary.
> Alfred C. aged 13, was brought up, having been found sleeping in some shavings, destitute, and no home; 6 months Penitentiary. . . .
> William S. aged 11, his father turned him out of the house, was found sleeping in a boat at night; 6 months Penitentiary. . . .
> John H. aged 13, was found at night sleeping on the side-walk, no parents; 6 months Penitentiary.

The House Is Founded

On the first day of January last [1825], the board met and opened the Institution, in presence of a considerable concourse of citizens . . . who assembled to witness the ceremony of the introduction of a number of juvenile convicts, the first in this city, if not in this country, into a place exclusively intended for their reformation and instruction. The ceremony was interesting in the highest degree. Nine of those poor outcasts from society, three boys and six girls, clothed in rags, with squalid countenances, were brought in from the Police Office, and placed before the audience. An address appropriate to so novel an occasion was made by a member of the board, and not an individual, it may safely be affirmed, was present, whose warmest feelings did not vibrate in unison with the philanthropic views which led to the foundation of this House of Refuge. . . .

The Promotion of Useful Skills

The employment of the girls, in addition to the needful domestic occupations, has been chiefly the plaiting of grass[2]; and although they have not yet advanced sufficiently to render their skill of much [financial] advantage, many of them have made attainments in this branch, which justify the belief that it may become a source of profit to the Institution, and the means of honest support to them when discharged.

The most considerable occupation of the boys, has been the clearing up of the premises, by the removal and disposal of the lumber, sheds, etc., clearing and cultivating a small garden, and more especially in waiting upon, and assisting the masons and carpenters that have been engaged in various repairs, elevating the wall, and erecting a new building within the enclosure. . . .

Devotion to Mental Improvement

About two hours in the day, one in the morning and one in the evening, are devoted to mental improvement. During the first hour, they are occupied in learning to spell, read, write, and cipher, and in this exercise the system of mutual instruction is followed, and they are divided into classes. . . .

On that system the
1st Class, learn the alphabet.
2nd Class, words and syllables of two letters.
3rd Class, words and syllables of three and four letters.
4th Class, words and sentences from Scripture of five and six letters.
5th Class, words and sentences from Scripture of two syllables.
6th Class, words and sentences from Scripture of three syllables.
7th Class, words and sentences from Scripture of four syllables.
8th Class includes the best readers, who spell and write words, with

---

[2] **plaiting of grass:** the braiding of reeds, such as bamboo or rattan, used chiefly for wickerwork.

their meanings attached, and read the Old and New Testaments. Arithmetic, as far as compound division. . . .

Rules and Regulations

[Among the rules and regulations adopted by the Society for the government of the House of Refuge are the following:]

The introduction of labor into the House of Refuge will be regarded principally with reference to the moral benefits, and not merely to the profits, to be derived from it.

Preference will be given to those trades, the knowledge of which may enable the delinquents to earn their subsistence, on their discharge from the House.

Food. — The children shall be fed with a sufficient quantity of coarse, but wholesome food, and in conformity with a dietary to be established by the Acting Committee. The greatest economy and plainness shall be used in furnishing food for the children. . . .

Clothing. — The children shall be clothed in coarse, but comfortable apparel, of the cheapest and most durable kind. The cloth to be of a uniform color, and the clothes of the same cut or fashion. All the clothes, garments, and shoes must, if practicable, be made on the premises, and by the children.

Kinds of punishments that may be used in the House of Refuge. — (1) Privation of play and exercise; (2) sent to bed supperless at sunset; (3) bread and water, for breakfast, dinner, and supper; (4) [thin, watery porridge] without salt, for breakfast, dinner, and supper; (5) . . . bitter herb tea, for breakfast, dinner, and supper; (6) confinement in solitary cells; (7) corporal [punishment], if absolutely necessary; (8) fetters and handcuffs, only in extreme cases.

6. Political Pressure for Common Schools[1]

✤ Working Men of Pennsylvania

The election of Andrew Jackson to the presidency was evidence of the rise of the workingman to a position of political power.

[1] "Address to the City and County Convention to the Working Men of the State" in John R. Commons *et al.* (eds.), *A Documentary History of American Industrial Society,* Vol. V [1910] (New York: Russell & Russell, 1958), pp. 114–115, 116–117. Reprinted by permission.

By 1830 numerous workingmen's associations had been formed in cities like New York, Boston, and Philadelphia. These organizations railed against creeping monopolies among industries and banks — which were seen as engines of corporate wealth and special privilege. In the same spirit, they decried the existing hodgepodge of "aristocratic" educational institutions — charity schools, church schools, private academies, and liberal arts colleges.

[*To realize the promises of democracy for their sons and daughters, these workingmen's groups lobbied impressively for a system of free, universal, public common schools.] Such schools, they argued, would lay the "axe of knowledge . . . at the root of aristocracy," and thus break up the "monopoly of talent." Such schools, in democratizing the "means of knowledge," would support equality of opportunity. To account for the rise and growth of common schools in America, one must note the importance of action by workingmen's associations, like the one cited below from Pennsylvania in 1830.* ■

FELLOW-CITIZENS: In offering to your consideration a subject of such importance, we shall state the ground which has led us to a separation from the two great political parties which have heretofore misruled and misrepresented the people. . . .

In assuming a title, our object is not to draw another useless line of distinction between our fellow-citizens for mere electioneering purposes — it is that all thinking as we do may rally under one banner, and by a unity in action produce the desired end.

Education for a Stable Republic

The main pillar of our system is general education; for it is an axiom no longer controverted, that the stability of a republic depends mainly upon the intelligence of its citizens — that in proportion as they become wise they become virtuous and happy — that the period for forming a good and useful citizen is in youth, ere ignorance and crime have deluded the mind by a lengthened dominion over it, and therefore that an early and suitable education for each child is of primary importance in maintaining the public [prosperity].

It is now forty years since the adoption of the constitution of Pennsylvania, and although that [document] strongly recommends that provision be made for the education of our youth at the public expense, yet during that long period, has the . . . patriotic obligation been disregarded by our legislative authority, and thousands are now suffering the consequences of this disregard to the public welfare on the part of our rulers.

It is true, that some attempts have been made to remedy the omission in two or three districts of the state, but they have proved ineffectual. The very spirit in which these provisions have been made not only defeats the object intended, but tends also to draw still broader the line of distinction between the rich and the poor. All who receive the limited knowledge imparted by the present system of public education are looked upon as paupers, drawing from a fount which they have in no wise contributed towards creating. . . .

It is in vain for the opponents of equal education to assert that the poor, if left to themselves, will use their exertions to educate their children, and that the expenses saved them by its being accomplished by public means, will be expended by the parent on less important subjects; for it is a lamentable fact, that persons destitute of education are ignorant of the loss they sustain, and hence, fail to avert the evil from their offspring. The ignorance of the parent generally extends to his children's children, while the blessings of a liberal education are handed down from father to son as a legacy which poverty cannot impoverish.

Education for Equality

We confidently anticipate the cordial co-operation of our brethren throughout the state in favor of this great object, so essential to our happiness as freemen. All must be aware of the necessity of the prompt interference of the people in behalf of those cardinal principles of republican liberty which were declared in '76, and which can only be sustained by the adoption of an ample system of public instruction, calculated to impart equality as well as mental culture — the establishment of institutions where the children of the poor and the rich may meet at that period of life, when the pomp and circumstance of wealth have not engendered pride; when the only distinction known, will be the celebrity each may acquire by their acts of good fellowship; when the best opportunity is afforded for forming associations that will endure through life, and where the [disgrace] attending the present system will not attach. The objection that the children of the wealthy will not be sent to these schools, is one of minor importance. Our main object is to secure the benefits of education for those who would otherwise be destitute, and to place them mentally on a level with the most favored in the world's gifts. As poverty is not a crime, neither is wealth a virtue. Why then so much anxiety to be associated with a particular portion of our citizens merely on account of their wealth? They form but a small portion of the entire population of our country, and as its safety must depend upon the majority, 'tis there our duty and our exertions should be directed.

It has been remarked, and with much plausibility, that if common schools were established, and provided with suitable instructors in the various departments of a thorough education, the numbers attending "colleges" would be much diminished. This position we admit and cheerfully assent to. Our object is not to raise the hue and cry against colleges — it is not to drag down and chain the intellect of others to the common extent of learning by endeavoring to enlist the public voice against them, but it is to make each avenue of learning the certain pathway to the entire field of science.

Let us unite then, fellow citizens, on a measure fraught with such momentous consequences — a measure involving the happiness or misery of posterity. We are all equally interested in preventing crime by contributing to the means of knowledge and virtue. Consider the responsibility which rests upon us as parents and citizens of a free state. We should constantly bear in mind that the prosperity and happiness of our beloved country essentially depend on the speedy adoption of an equal and republican system of mental instruction.

VI. Christianizing the Common School

The Jeffersonian ideal of a free, public, common school system, which men like Horace Mann worked to make a reality, was eventually accepted — with modifications — by its leading opponents. Members of the propertied class became convinced of its worth on economic grounds; eventually they came to believe that an increase in national wealth would accompany increased education for the masses. [The Protestant churches saw the common school as an agency to encourage the values of Protestantism — and to guard against the spread of Catholicism.] Many church leaders believed that the constitutional doctrine of church-state separation would not be violated if public schools taught the values of non-denominational Protestant Christianity. Such leaders tended to equate Protestantism with Americanism. For decades these values were taught through the McGuffey readers. When compulsory attendance laws eventually brought large numbers of Irish Catholic children into the common schools, Americans began to realize the extent to which the wall of separation between church and state had been breached. Said one Catholic spokesman, "The Catholic Church tells her children that they must be taught by authority. The sects say, read the Bible, judge for yourselves. The Bible is read in the public schools. The children are allowed to judge for themselves. The Protestant principle is therefore acted upon, silently inculcated, and the schools are sectarian."

Children who refused to participate in school-sponsored religious exercises were often whipped. Soon parents' and citizens' organizations called upon the courts to rule on the legality of religious exercises.

Of the nineteenth century textbooks, David B. Tyack says in Turning Points in American Educational History, ". . . . increasingly in the latter half-century — and usually unconsciously and by indirection — Americanism was defined in such a way that it could fit only the white, middle-class, Protestant, native-born citizen. Through uncomplimentary stereotypes, the Negro, the Catholic, the Jew, and foreigners of many nations were read out of the clan." ■

1. The Schoolchild's "Bible"

✣ William Holmes McGuffey

If the children of Irish and German immigrants, as well as those of native-born settlers, were socialized into Protestant America, it was due in no small part to schoolbooks such as those written by William Holmes McGuffey. McGuffey's readers were graded for vocabulary and level of comprehension: First Reader, Second Reader, and so on. Approximately 122 million copies of these books were sold between 1836 and 1922; they formed the backbone of the curriculum of the common school.
[The McGuffey readers inculcated the basic ideals of Protestantism and a politically conservative view of American government.] The following pieces — strongly moralistic in nature — are taken from the Third, Fourth, and the Fifth Readers. Notice how the values of hard work, honesty, individualism, thrift, and obedience permeate the teachings. ■

A. ALL MUST WORK[1]

The Child

1. Stop, little stream, and tell me why
    Thou art running on so fast,
   Forever gliding swiftly by,
    And yet art never past!

2. Thou must be very happy here,
    With nothing else to do,
   But running by these mossy banks,
    Beneath the greenwood, too.

3. The pretty robin sings to thee
    His cheerful morning song;
   Amid the leaves the squirrel peeps,
    And frolics all day long.

---

[1] William Holmes McGuffey, *New Third Eclectic Reader* (Cincinnati: Wilson, Hinkle & Co., 1865, pp. 165–167.

The Stream

4. 'Tis true, I've squirrels, birds, and flowers,
     To cheer me on my way;
   And very pleasant is my lot,
     But still I must not stay.

5. Like truth, I have my work to do,
     My errand to fulfill;
   I cool the weary traveler's lips,
     And help the sea to fill.

6. If I should stop, and idly lie
     Upon my pebbly bed,
   Soon all my freshness would be gone,
     My verdant banks be dead.

7. Our heavenly Father gives to all
     His blessings most profuse;
   And not the least, in wisdom gives
     The kindly law of use.

8. So, little child, your duty do
     In cheerfulness all day;
   And you, like me, shall soon be blest
     With flowers upon your way.

B. THE BIBLE[2]

Behold the book whose leaves display
The truth, the life, the light, the way.
The mines of earth no treasures give
  That could this volume buy:
In teaching me the way to live,
  It teaches how to die.

---

[2] William Holmes McGuffey, *New Fourth Eclectic Reader* (Cincinnati: Wilson, Hinkle & Co., 1866), p. 60.

C. RESPECT FOR THE SABBATH REWARDED[3]

1. In the city of Bath, not many years since, lived a barber, who made a practice of following his ordinary occupation on the Lord's day. As he was pursuing his morning's employment, he happened to look into some place of worship, just as the minister was giving out his text, "Remember the Sabbath-day, to keep it holy." He listened long enough to be convinced that he was constantly breaking the laws of God and man, by shaving and dressing his customers on the Lord's day. He became uneasy, and went with a heavy heart to his Sabbath task.

2. At length he took courage, and opened his mind to his minister, who advised him to give up Sabbath dressing, and worship God. He replied, that beggary would be the consequence. He had a flourishing trade, but it would almost all be lost. At length, after many a sleepless night spent in weeping and praying, he was determined to cast all his care upon God, as the more he reflected, the more his duty became apparent.

3. He discontinued Sabbath dressing, went constantly and early to the public services of religion, and soon enjoyed that satisfaction of mind which is one of the rewards of doing our duty, and that peace [of God] which the world can neither give nor take away. The consequences he foresaw, actually followed. His genteel customers left him, and he was nicknamed a Puritan, or Methodist. He was obliged to give up his fashionable shop, and, in the course of years, became so reduced, as to take a cellar under the old market-house, and shave the common people.

4. One Saturday evening, between light and dark, a stranger from one of the coaches, asking for a barber, was directed by the [stableman] to the cellar opposite. Coming in hastily, he requested to be shaved quickly, while they changed horses, *as he did not like to violate the Sabbath*. This was touching the barber on a tender chord. He burst into tears, asked the stranger to lend him a half-penny to buy a candle, as it was not light enough to shave him with safety. He did so, revolving in his mind the extreme poverty to which the poor man must be reduced.

5. When shaved, he said, "There must be something extraordinary

---

[3] William Holmes McGuffey, *New Fifth Eclectic Reader* (Cincinnati: Wilson, Hinkle and Co., 1866) pp. 105–107.

in your history, which I have not now time to hear. Here is half a crown for you. When I return, I will call and investigate your case. What is your name?" "William Reed," said the astonished barber. "William Reed!" echoed the stranger: "William Reed! by your dialect you are from the West." "Yes, sir, from Kingston, near Taunton." "William Reed, from Kingston, near Taunton! What was your father's name?" "Thomas." "Had he any brother?" "Yes, sir; one after whom I was named; but he went to the Indies, and, as we never heard from him we supposed him to be dead."

6. "Come along, follow me," said the stranger, "I am going to see a person who says *his* name is William Reed, of Kingston, near Taunton. Come and confront him. If you prove to be indeed he who you say you are, I have glorious news for you. Your uncle is dead, and has left an immense fortune, which I will put you in possession of, when all legal doubts are removed."

7. They went by the coach; saw the pretended William Reed, and proved him to be an impostor. The stranger, who was a pious attorney, was soon legally satisfied of the barber's identity, and told him that he had advertised him in vain. Providence had now thrown him in his way in a most extraordinary manner, and he had great pleasure in transferring a great many thousand pounds to a worthy man, the rightful heir of the property. Thus was man's extremity, God's opportunity. Had the poor barber possessed one *half-penny*, or even had credit for a *candle*, he might have remained unknown for years; but he trusted God, who never said, "Seek ye my face" in vain.

he still gets rewarded with money.

2. Religious Exercises Challenged

The ethnic, cultural, and religious diversity becoming more apparent among the American people during the nineteenth century was reflected in the common schools. In cities like Boston, New York, and Philadelphia, Catholic parents objected to the common inclusion of Protestant teachings in the public schools. This controversy often erupted into riots. Catholic seminaries were burned and entire blocks of Irish homes were destroyed. Deaths were frequent.

Ethnic and religious minorities sometimes sought redress of their grievances in the courts. In the Cincinnati common schools,

Bible reading had been a regular exercise since 1829. When the Board of Education resolved in 1869 to discontinue religious instruction, a number of citizens complained to the court. The first selection below is taken from the decision of the Superior Court of Cincinnati which ruled in favor of continuing Bible readings. Although the decision was later overruled, it nevertheless represents a widely-held viewpoint of the times. The second selection by Reverend Henry Ward Beecher gives opposing arguments in the national controversy. ■

A. THE COMMON SCHOOL MAY CONTINUE BIBLE READINGS[1]

✣ Minor v. Board of Education of Cincinnati

... What, then, does our present Constitution prescribe? By sec. 7, art. 1, it is ordained that "Religion, morality, and knowledge being essential to good government, it shall be the duty of the General Assembly to pass suitable laws to protect all religious denominations in the peaceable enjoyment of their own mode of public worship, and to encourage schools and the means of instruction." The section commences with the assertion that "all men have a natural and [undeniable] right to worship Almighty God according to the dictates of their own conscience. No persons shall be compelled to, erect or support any place of worship, or maintain any form of worship, and no preference shall be given by law to any religious society, nor shall any interference with the rights of conscience be permitted...."

Now it will be admitted that no preference can be given to religious sects, as such, as difference of opinion upon religious subjects is not only tolerated, but the right to enjoy it is given to its fullest extent. There is a manifest distinction, however, between religion and religious denominations, as they present all shades of theoretic as well as practical belief. Hence it is we may recur to the clause so prominently presented in the section of our Bill of Rights that secures to all the worship of Almighty God, as the exponent of what we may rationally conclude the founders of the Constitution intended by the general term religion....

---

[1] Opinion of Judge Storer, published in *The Bible in the Common Schools* (Cincinnati: Robert Clarke & Co., 1870), pp. 376, 381, 382, 385.

A Common Unity of Man

The whole argument that seems to us reaches the real question before us is predicated upon the supposition that the Bible is a volume whose teachings lead to sectarianism, and which ought not, therefore, to remain in the schools.

We do not admit the assertion, either in whole or in part. What we understand by sectarianism is the work of man, not of the Almighty. We are taught in the Scriptures that we are all the children of a common Parent, who is our Father and our Friend; that we are all of the same blood, a common unity pervading the race. Such, however, is not the human lesson. Learned men are not satisfied with the plain statement of revelation. They have divided the human family into distinct parts, giving to each a separate origin. We learn from the Bible to forgive injuries, to deal justly, to elevate our conceptions above the objects that surround us, and feel we were born to be immortal. Not so are we thoroughly taught by the profoundest system of human philosophy....

It is urged, however, that the conscience of the Catholic parent cannot permit the ordinary version to be read as an exercise, as no religious teaching is permitted by his church, unless it is directed by the clergy or authorized by the church itself, and it is, therefore, offensive to the moral sense of those who are compelled to listen when any portion of the Bible is read; but the rule has long since been abolished requiring children to be present, or to read from the version now in use, if it should be the expressed wish of the parents first communicated to the teachers.

The reason of the objection, then, would seem to have ceased. More than this, it is in evidence before us that our Catholic friends have their own separate schools, and very few of their children attend the common schools, while in one of these schools the Douay translation of the Bible is read as a daily exercise....

Nor do we think that the mere reading of the Scriptures without note or comment, and in detached sentences, can be deemed an act of worship, in its commonly received definition. The lessons selected are, in all probability, those which elevate the mind and soften the heart — an exercise not only proper, but desirable to calm the temper of children, while it impresses the truth of personal responsibility for good or evil conduct.... No prayer is required of the teacher or the scholar, though the simple and beautiful [Lord's Prayer] would not, we believe, be out of place.

If, then, "no religious test," to use the language of the Bill of Rights, is required of teacher or scholar, if no act of worship, in a sectarian sense, is performed, if no sectarian or denominational teaching is introduced, and even the possibility of either is prevented by the resolution long since [made official], that those who desire it may be exempted from the general rule, we cannot see how the defendants can justify the exclusion from the schools of what has been permitted there for nearly half a century without rebuke.

B. THE COMMON SCHOOL MUST PROMOTE NATIONAL UNITY[2]

✦ *Rev. Henry Ward Beecher*

I mention next, the ministration of the free common school, as vital to our hope as a great united republic covering a whole continent....

These schools should not only be free and common, but they should be *unsectarian*. If it be needful that the teaching of technical religion should be excluded from our common schools for the sake of maintaining their universality, I vote to exclude it. If it be needful that the Bible should not be read in the common schools in order to maintain their universality, their freedom, and their commonness, I should vote not to read it. Because I disesteem it? I, the son of a Puritan, and a Puritan myself . . . — *I disesteem the Bible?* Most venerable is it of all the memorials that have come down through all time to our day. More joy is in it for the common people, more comfort has it for the afflicted, than any other book.... It is the common people's book; and there is no class of people that need to read it so much as the children of the poor and the needy.... And yet, I would not force it upon any.... It was because they would not suffer others to impose their faith upon them that our fathers came hither; and shall we, now that the power is with us, take the ground that we may impose our faith upon those who do not believe as we do, because they are in the minority? Shall we, after a hundred years, with all the growing light and knowledge which have come down to

---

[2] Henry Ward Beecher, ed., *The Bible in the Public Schools* (New York: J. W. Schermerhorn & Co., 1870), pp. 3, 8–10.

us on this subject, commit the fatal blunder that sent the Pilgrims across the sea in winter, to lay the foundations of this noble republic? We believe in the freedom of religion, and do not believe in forcing one man's faith upon another man. And this being so, how can you organize the common school, which is supported by the public funds, in such a way as to force the Bible on the Jews, who do not believe in the New Testament, or upon sceptical men who do not believe in either the Old Testament or the New? . . . To say that a Christian nation has a right to have Christianity taught in the schools, even if it be distasteful to a minority, is to put forth a formula for arrogant sects as soon as they are in the majority. Put the term Catholic in the place of the word Christian in the foregoing sentence, and how would the logic suit a Protestant?

VII. Character and Conduct of the Common School

A wide gap existed between the goals envisioned for the common school and the way most common schools functioned. This was due in large part to inadequate financial support. Many people of wealth used their political influence to keep school taxes low. The advocates of private schools used the double tax argument to oppose large appropriations. The exorbitant costs of the Civil War and the relatively low priority placed by most Americans on the establishment of common schools also helped create the vast difference between the ideal and the reality. Meager financial support attracted poorly qualified teachers, provided inadequate school buildings and supplies, and necessarily reduced the school's overall educational effectiveness. ■

1. Teacher Training[1]

✣ Michigan Teachers' Institute

Since liberal arts colleges were not interested in preparing teachers for the common school, such educational leaders as James G. Carter of Massachusetts began to develop state-supported normal schools for the express purpose of teacher preparation. The educational theory upon which normal schools were founded was simple yet to the point. Said Carter, "Though a teacher cannot communicate more knowledge than he possesses, yet he may possess much and still be able to impart but little." Normal schools were conceived by their sponsors as an agency for scientifically studying the processes of teaching and learning, much as the new agricultural and mechanical colleges studied the processes of farming. By 1860 twelve public normal schools had been established in states from Massachusetts to Illinois.

[1] Harry A. Kersey, "Michigan Teachers' Institutes in the Mid-Nineteenth Century: A Representative Document," in *History of Education Quarterly*, V (March 1965), pp. 48–51. Reprinted by permission.

Before 1885, however, most common school teachers never entered the doors of a normal school. Two years at such a school was considered much too long and too expensive to prepare a fourteen- to eighteen-year-old girl to be a common school teacher. The conventional wisdom held that a young woman, raised to be a mother and housewife, was already by her rearing prepared politically and morally to teach. It was anticipated that she would work only for a few years until she married and became a homemaker.

So many young ladies became teachers in the nineteenth century that teaching was dubbed the "petticoat profession." Their preparation typically consisted of a two-week Teachers' Institute upon graduation from a public common school. More than 1200 teachers were trained for the common schools of Michigan in 1859 in such institutes as the one described below. ■

Record of Proceedings of the State Teachers' Institute at Charlotte

Monday evening. The introductory lecture was delivered at the Methodist Church by J. M. Gregory, Supt. of Public Instruction. *Subject*: The special education of teachers, its necessity and value.

Tuesday, Sept. 20

Morning

8:45. The institute met at the lower hall of the Charlotte Academy. Reading of Scripture, Prayer, and singing.

Enrolling names of members.

9:15. Prof. Sill introduced the subject of Grammar, showing that the study of grammar should begin with the *sentence* rather than with the *word*, because in the English language the class to which a word belongs cannot be invariably determined without first knowing its office in the sentence.

Redefined the sentence and its principal parts, and classified sentences into Dependent and Independent.

10:15. Mr. Gregory introduced the subject of Reading remarking upon its importance as a common school study.

Reading is of two kinds, *silent* and *spoken*.

In silent reading, the book or its author speaks to the reader; in the second kind of reading, the reader gives voice to the book — talks for the author.

The first should always precede the second, since we must first understand a passage before we can properly give utterance to it.

The lecturer proceeded to exhibit and classify the elementary sounds of the language, and to exercise the class in their utterance, saying that a distinct articulation is an essential requisite for good elocutionary reading.

11:15. Prof. Sill resumed the subject of the sentence, giving the classification of sentences into Transitive, Intransitive and Neuter, and describing, fully, each class.

Afternoon
1:30. Elocution with exercises in articulation.
2:15. Grammar. The *phrase* described. The Word, the third and last element of language, was then taken up and the various classes of words were shown. The noun was discussed.
3:15. Education as a science was taken up and its discussion begun with a division into the two departments of training, and teaching. The duty of teachers to train the physical powers, and care for the health of their pupils was strongly enforced.
4:15. Prof. Sill continued grammar, the pronouns were examined.

Evening
Lecture at the Methodist Church, "Education life long."

It was rainy, but a good audience gathered.

Seventy six names were enrolled this first day and a high degree of interest was shown at the outset.

* * * * *

Saturday, Sept. 24

Morning
8:45. Reading Scripture, Prayer and Singing.
9:15. Hon. J. M. Gregory — Education and discipline — mode of teaching the young — explanation of the word system — the teacher should be a model of order himself — should guard against the least appearance of disorder as the great enemy of the school — advice to teachers as to the course to be pursued in regard to the introduction in their teaching, of the methods of which they have heard something in this Institute — Grammar for instance — Concluding remarks —

Teacher Training

10:15. Grammar Prof. Sill. Recapitulation in brief with concluding remarks.
11:15. Geography exercise and Reading exercise conducted by Messres (sic) Mood and Inghram.

Afternoon
Consumed in organizing a County Teachers' Association.

* * * * *

Wednesday, Sept. 28

Morning
Singing and read Scripture and Prayer — Pres. Fairfield.
9:30. Arithmetic — Multiple least common fractions — def. modes of teaching — Pres. Fairfield.
10:15. Currents of the Seas — D. P. Mayhew.
11:15. Fractions —

Afternoon
Institute did not assemble in afternoon on acct. of the County Fair — and for the purpose of listening of the address before the Ag[ricultural] Society by Pres. Fairfield of Olivet.

* * * * *

Friday, Sept. 30th

Morning
8:45. Devotional Exercises by Pres. Fairfield.
9:15. Arithmetic — Analysis showing methods of and proportion modes of statement Pres. Fairfield.
10:15. How to teach Geography — Chart of Definitions — and how to use it (Mayhew).
11:15. Roots — Square and Cube.

Afternoon
1:30. Meridians and Parallels — Zones, what determines them, Cause of Change of seasons. . . .
2:15. Pres. Fairfield lectured upon Responsibilities and Dignity of Teachers' Profession.
3:15. How to teach Socal (sic) Geography. How to teach Descriptive by Topics (Mayhew).

Evening
Social Gathering and Public Meeting — Interesting.

2. The Teacher at Work[1]

✤ D. S. Domer

The following account of teaching in the common school was given by a beginning teacher in 1888. D. S. Domer began his career in a small Pennsylvania town where "grades," "method," and "psychological teaching" were unknown. Without benefit of normal school training, Domer relied upon methods which had been used for the past forty years and by which he had been taught. His description also sheds light on the cultural values underlying instruction in the one-room country school. ■

Getting my first school proved to be an experience never to be forgotten. After receiving a certificate, one looked for a school — unless it had been promised earlier on condition of passing. I had no such promise, but the County Superintendent suggested several places to look up. I selected one and notified the Board I would present myself.

A word on the administration of common schools may be useful. Lancaster County had township organization. The township I first taught in had forty districts, all under the direction of six school trustees, chosen annually. Each trustee had an area, or number of schools under his oversight, and he reported to the Board each month. At such meetings the trustees also examined teachers' reports and paid their salaries. The Board could be quite autocratic, might disregard even the suggestions of the County Superintendent, for he himself held office at their pleasure.

The Board I approached wanted a "man" teacher. They met on a Saturday in August (1888), twenty days before the beginning of school, to hire the teacher. These six representatives of the community were indeed an august body — but their names are all forgotten now, save those of the president and one other. It was with some trepidation that I came before this body, for they met in the back end of a barroom in the village of Schoeneck. As I entered the room, I met the gaze, the inspection, and then the quiz of these patriarchs of education.

I had applied in writing for a school a short way from the village,

---

[1] Thomas Woody, "Country Schoolmaster of Long Ago," in *History of Education Journal*, 5, Winter, 1954, pp. 41-53. Copyright owner unknown.

and the application was filed here with [the] others. When I was seated at one end of the long table around which the Board sat, I was asked by the chairman whether I believed in the "three R's"; but he, to relieve me of any fear, at once assured me they stood for "Radcliffe's Ready Relief." Of course, they had already read the applications and had really decided by a previous vote to let me have the school at the munificent salary of $28.00 a month for a term of six months. I was to be my own janitor, sweep out, and keep fires going. . . .

I went to the schoolhouse alone the Saturday before school began. The building, located on an acre for a playground, was not significantly different from the one where I first went to school. It was of brick, dirt cheap. . . . The inside was as dull as a leaden sky in December, save as it was sometimes brightened by leaves in autumn, or some pictures [that] could be borrowed from the pupils' homes. The desks were a little better than I had first used at school, but single seats had not yet appeared. The double-seated desks were a source of trouble: they induced whispering, idle mischief, neglect and dishonesty in studies; books got mixed up, articles were stolen, and property destroyed. I counted the seats, made up a tentative program, set the clock, put shoe mats in place, had two water buckets (one for waste, for there was no drain) and two tin cups ready for thirsty children. Sanitary rules were then unknown in country districts, and often in small towns, too. Water was brought from the nearest farmer's well. With 60 children, a bucket full would not last long. Sometimes trustees paid a monthly tax to the farmer for the water used at school. Toilets were outdoors, and exposed to public view. A partition separated boys and girls. Obscenity was bound to result from such conditions. More than one problem arose from this source to confront me in my early teaching.

School Begins

Monday, the first day of school, came. It was with no little emotion that I faced a small army of motley-dressed boys and girls. They had arranged themselves in two rows of about equal length along the pathway, and I had to run the gauntlet of inspection. No sooner was the door opened than a rush for seats was made; for it was customary there, that the first arrivals should have the choice of seats. One can imagine the tumult: about 60 pupils, six to twenty, dashing through the door before I could say "Stop!" Such a scramble meant that half the seats were unsuitable to those who first claimed them, so teacher's job, and a lot of trouble it was, too, loomed before him. But with a show of being master, after an hour's work the "seating" of the school was completed, the small ones up front, the rest, according to size, reaching back to the rear.

Classifying pupils was the next task that taxed my ingenuity. I had them write their names, if they could, and the Reader they were "in" at the previous school term. This showed me at once who were the writers. Some who could not write, printed their names. The beginners were interviewed personally, to get their names. These would be the A B C class. Placing the others was more difficult. Some brought an advanced Reader, but could not read it at all, when put to the test. The promotions and demotions made some parents glad and others mad; mothers came and wanted their children changed. I made enemies the first day. I was [firm]; I was running the school, and I would not change pupils unless I was convinced they could do the work that was assigned them. I handled some cases by calling the pupils to read in the presence of their parents, who could then see and hear [that] the child could not read, or do the other work of the class they had wanted to enter. The oldest pupils, whose records I could learn from the register left by my predecessor, I simply directed to the program placed earlier on the blackboard.

The program went like this: I opened with Bible reading, repeating the Lord's Prayer, and singing a familiar song. Then came, first, the beginners; then arithmetic; reading classes; grammar, elementary and advanced; geography; history; physiology; and finally three or four spelling classes. The beginners recited three or four times a day; altogether thirty-three classes were heard in about 310 minutes, an average of less than ten minutes to each.

Rules, all of which I thought very necessary at the time, were posted in a conspicuous place for the observation of all. Among them were: no whispering, sharpening pencils, throwing stones, name-calling. They were to raise their hands when anything was wanted; they were to stand, pass, and be seated, as I counted one, two, three, or tapped a small bell. . . .

Discipline Requires Physical Strength

Discipline, when I began teaching, depended more on physical strength, the ability and the will to give punishment, than any other thing. One of the first questions I was asked upon applying for the school, was whether I believed in "licking," and whether I was afraid of the boys in school. A negative answer to the first question, or an affirmative answer to the second, would have ended my career then and there. ...

[M]uch of my time was spent showing boys, and girls too, how strong I was, and what feats of strength I could perform. It was a day of weight-lifting. I became adept at lifting with my arms and gripping with teeth and hands. It was no small trick to place a twenty-five pound bag of shot on my left shoulder, and then reach my right hand over my head and lift the weight single handed to the right shoulder. I moved the big stove around the school room, held pupils in or out of the room by bracing myself against them in the doorway; let the pupils hang on my arm, extended against the wall; had pupils strike my chest; lifted heavy objects on the school grounds, and did feats of strength at neighborhood gatherings, such as lifting bags of wheat with my teeth, and wheeling heavy loads in a wheelbarrow. These I did when "living round" with patrons of a district.

By such demonstrations I showed I would be physically able to punish boys as old and big as I was, and the girls too, for they were sometimes hard to keep obedient to the rules laid down. It was sometimes necessary to demonstrate competence. I did not hold to the notion that it was always necessary to thrash pupils to make them mind, but it was sometimes necessary, seemed a fairly effective remedy, and, in fact, was mandatory from headquarters. Several teachers had been run out before I came. Laws governing conduct of pupils in the late [1880's], save by such means as have been named, were not thought of, and the teacher had to be a law unto himself when emergencies demanded quick action.

3. The Curriculum[1]
✤ Marshall Barber

The following recollections — from a student's point of view — describe the daily routine of a common school on the Kansas frontier in the 1870's. Practicality was a major factor considered

[1] Marshall A. Barber, The Schoolhouse at Prairie View (Lawrence, Kansas: University of Kansas Press, 1938), pp. 30–32, 34–35, 37. Permission granted by the University Press of Kansas.

in determining the curriculum. Arithmetic, reading, writing, and spelling ranked high in importance, and memorization was the primary means of instruction. The common school, by transmitting local culture, helped home and church exercise social control by defining the boundaries of acceptable attitudes and actions. ■

Arithmetic ranked high in our curriculum because it was considered so practical. That was why it was recited early in the day while the pupil's mind was fresh. We began arithmetic with the simplest sums in addition and subtraction and went up to the dizzy level where one extracted cube root. We had little nests of long and cubical blocks which were supposed to clarify the process of extraction, but I never understood the blocks. Arithmetic was a difficult subject for most of us, and we had one teacher who tried to make it more palatable by a simple game. Here were the rules: A problem was presented to two pupils who tried to "work" it and get the correct answer in the shortest possible time. The winner was pitted against a new problem and a new antagonist, whose privilege it was to select the kind of problem which was to be given out by the teacher. I had that choice one day and promptly chose "subtraction," a subject in which I then shone but dimly, but it was my best chance of beating Tommy Green, who was put against me. But that false teacher ignored my just choice and put in another sort of sum in which Tommy had been recently coached. She wanted to "show off" Tommy before the school and, of course, she had her way and Tommy won.

I felt much more kindly towards a teacher who explained common fractions by an apple neatly cut into segments in the presence of the class. I really understood fractions for the first time that day, and I was so interested that I forgot what became of the apple.

The Gateway to All Knowledge

Reading was the subject next in importance, for it was thought the gateway to all knowledge. I had learned to read a little before I entered school and I soon got into the Third Reader. I wish I could remember the name of that reader. It fell into the post-McGuffey period or may have been McGuffey itself or strongly influenced by that famous writer. Maybe some reader can identify it by one poem on tobacco which it contained:

> Tobacco is a filthy weed,
> It was the Devil sowed the seed,
> It leaves a stench where'er it goes,
> It makes a chimney of the nose.

* * * * *

Writing perhaps came next in importance. It was largely an affair of copybooks and Mr. Spencer[2] and I hated it. We early affected a more level script which we called a "business hand"; why I do not know — maybe because we thought a business man had no time for Spencerian curlicues or shaded pothooks. Surely no business man would care for those Spencerian birds admired by all of us but attempted by only the more gifted pupils....

The Virtue of Correct Spelling

Spelling ranked high in our curriculum. There was perhaps more disgrace attached to misspelling in those times than at present; correct spelling was the mark of an educated person. And the subject was easy to study and easy to teach. It was largely a memory exercise for the pupil, and the teacher had only to call out the words from his spelling book and assign good or bad marks or other measure of standing to the pupil. The simplest way to conduct a recitation was to line the pupils along a board in the schoolroom floor. A word was called out and if the pupil missed it, it was repeated to the pupil next in line. If he got it right, he went above (to the right in our school) the misspeller, and in the course of the recitation might get to the head of the class — he did not need to be graded, his "standing" was evidence that he knew his lesson. There was a touch of the dramatic in standing up for oral recitation. I still have a picture in my mind of the correct speller marching head up to the top of the class and the misspellers shuffling downwards with eyes on their toes....

A Noncontroversial Treatment of History

History was largely taught from a single textbook. Our teachers did not stray far from the book; perhaps some of them feared to get into politics, which would hardly do for a public school. But the

---

[2] **Mr. Spencer:** Platt Rogers Spencer (1800–1864), an American calligrapher who originated an ornate style of penmanship, which employed evenly rounded letters slanted to the right.

teacher ran little risk. It was generally assumed by our community that the Union and Republican party were right; the Prohibition and Populist parties had not come in prominence at that time, so that there was little of a political nature for us to quarrel about.

Our book was fair enough; there was little or no attempt at propaganda in it. It was full of pictures, chiefly of people notable in the history of the United States or of the colonies. I remember well a woodcut of a [fortification] used by the colonists during King Philip's War. A bold Indian, maybe King Philip himself, was shown wandering around outside the enclosure, reminding one of a boy seeking a knothole during a baseball game. We recited Presidents and some of the chief events of their administrations — there were not nearly so many ex-Presidents, living or dead, at that time.

The Civil War was a safe topic for the most timid teacher, for our neighborhood was almost unanimously Union. Many of the fathers of our pupils, perhaps a majority of them, were "Old Soldiers" who marched in procession on Memorial Day. Some of them were buried right by the schoolhouse, and the children used to put flags and flowers on their graves. One of our neighbors, the portly Mr. Foster, had been a prisoner in a Confederate camp, and his children told us how thin he was when he returned home after the War.

We hardly dreamed of war as a thing which could affect our lives, unless we joined the Army and fought Indians, who occasionally left their reservations and started some very lively skirmishes. The Civil War was only ten years past and the sky had not wholly cleared after that mighty storm. . . . But for us children the war god was asleep and probably would never awaken again; the world had had enough of him. . . .

We knew a world of natural history, about all sorts of plants, especially those which bore edible fruits, about wild birds and mammals and those tame ones we saw daily on the farm. Farming itself was an important study in science. But that was learning which we were supposed to get at home, not in school. It should be acquired by experience or taught us by our elders, who probably knew much more about it than the teacher did, anyhow a lady teacher; she might be criticized if she took up school time for formal instruction on such things as animals or plants.

Probably the neighborhood sentiment was right — we needed instruction in things our parents could not or would not teach us, and we were getting about enough science on the farm.

VIII. Beginning of Black Education

It was not until after the end of legally-sanctioned slavery that Negro education had its real beginning. Prior to the Civil War educational benefits had been systematically closed to black children. Only rarely did slaves, such as Frederick Douglass, learn to read or write. The minimal educational achievements of the mass of black freedmen stood in stark opposition to the claims many whites had made — that the slave system was an effective means of civilizing the "savage" African. More accurately, slavery had robbed the Negro of his own culture and self-esteem and trained him to assume a state of dependency.

In the years immediately following the Civil War, states throughout the South began to amend their constitutions to provide for the establishment of free public schools, racially integrated. However, by the end of the nineteenth century racist attitudes had prevailed and state constitutions were again amended to establish a dual system of schools — one for whites and one for blacks. Much of the early progress made in developing mass education for the Negro was due to the efforts of the Freedmen's Bureau and various religious and civic groups. In the absence of strong Southern support, Northern philanthropic organizations aided in the establishment of some private grammar schools, technical institutes, and colleges for the freedman. The following documents afford an insight into some of these early educational efforts in behalf of black Americans. ■

1. Slavery and Education Incompatible[1]
✤ Frederick Douglass

Few people could express the indignities of slavery as well as Frederick Douglass. Born a slave himself in 1817, he knew firsthand what it meant to be completely without rights save those

[1] Frederick Douglass, *Narrative of the Life of Frederick Douglass, Written by Himself* (Boston: Published at the Anti-Slavery Office, 1845), pp. 33, 34, 38, 43.

The education of blacks in the 19th century was a controversial issue even in the North, as is illustrated above. In the 1840's, free Negroes in Ohio were taxed to support public schools but were barred from attending them. During Reconstruction, thousands of white Northerners flocked to the South to give the freedmen their first taste of formal education. Obstacles to success, however, proved insurmountable. Hostility of white Southerners to Negro advancement, inadequate tax revenue, poorly equipped buildings, and ill-trained teachers meant that most blacks by the close of the century had received only the rudiments of education.

Tuskegee Institute, a Negro normal school in Alabama, was founded by Booker T. Washington in 1881. Beginning with 40 students meeting in a "dilapidated shanty," by 1915 the school had 1500 students and an endowment of nearly two million dollars. Washington strongly advocated a program of industrial and domestic training, with a measure of liberal arts instruction, in order to create a firm base for future Negro progress. Some black leaders blamed Washington for neglecting the Negro's intellect.

which his master chose to grant him. In short, the slavemaster owned not only the slave's labor, but his mind as well. To educate a slave was antithetical to the whole idea of slavery. In this passage from the autobiography of Douglass, he describes how he came to understand that the "pathway from slavery to freedom" was in the acquisition of an education. ■

Very soon after I went to live with Mr. and Mrs. Auld, she very kindly commenced to teach me the A,B,C. After I had learned this, she assisted me in learning to spell words of three or four letters. Just at this point of my progress, Mr. Auld found out what was going on, and at once forbade Mrs. Auld to instruct me further, telling her, among other things, that it was unlawful, as well as unsafe, to teach a slave to read. To use his own words, further, he said, "If you give a nigger an inch, he will take an ell[2]. A nigger should know nothing but to obey his master — to do as he is told to do. Learning would *spoil* the best nigger in the world. Now," said he, "if you teach that nigger (speaking of myself) how to read, there would be no keeping him. It would forever unfit him to be a slave. He would at once become unmanageable, and of no value to his master. As to himself, it could do him no good, but a great deal of harm. It would make him discontented and unhappy." These words sank deep into my heart, stirred up sentiments within that lay slumbering, and called into existence an entirely new train of thought. It was a new and special revelation, explaining dark and mysterious things, with which my youthful understanding had struggled, but struggled in vain. I now understood what had been to me a most perplexing difficulty — to wit, the white man's power to enslave the black man. It was a grand achievement, and I prized it highly. From that moment, I understood the pathway from slavery to freedom. . . . In learning to read, I owe almost as much to the bitter opposition of my master, as to the kindly aid of my mistress. I acknowledge the benefit of both. . . .

Learning Despite Opposition

From this time I was most narrowly watched. If I was in a separate room any considerable length of time, I was sure to be suspected of having a book, and was at once called to give an account of myself. All this, however, was too late. The first step had been taken. Mis-

[2] **ell:** an English measurement equal to 45 inches.

tress, in teaching me the alphabet, had given me the *inch*, and no precaution could prevent me from taking the *ell*.

The plan which I adopted, and the one by which I was most successful, was that of making friends of all the little white boys whom I met in the street. As many of these as I could, I converted into teachers. With their kindly aid, obtained at different times and in different places, I finally succeeded in learning to read. When I was sent of errands, I always took my book with me, and by going one part of my errand quickly, I found time to get a lesson before my return. I used also to carry bread with me, enough of which was always in the house, and to which I was always welcome; for I was much better off in this regard than many of the poor white children in our neighborhood. This bread I used to bestow upon the hungry little urchins, who, in return, would give me that more valuable bread of knowledge. I am strongly tempted to give the names of two or three of those little boys, as a testimonial of the gratitude and affection I bear them; but prudence forbids;—not that it would injure me, but it might embarrass them; for it is almost an unpardonable offence to teach slaves to read in this Christian country....

Learning to Write

The idea as to how I might learn to write was suggested to me by being in Durgin and Bailey's shipyard, and frequently seeing the ship carpenters, after hewing, and getting a piece of timber ready for use, write on the timber the name of that part of the ship for which it was intended. When a piece of timber was intended for the larboard side, it would be marked thus—"L." When a piece was for the starboard side, it would be marked thus—"S." A piece for the larboard side forward, would be marked thus—"L.F." When a piece was for starboard side forward, it would be marked thus—"S.F." For larboard aft, it would be marked thus—"L.A." For starboard aft, it would be marked thus—"S.A." I soon learned the names of these letters, and for what they were intended when placed upon a piece of timber in the shipyard. I immediately commenced copying them, and in a short time was able to make the four letters named. After that, when I met with any boy who I knew could write, I would tell him I could write as well as he. The next word would be, "I don't believe you. Let me see you try it." I would then make the letters which I had been so fortunate as to learn, and ask him to beat that. In this way I got a good many lessons in writing, which it is quite possible I should never have gotten in any other way. During this time, my copy-book was the board fence, brick wall, and pavement; my pen and ink was a lump of chalk. With these, I learned mainly how to write. I then commenced and continued copying the Italics in Webster's Spelling Book, until I could make them all without looking on the book. By this time, my little Master Thomas had gone to school, and learned how to write, and had written over a number of copy-books. These had been brought home, and shown to some of our near neighbors, and then laid aside. My mistress used to go to class meeting at the Wilk Street meeting-house every Monday afternoon, and leave me to take care of the house. When left thus, I used to spend the time in writing in the spaces left in Master Thomas's copy-book, copying what he had written. I continued to do this until I could write a hand very similar to that of Master Thomas. Thus, after a long, tedious effort for years, I finally succeeded in learning how to write.

2. Constitutional Provisions for Racial Segregation (1864-1898)[1]

The passage of the Thirteenth and Fourteenth Amendments held out high hopes for the ex-slave. By 1876 the state legislatures in South Carolina, Florida, Mississipi, Louisiana, and Alabama were virtually controlled by black politicians. As a move toward a racially integrated society, constitutions in these states were revised to establish free public schools for all children.

But by 1880, the intimidations of blacks by the Ku Klux Klan and other secret societies, and the absence of strong support for integration among whites, led to a new pattern of racial segregation. State constitutions were again amended to set up racially segregated public schools. And in 1896, the Supreme Court in Plessy v. Ferguson upheld a Louisiana law which provided for "separate but equal" railroad accommodations. It was this landmark decision that gave legal sanction to segregated transportation facilities, hotels, restaurants, theaters, parks — and schools. ■

[1] Francis N. Thorpe, ed., *The Federal and State Constitutions, Colonial Charters, and Other Organic Laws of the States, Territories, and Colonies Now or Heretofore Forming the United States* (Washington, D.C.: U.S. Government Printing Office, 1909). III, 1446, 1465, 1508, 1575–76; V, 2817; VI, 3300–01, 3338–39, 3469.

Constitution of Louisiana, 1864

ARTICLE 141. The legislature shall provide for the education of all children of the state, between the ages of six and eighteen years, by maintenance of free public schools by taxation or otherwise.

Constitution of Louisiana, 1868

ARTICLE 135. The general assembly shall establish at least one free public school in every parish throughout the state, and shall provide for its support by taxation or otherwise. All children of this state between the years of six and twenty-one shall be admitted to the public schools or other institutions of learning sustained or established by the state in common, without distinction of race, color, or previous condition. There shall be no separate schools or institutions of learning established exclusively for any race by the state of Louisiana.

Constitution of Louisiana, 1879

ARTICLE 224. There shall be free public schools established by the General Assembly throughout the state for the education of all children of the state between the ages of six and eighteen years; and the General Assembly shall provide for their establishment, maintenance, and support by taxation or otherwise. And all moneys so raised, except the poll tax, shall be distributed to each parish in proportion to the number of children between the ages of six and eighteen years.

Constitution of Louisiana, 1898

ARTICLE 248. There shall be free public schools for the white and colored races, separately established by the General Assembly, throughout the state, for the education of all the children of the state between the ages of six and eighteen years; provided, that where kindergarten schools exist, children between the ages of four and six may be admitted into said schools. All funds raised by the state for the support of public schools, except the poll tax, shall be distributed to each parish in proportion to the number of children therein between the ages of six and eighteen years.

Constitution of North Carolina, 1868

ARTICLE IX, SEC. 1. Religion, morality, and knowledge being necessary to good government and happiness of mankind, schools and the means of education shall forever be encouraged.

Sec. 2. The general assembly, at its first session under this constitution, shall provide, by taxation and otherwise, for a general and uniform system of public schools, wherein tuition shall be free of charge to all the children of the state between the ages of six and twenty-one years.

Constitution of North Carolina, 1876

Article IX, Sec. 1. Religion, morality and knowledge being necessary to good government and the happiness of mankind, schools and the means of education shall forever be encouraged.

Sec. 2. The General Assembly, at its first session under this Constitution, shall provide by taxation and otherwise for a general and uniform system of public schools, wherein tuition shall be free of charge to all the children of the state between the ages of six and twenty-one years. And the children of the white race and the children of the colored race shall be taught in separate public schools; but there shall be no discrimination in favor of or to the prejudice of either race.

Constitution of South Carolina, 1868

Article X, Sec. 3. The general assembly shall, as soon as practicable after the adoption of this Constitution, provide for a liberal and uniform system of free public schools throughout the state, and shall also make provision for the division of the state into suitable school districts. There shall be kept open, at least six months in each year, one or more schools in each school district.

Article X, Sec. 10. All the public schools, colleges, and universities of this state, supported in whole or in part by the public funds, shall be free and open to all the children and youths of the state, without regard to race or color.

Constitution of South Carolina, 1895

Article XI, Sec. 5. The General Assembly shall provide for a liberal system of free public schools for all children between the ages of six and twenty-one years, and for the division of the counties into suitable school districts, as compact in form as practicable, having regard to natural boundaries, and not to exceed forty-nine nor be less than nine square miles in area. . . .

Article XI, Sec. 7. Separate schools shall be provided for children of the white and colored races, and no child of either race shall ever be permitted to attend a school provided for children of the other race.

3. A Yankee Teacher in the South[1]
✤ Elizabeth G. Rice

Following the Civil War, thousands of ex-slaves passionately desired a formal education. Education, it was envisioned, was the key to unlimited opportunity. Sharing this optimism were a battalion of Yankee schoolteachers who descended upon the South in the early days of Reconstruction to teach the Negro the meaning of freedom. As this passage by Elizabeth Rice demonstrates, many of these volunteers, though well-meaning in their intentions, lacked an understanding of the problems created by 200 years of slavery. As they described their observations, the Northerners often perpetuated demeaning racial stereotypes. ■

Six weeks from the day that General Beauregard evacuated Charleston [early 1865], a party of New England men and women, including myself, entered the city as volunteer teachers for the colored schools that had been organized under the superintendence of Mr. James Redpath. We had been sent out by a society in Boston, who paid us a small sum above our necessary expenses, the government providing, as far as possible, transportation, rations, and military protection.

Everywhere were to be seen ruins, new and old; and the sense of disaster was greatly increased by the fires that took place the night that the city was evacuated. When the Union troops entered, their first effort was to extinguish these fires. Then the officers took possession of the vacant houses, which had already been emptied of everything of much value. Our party of twelve looked about to find a vacant house that pleased us, and soon selected a large brownstone mansion. . . .

All the available school buildings were put in use as fast as teachers, either Northern or native, could be found. Pupils who did not know a letter of the alphabet or a figure in arithmetic were separated from those who did, and those who could read from those who could not. Our places as teachers were assigned by lot, and the task that fell to me was a hard one. My school met in the third floor of the fine old

[1] "A Yankee Teacher in the South," *The Century Illustrated Monthly Magazine*, new ser., Vol. XL (May, 1901 to October, 1901), pp. 151, 152–153, 154.

State Normal School building. The room had formerly been used as a hall for lectures, and was fitted with [long wooden benches] for four hundred. There I never had a pupil who knew the alphabet or could count correctly to ten.

To Be Educated Like White Men

Charleston was a great gathering-place for the suddenly freed people from plantations for miles and miles around. To them freedom meant liberty to rove about as they liked, and they wandered aimlessly into the city by hundreds and thousands, destitute of nearly everything.... To them being free meant being educated like white men. One of their first impulses, therefore, was to go to school.

Many among those who had been brought up in towns could read, but the great throng of plantation and rice-swamp workers were in the densest ignorance, and often spoke such bad English that it was impossible to get at their meaning. As they passed in crowds through the city, many would stop at the school doors and ask admittance. Any applicant, man, woman, or child, not knowing the alphabet, was sent to my school; and when the four hundred seats were full, as they always were, subsequent comers had to be sent away. Consequently my room was filled each day with a constantly changing set of people. Many, probably, never came the second time. They had no idea of school life, and found sitting still and mental application the most laborious task they had ever been set to do. They wanted to talk, or to get up and walk round the room; and they fell asleep in their seats, even falling upon the floor, as easily as babes. My room was searched weekly for deserters from the army, so many men were there among the women and children.

My own rearing had been in a quiet New England town, and I hardly think I had ever seen a hundred colored people when I went South on this mission. My sense of helplessness was complete when I first stood on the platform and faced the dark crowd in motley apparel. I hardly knew whether to cry or laugh. There seemed to be no other individuality than sex. All the men looked just alike, and so did all the women and girls, except when some peculiar arrangement of the kinks of curls on their heads was distinctive.... The school session lasted only three hours each day, and that included a generous recess, for the confinement was as tedious to those grown-up children as to an ordinary three-year-old.

A soldier was detailed daily to stand at the outer entrance of the building to keep out unruly persons, and another was stationed by my door on the upper floor, and sometimes I had to call upon him for aid in ejecting disturbers.

Teaching the Alphabet

I was given the assistance of eight colored girls who had had some schooling. One of them had been a teacher and was really helpful. To each of these eight assistants I assigned the care of fifty pupils. I printed the alphabet and a few numerals with chalk on blackboards in each of the four corners of the room, and four assistants alternated their sections in classes of twenty-five each, standing before these boards and trying to make them see the different shapes of the letters and learn their names. Two of the teachers heard their classes in two small anterooms and two more on the broad landing of the staircase entry, while I tried to keep order among the two hundred who were resting in their seats, and conducted general exercises between the changing of the classes.

Singing and marching were the general exercises they liked best; all others were usually failures. For instance, I would say to the school, "To-day is Wednesday. What day will to-morrow be?" and when someone had guessed the right answer, I would have them repeat it several times in concert; yet the chances were that in a few minutes the same question would call forth the same series of guesses. Still, because they had an instinctive ear for rhythm, they would repeat in order the days of the week in concert, or would count to ten together, or partly get through the letters of the alphabet. Yet if I should ask suddenly, "What number comes after seven?" or any such question, the whole list would be guessed over again. If a pupil came regularly enough to learn the alphabet, he was at once promoted to a room where reading was taught.

The problem of keeping order in such a body was serious. It is fair to say that, in a general way, all were anxious to please me and to learn; but they reasoned that, if they were free, they could talk when they wanted to, or they could go out and come in as they liked. . . . I found it impossible to enforce authority without using punishments such as sitting on the floor in front of my desk with legs kept straight and feet turned up, or standing and toeing a line. They seemed to dislike having attention drawn to their feet, which were always bare. Occasionally I found use for a small [switch] which someone had left in the teacher's desk.

The days grew steadily hotter, and the sleepy crowd grew sleepier as they sat wearily on their [benches] in school. It was no use to give them books, for they could not read a word, and we had few picture-books or illustrated papers. We taught on with flagging courage till early in July, when we were very glad to avail ourselves of a government permit for transportation at half-rates to New York. Some teachers returned in the fall to continue the work, which went on, under more usual and orderly conditions, until the military rule was over and the former civil authority was resumed in the city, and with it the care of its own school system.

4. Hostility Towards White Teachers of Negroes[1]
✤ Cornelius McBride

> To educate the Negro in post-Civil War years was to threaten the entire social and economic system upon which the South had been based. The Southern advocates of slavery had convinced many that the Negro was innately childlike and inferior. To spend tax dollars on black education was a "waste," argued one Southern governor, because one was attempting to "make of the Negro what God Almighty never intended." White antagonism to education for blacks was expressed by burning schoolhouses and intimidating the teachers. The selection below demonstrates some of the hostility experienced by one white teacher in Georgia. ■

The last week in March there was a raid made over several counties there. I had several warnings, in the shape of several school-houses being burned there; but inasmuch as I was on good terms with the people in the neighborhood where I was teaching, I did not apprehend any difficulty. There was a school-house burned down not far off from where I lived; Mr. Burt Moore was teaching the school there, and they threatened his life if he did not stop teaching. At Houston several teachers of colored schools were attacked; one of them told me that they ordered him to leave in three days or they would take his

---

[1] Cornelius McBride, quoted in "Report on the Conditions of Affairs in the Late Insurrectionary States," February 19, 1872, in *Senate Reports*, 42nd Congress, 2nd Session, Vol. II, part 1, pp. 78–79.

life. His wife was about to [bear a child], but he had to leave. But I did not fear any difficulty for myself, inasmuch as I had opened the school there with the consent of the white people in the neighborhood. During the last week in March some of my scholars told me they had heard that the Ku-Klux were out after me, but I did not pay any attention to it. I boarded with Mr. Thomas Johnson, an old gentleman; he was then in Alabama, and I was alone in the big house, and I had no arms in the house. There were some colored people living in cabins in the yard, but there was no one with me in Mr. Johnson's house.

A Matter of Life and Death

Between 12 and 1 o'clock on Thursday night, in the last week of March, a body of men came to the house, burst in the doors and windows, and presented their rifles at me. I asked them, "What are you all coming here this time of night for, making this row?" The leader of the party said, "You damn Yankee, come out here." Well, I realized my position at once; I knew it was a matter of life and death; I did not believe those men came there merely to whip me and then leave me, as they did colored men; I thought they meant to kill me, and I made up my mind to make an effort to escape. There were two men standing at the window with their rifles presented at me. . . .

I jumped out of the window and ran to the house of a colored man in the yard, where there was a double-barreled gun; I was determined to get that, if I could, and defend myself. I had no time to wait for the colored woman to open the door, but I just burst right in. While I was running down the yard, they fired at me a number of times, crying out, ". . . Stop, or we will blow your damned brains out. . . ."

While I was in the cabin trying to find the gun, these men came in before I could find it. There were two rooms in the house of the colored man, and I went into one of them and tried to hide. They came in and searched for me and got me. The colored people prayed to them, "O, don't hurt Mr. Mac; for God's sake let him alone." They said, "Don't make that noise; keep quiet; we will not hurt you; hold your tongues." They took me out of the house and across the yard; I asked them in what way I had injured them to justify that attack on me. They cursed me, told me to stop talking, struck me in the side with their bowie-knives[2] that had their scabbards[3] on, and with the

[2] **bowie knife:** a single-edged steel hunting knife, about 15 inches in length.
[3] **scabbard:** a sheath or container for a dagger or hunting knife.

butt-ends of their pistols. They took me scarcely a quarter of a mile from the house, to a field near the road, and told me to take off my shirt, which I refused to do. Then one fellow struck me on the head with a pistol, cut my head, and knocked me down, and then pulled off my shirt. . . .

White Man's Country

One of them took the bundle of switches and commenced to whip me. They said they were going to give me a hundred each. I do not know how many men there were; I counted only five around me, but I believe there were more than a dozen there. They agreed to give me a hundred lashes each. . . . I asked them while they were whipping me what I had done to merit that treatment. They said I wanted to make these niggers equal to the white men; that this was a white man's country. They said, ". . . Don't you know this is a white man's country?" I said, "The white people in the neighborhood are satisfied with my conduct and the manner I have been conducting the school here. They have shown it by selecting me to take charge of their Sunday-school." They said, "Yes, . . . that is the worst feature in it, having a nigger teacher to teach the white school on Sunday!" I was fighting them all the time as well as I could — kicking at them and doing what I could — for the torture was horrible. . . . One of them came up to me with his pistol and asked me if I wanted to be shot. I said, "Yes; I can't stand this." The leader of the party said, "Shooting is too good for this fellow. We will hang him when we get through whipping him." I saw a rope hanging from a limb of a tree by the side of the road. . . . I asked him whether they would let me off if I would promise to leave in the morning.

A Narrow Escape

All this time they were whipping me, but I managed to partly raise myself. I was half way up, on my hand and knee; I made a spring. . . . The way was then clear to the fence, and I leaped the fence. As I did so they swore terribly and fired at me, and the shots went just over my head, scattering the leaves all around me. As I went across the field they kept firing at me and followed me a short distance. By that time the neighborhood was alarmed, hearing my screams and the shooting. I went back to the house to get the gun I was after in the first place; but the colored people had hidden it, thinking that if I got it and shot at them they would kill me, but that without it they would let me off with a whipping. I went to the house of a neighbor there, Mr. Walser, and remained there during the rest of the night. Mr. Walser of course sympathized with me; he was my near neighbor and my friend. He said, "My God! Has it come to this now, that no man is safe, when you are attacked!" It was a very cold night, that night was — piercing cold.... The blood was running down my back, and my suffering was fearful. Mr. Walser was afraid if I stayed at his house they might come there; but I remained there that night.

The next day I taught my school as usual. They had threatened me while they were whipping me that if I held the examination I had advertised — they spoke something about the examination, and said they were preparing me for examination in another way. Some colored people brought me word that if I held that examination the Ku-Klux would come again and kill me that time sure; but I held my examination the following Monday notwithstanding the threats. I went there with a gun over my shoulder, and several people came there and brought their guns, and I held the examination. That night several white men and some colored men and myself laid out in the woods expecting that the Ku-Klux would come.

5. Accommodation with White Power[1]
✤ Booker T. Washington

The legal sanction of segregated schooling had dimmed the Negro's early hopes to rise through education. During the 1890's Booker T. Washington, an ex-slave and the head of Tuskegee Institute, became the spokesman for his people. Preaching a message of patient endurance, he stressed the need for a practical education for blacks and minimized the idea of forced social and political integration. In a speech before a largely white audience in Atlanta in 1895, Washington argued that "the opportunity to earn a dollar in a factory is worth infinitely more than the opportunity to spend a dollar in the opera house." His words were warmly received by both Northern and

---

[1] Booker T. Washington, *My Larger Education* (New York: Doubleday, Page, & Co., 1911), pp. 296–297, 299–303, 310.

Southern whites. Although bitterly criticized by more militant Negroes, his views represented a majority of the thinking in the black community in the 1890's. In this passage below, Washington expands on his views. ■

We have in the South, in general, five types of Negro schools. There are (1) the common schools, supported in large part by state funds supplemented in many cases by contributions from the colored people; (2) academies and so-called colleges, or universities, supported partly by . . . Negro religious denominations and partly by the contributions of philanthropic persons and organizations; (3) the state normal, mechanical, and agricultural colleges, supported in part by the state and in part by funds provided by the federal government; (4) medical schools, which are usually attached to some one or other of the colleges, but really maintain a more or less independent existence; (5) industrial schools, on the model of Hampton and Tuskegee. . . .

One of the chief hindrances to the progress of Negro education in the public schools in the South is in my opinion due to the fact that the Negro colleges in which so many of the teachers are prepared have not realized the importance of convincing the Southern white people that education makes the same improvement in the Negro that it does in the white man; makes him so much more useful in his labor, so much better a citizen, and so much more dependable in all the relations of life, that it is worthwhile to spend the money to give him an education. As long as the masses of the Southern white people remain unconvinced by the results of the education which they see about them that education makes the Negro a better man or woman, so long will the masses of the Negro people who are dependent upon the public schools for their instruction remain to a greater or less extent in ignorance.

No Need for Greek or Latin

Some of the schools of the strictly academic type have declared that their purpose in sticking to the old-fashioned scholastic studies was to make of their students Christian gentlemen. Of course, every man and every woman should be a Christian and, if possible, a gentleman or a lady; but it is not necessary to study Greek or Latin to be a Christian. More than that, a school that is content with merely turning out ladies and gentlemen who are not at the same time something else — who are not lawyers, doctors, business men, bankers, carpenters, farmers, teachers, not even housewives, but merely ladies and gentlemen — such a school is bound, in my estimation, to be more or less of a failure. There is no room in this country, and never has been, for the class of people who are merely gentlemen. . . .

In the majority of cases I have found that the smaller Negro colleges have been modeled on the schools started in the South by the anti-slavery people from the North directly after the war. Perhaps there were too many institutions started at that time for teaching Greek and Latin, considering that the foundation had not yet been laid in a good common-school system. It should be remembered, however, that the people who started these schools had a somewhat different purpose from that for which schools ordinarily exist today. They believed that it was necessary to complete the emancipation of the Negro by demonstrating to the world that the black man was just as able to learn from books as the white man, a thing that had been frequently denied during the long anti-slavery controversy.

I think it is safe to say that that has now been demonstrated. What remains to be shown is that the Negro can go as far as the white man in using his education, of whatever kind it may be, to make himself a more useful and valuable member of society. Especially is it necessary to convince the Southern white man that education, in the case of the colored man, is a necessary step in the progress and upbuilding, not merely of the Negro, but of the South.

It should be remembered in this connection that there are thousands of white men in the South who are perfectly friendly to the Negro and would like to do something to help him, but who have not yet been convinced that education has actually done the Negro any good. Nothing will change their minds but an opportunity to see results for themselves.

The Need for a Practical Curriculum

The reason more progress has not been made in this direction is that the schools planted in the South by the Northern white people have remained — not always through their own fault to be sure — in a certain sense, alien institutions. They have not considered, in planning their courses of instruction, the actual needs either of the Negro or of the South. Not infrequently young men and women have gotten so out of touch during the time that they were in these schools with the actual conditions and needs of the Negro and the

South that it has taken years before they were able to get back to earth and find places where they would be useful and happy in some form or other of necessary and useful labor. . . .

I have long been of the opinion that the persons in charge of the Negro colleges do not realize the extent to which it is possible to create in every part of the South a friendly sentiment toward Negro education, provided it can be shown that this education has actually benefited and helped in some practical way the masses of the Negro people with whom the white man in the South comes most in contact. We should not forget that as a rule in the South it is not the educated Negro, but the masses of the people, the farmers, laborers, and servants, with whom the white people come in daily contact. . . .

I was asked the other day by a gentleman who has long been interested in the welfare of the colored people what I thought the Negro needed most after nearly fifty years of freedom. I promptly answered him that the Negro needed now what he needed fifty years ago, namely, education.

Part Three

Introduction
IX. Inadequate Schooling
X. Educational Reform
XI. Debate over the Curriculum
XII. Striving for Equal Opportunity
XIII. Separation of Church and State
XIV. Continuing Criticism

Urbanization of American Education: 1900 to the Present

Part Three: Introduction

In the late nineteenth century, new patterns of living were adopted by the residents of expanding industrial cities, and a new urban life style developed. Gone were the quiet scenes of the countryside. Gone also was the sense of community among those in the small village. Instead, massive skyscrapers dotted the urban landscape. People worked and played amidst a ceaseless din. The almighty machine dictated the routine of sleep and work. The growth of cities also presented challenges to traditional American education.

Ethnic Diversity of City Life

Between 1885 and 1915, millions of villagers and European immigrants flocked to the American cities. Seeking a new life, these predominantly rural migrants — polyglot in language and pluralistic in life style — often found shelter in dingy tenements near the factories which provided them with dirty, repetitive, and often dangerous work.

The city fostered social change. Its diversity challenged the adequacy of agrarian values. In cities, the one-room school no longer sufficed. Pleas for social and educational reform begun in the 1890's became vociferous demands by 1910. Statesmen such as Theodore Roosevelt and Woodrow Wilson and educators such as John Dewey and William Heard Kilpatrick were confronted with the problem of how to achieve a democracy in an urban industrial society.

Journalists aroused the public with lurid accounts of children who labored in factory sweatshops and coal mines and pointed out the physical and mental dangers of such conditions. Social reformers such as Jane Addams and Lillian Wald joined the vigorous campaign to enact child labor legislation. By 1915 child labor laws had been enacted in most states, though they were not universally enforced.

Compulsory Education Laws

By 1900 most states had developed a system of public elementary graded schools through the eighth grade. The public high school, however, was not so well established. Fewer than 5 per cent of American youth aged fourteen to seventeen attended secondary schools.

Criticism of American education increased — particularly subject to attack was the outdated curriculum. Leaders in government and education slowly responded by centralizing schools, professionalizing teachers, and economizing on administration. Educators sought to make the traditional course of study more relevant, both socially and vocationally. They developed programs to Americanize the immigrant — emphasizing the values of cleanliness, patriotism, and conformity to society's existing patterns of living and working. Curriculum reforms were undertaken in an effort to solve the dropout problem. By 1920, most states had compulsory attendance laws to age sixteen.

With the decline of the apprenticeship, the growth of mass production, and the increased complexity of urban life, the high school was called upon to do its part in solving the multitude of problems which had been unforeseen by earlier generations. By 1920 the high school had become part of the common public school system. With this extension to the twelfth grade, the public school provided an additional four years to prepare youth for an industrial democracy.

Changing Images of the Ideal

The rise of the city not only brought about changes in the nation's education; it also challenged the traditional image of the good American. The nineteenth century Protestant-American ideal reflected in McGuffey's readers was in conflict with the pluralism of the early twentieth century in which numerous distinct ethnic, religious and cultural groups coexisted in the United States. Though the traditional image was not fully discarded, educational leaders came to recognize as valid still other ideals held by some Americans. Into the national dialogue over the appropriate image of the twentieth century American also would come such diverse images as the scientist-humanist, the world-citizen, and the Afro-American.

The Black Struggle for Equal Opportunity

The Thirteenth Amendment abolished slavery without providing the freed Negro with land, money, or training to allow him to take his rightful place in American society. He was soon to learn that, though legally free, his economic, political, social, and educational opportunities had not greatly improved. The racist attitudes of many white Americans sanctioned the use of ostracism to segregate blacks in both North and South. By 1900, racial segregation had become the prevalent way of life for white and black Americans. In the South this pattern was enforced by provisions in state constitutions for a dual system of public schools; in the North the pattern was enforced by *de facto* segregation in housing.

Despite subtle and overt practices of discrimination, black leaders persisted in seeking redress of their grievances. Black Americans such as Booker T. Washington, W. E. B. DuBois, Marcus Garvey, and Martin Luther King, Jr., expressed diverse views about the best course of action. They were agreed, nevertheless, that the promises of American democracy had been largely unfulfilled.

In 1954 the legal basis for racially segregated public education was removed. The Supreme Court — petitioned by the National Association for the Advancement of Colored People (NAACP) in behalf of Linda Brown of Topeka, Kansas — overturned the 1896 decision which sanctioned the doctrine of "separate but equal." After 1954, however, barriers to racial equality still remained; many Negro children in both North and South still attended racially segregated schools.

Education in the 1970's

As America's population climbed to over 200,000,000 by 1970, the number of Americans enrolled in public and private schools reached beyond 60,000,000. This burgeoning school population stimulated a boom in the construction of new school buildings, created lucrative markets for textbook and test publishers, and nurtured teaching into one of the largest professions in the society. From its obscure beginnings in rural America, education by the last half of the twentieth century had become a major enterprise. Given its size and its importance to society it was destined to become the object of praise and hope. Given its economic and pedagogical inadequacies the school system would also frustrate thousands of its diverse clients and become the scapegoat for many of America's ills.

By the 1970's new educational reforms were called for. Youth demanded that the school system be responsive and relevant to their needs. Business leaders, under the banner of accountability, demanded that the schools be operated more economically and efficiently. Blacks marched in protest against the system's institutionalized racism. Teachers sought greater autonomy and control over the operation of the schools. And some, in despair, even called for the system's demise — a wholesale deschooling of the society. However, most Americans continued to support the educational system. ■

Compulsory attendance laws imposed new burdens on the public schools in the early 20th century. Faced with an increasing diversity of American life, schools were called upon to create a social and cultural unity, to provide children with a standard school experience. The public high school became an integral part of the educational system by the 1930's. At the other end, the kindergarten was promoted as a means of influencing the early growth of the child. Leaders of the progressive movement were appalled by the regimentation and rote methods of instruction. They stressed the need to appeal to the child's interests in fostering constructive and creative learning activities.

IX. Inadequate Schooling

Urban schools at the beginning of the twentieth century were essentially agrarian schools grown large. Originally intended for a relatively homogeneous population, these schools largely ignored the growth of pluralism in American society as thousands of immigrants settled in the large cities.

Many people became disenchanted with schools which were insufficiently related to the needs of children and youth. They were also concerned about the schools' lack of attention to the problems of industrial America. Their criticisms were vigorous and intense. However, they sometimes failed to consider the lack of sufficient financing; inadequate support of schools contributed to many of the failures of education at the turn of the twentieth century. ■

1. Traditional High School Curriculum[1]

The typical course of study in American high schools at the turn of the century was oriented toward college preparation. Since most colleges stressed the classics, focusing on the literature of Rome and Greece, they usually required a mastery of Latin and sometimes of Greek. The following Chicago course of study was offered youth in the late nineteenth century. By the twentieth century, high school programs of this kind had caused thousands of sons and daughters of the common man and of the "new immigrant" to drop out of school. ■

---

[1] John Addison Clement, *Principles and Practices of Secondary Education* (New York: Appleton-Century-Crofts, Inc., 1924) p. 18. By courtesy of Appleton-Century-Crofts, Educational Division, Meredith Corporation.

Traditional High School Curriculum **125**

**HIGH SCHOOL DEPARTMENT FULL COURSE
FOUR YEARS (ADOPTED IN 1884)**

	First Term	Second Term	Third Term
1st Year	Algebra Physiology Latin or German	Algebra Physical Geography Latin or German Physiology	Algebra Physical Geography Latin or German
2nd Year	Geometry History Latin or German Natural History	Geometry History Latin or German Natural History Botany	Geometry History Latin or German Botany
3rd Year	Natural Philosophy Rhetoric Latin, German, or French Chemistry	Natural Philosophy English Literature Latin, German, or French Chemistry	Natural Philosophy English Literature Latin, German, or French
4th Year	Astronomy Civil Government Latin, German, or French Study of Authors	Astronomy Geology Mental Science Latin, German, or French Reviews	Geology Political Economy Latin, German, or French Reviews

Composition, Declamation and Select Readings through the course. Drawing and Singing optional through the course. Greek elective after the first year. Bookkeeping optional during the last year.

2. Mindless Rote Learning[1]
✤ *Joseph M. Rice*

In 1892, Dr. Joseph Rice, a physician, spent six months visiting public school classrooms in 36 American cities. He reported his

[1] J. M. Rice, "Our Public-School System: Evils in Baltimore" in *The Forum*, XIV (1892), pp. 147, 152–153, 154–155; and "The Public Schools of Chicago and St. Paul" in *The Forum*, XV (1893), pp. 202–203.

observations in a series of articles published in The Forum, *thus launching a massive attack on the mechanical methods of teaching and the academically irrelevant education provided in these schools. He placed much of the blame on the superficial training of teachers and the lack of professional administration.* ■

The characteristic feature of our school system may perhaps be best defined by the single word "chaos," as it lies in the fact that each city, each county, and in some states each country district, has practically the privilege of conducting its schools in accordance with any whim upon which it may decide, being restricted only by certain state laws of secondary importance. Consequently, unless chaos be preferable to law and order, there is no foundation for the opinion held by so many that our public schools are the best in the world. . . .

Arithmetic

I have selected for the opening the schools of Baltimore, because they were the first of a group of schools of a certain order that came under my observation. My first illustration will be that of an arithmetic lesson which I witnessed in an "advanced first grade" (actually the second school year) in one of Baltimore's schools. This lesson will indicate, to a great extent, in what a soul-inspiring manner from one-fourth to one-third of the time is spent in the average primary school of that city during the first two years of school life.

On entering this classroom a large blackboard entirely covered with problems in addition, in endless variety, struck my eye. First there were such columns as —

$1 + 1 =$ $\qquad$ $1 + 2 =$
$2 + 1 =$ $\qquad$ $2 + 2 =$
$3 + 1 =$ $\qquad$ $3 + 2 =$

running down to $10 + 1 =$ and $10 + 2 =$, respectively.

Then there were columns with mixed figures, four lines deep, five lines deep, and ten lines deep; next, examples in horizontal lines, such as $3 + 6 + 8 + 4 =$, and columns where each succeeding figure was 5 greater than the one before: thus, 1, 6, 11, 16; 2, 7, 12, 17; and so on.

"We are just adding," the teacher said to me. "I am very particular with their adding. I devote from one and a half to one and three-quarter hours a day to this subject, and I will tell you," she continued, growing quite enthusiastic, "my pupils can add."

Then she faced the class and said, "Start that column over again."

A little boy (apparently the leader of the orchestra) then began to tap on the blackboard with a stick, beating time upon the figures, while the class sang in perfect rhythm: "1 and 1 are 2; 2 and 1 are 3; 3 and 1 are 4," and so on, until the column was completed; next they began with 2 and 1, 2 and 2, etc. (When later they came to 5 and 8 are 13, 5 and 9 are 14, the rhythm was retained, but the effect was changed.) Next came a column of 2s, the children adding "2 and 2 are 4; 4 and 2 are 6," and so on.

The teacher here said to me, "Now I shall let them add that column mentally." Upon receiving such an order, the children cried out, "2, 4, 6, 8, 10."

I discovered, therefore, that this teacher's idea of the difference between written and mental arithmetic consisted in nothing further than that in mental arithmetic the "and (2) are" is left out. Thus 2, 4, 6, 8, 10 is mental arithmetic, while 2 and 2 are 4, 4 and 2 are 6 is the other kind. . . .

I asked one of the primary principals whether she believed in the professional training of teachers.

"I do *not*," she answered emphatically. "I speak from experience. A graduate of the Maryland Normal School once taught under me, and she wasn't as good a teacher as those from the High School."

One of the primary teachers said to me: "I formerly taught in the higher grades, but I had an attack of nervous prostration some time ago, and the doctor recommended rest. So I now teach in the primary, because teaching primary children does not tax the mind. . . ."

Science

I met one principal who was quite enthusiastic, but as she was hampered in her work by lack of professional training, the teaching throughout her school did not differ much from that of other schools. She informed me, while speaking of natural-science work, that physics was studied quite thoroughly in the schools of Baltimore.

"Do the children experiment for themselves," I asked, "or do the teachers perform the experiments?"

"Oh, we have no experiments," she said. "We learn our physics from books. The city supplies us with no apparatus. We are at liberty to experiment if we desire. A friend of mine, a principal, informed me that she tried an experiment once, but it was a failure, and she vowed that she would never dream of making another one."

Inadequate Schooling

In one class, where they were having some physiology, in answer to the question, "What is the effect of alcohol on the system?" I heard a ten-year-old cry out at the top of his voice and at the rate of a hundred miles an hour, "It — dwarfs — the — body, — mind, — and — soul, — weakens — the — heart, — and — enfeebles — the — memory."

"And what are the effects of tobacco?" asked the teacher.

In answer to this, one boy called off, in rapid succession, a longer list of diseases than most physicians are acquainted with.

"What brings on these diseases, excessive or moderate smoking?"

"Moderate smoking," was the prompt reply.

Now, what do these illustrations mean? Simply that I did not succeed in discovering any evidence that the science of education had as yet found its way into the public schools of Baltimore.

* * * * *

Reading

In the first school visited [in Chicago], I attended lessons in several grades, some of which I shall now describe. In the lowest grade the proceedings were such as to remind me of a room used for playing school. . . . Some of the pupils were copying words from their reading-books on their slates, and the writing in some instances might have been mistaken for the footmarks of flies with chalk legs.

I heard some of the pupils read, and their reading was anything but good. I learned from the teacher that the children, during much of the time, had no opportunity to do any sight-reading. The city furnished them with only one reading-book, so that they were obliged to read the same book over and over again until the end of the term. The reading-lesson itself presented many absurdities. The teacher made an attempt to teach phonics, but while the pupils had learned the sounds of the letters they did not possess much power to combine them, so after sounding all the letters in a word they frequently remained unable to name the word. When the pupils began a new lesson they pronounced all the words in the column placed at the top of the lesson before going to the text. In pronouncing these words each child was obliged to go through a set formula, thus: "That word is 'moon,'" "That word is 'dark,'" etc. When a pupil simply named a word without repeating the formula, "That word is," the teacher said, "Well, tell me so," whereupon the child would say, "That word is 'mice,'" or whatever it happened to be.

3. The Deadening Classroom Routine[1]
✤ Randolph S. Bourne

>Between 1885 and 1910 the schools lost touch with the realities of an urban society. Yet child labor laws and compulsory school attendance laws compelled millions of youth to attend school in the cities. Jane Addams in 1905 observed as many as fifty-five pupils and one teacher per class in the Chicago schools. Criticism of the traditional curriculum mounted. Social reformers such as Randolph Bourne wrote scathing indictments of the artificial atmosphere prevalent in the American classroom. ■

The other day I amused myself by slipping into a recitation at the suburban high school where I had once studied as a boy. The teacher let me sit, like one of the pupils, at an empty desk in the back of the room, and for an hour I had before my eyes the interesting drama of the American school as it unfolds itself day after day in how many thousands of classrooms throughout the land. I had gone primarily to study the teacher, but I soon found that the pupils, after they had forgotten my presence, demanded most of my attention.

Passive Acceptance

Their attitude towards the teacher, a young man just out of college and amazingly conscientious and persevering, was that good-humored tolerance which has to take the place of enthusiastic interest in our American school. They seemed to like the teacher and recognize fully his good intentions, but their attitude was a delightful one of all making the best of a bad bargain, and co-operating loyally with him in slowly putting the hour out of its agony. This good-natured acceptance of the inevitable, this perfunctory going through . . . the ritual of education, was my first striking impression, and the key to the reflections that I began to weave.

As I sank down to my seat I felt all that queer sense of depression, still familiar after ten years, that sensation, in coming into the schoolroom, of suddenly passing into a helpless, impersonal world, where expression could be achieved and curiosity asserted only in the most

[1] Randolph S. Bourne, "In a Schoolroom," *New Republic*, I (1914–1915), pp. 23–24.

formal and difficult way. And the class began immediately to divide itself for me, as I looked around it, into the artificially depressed like myself, commonly called the "good" children, and the artificially stimulated, commonly known as the "bad," and the envy and despair of every "good" child. For to these "bad" children, who are, of course, simply those with more self-assertion and initiative than the rest, all the careful network of discipline and order is simply a direct and irresistible challenge. I remembered the fearful awe with which I used to watch the exhaustless ingenuity of the "bad" boys of my class to disrupt the peacefully dragging recitation; and behold, I found myself watching intently, along with all the children in my immediate neighborhood, the patient activity of a boy who spent his entire hour in so completely sharpening a lead-pencil that there was nothing left at the end but the lead. Now what normal boy would do so silly a thing or who would look at him in real life? But here, in this artificial atmosphere, his action had a sort of symbolic quality; it was assertion against a stupid authority, a sort of blind resistance against the attempt of the schoolroom to impersonalize him. The most trivial incident assumed importance; the chiming of the town-clock, the passing automobile, a slip of the tongue, a passing footstep in the hall, would polarize the wandering attention of the entire class like an electric shock. Indeed, a large part of the teacher's business seemed to be to demagnetize, by some little ingenious touch, his little flock into their original inert and static elements.

An Artificial Atmosphere

For the whole machinery of the classroom was dependent evidently upon this segregation. Here were these thirty children, all more or less acquainted, and so congenial and sympathetic that the slightest touch threw them all together into a solid mass of attention and feeling. Yet they were forced, in accordance with some principle of order, to sit at these stiff little desks, equidistantly apart, and prevented under penalty from communicating with each other. All the lines between them were supposed to be broken. Each existed for the teacher alone. In this incorrigibly social atmosphere, with all the personal influences playing around, they were supposed to be, not a network or a group, but a collection of things, in relation only with the teacher....

While these reflections were running through my head, the hour dragged to its close. As the bell rang for dismissal, a sort of thrill of rejuvenation ran through the building. The "good" children straightened up, threw off their depression and took back their self-respect, the "bad" sobered up, threw off their swollen egotism, and prepared to leave behind them their mischievousness in the room that had created it. Everything suddenly became human again. The brakes were off, and life, with all its fascinations of intrigue and amusement, was flowing once more. The school streamed away in personal and intensely interested little groups....

Is it not very curious that we spend so much time on the practice and methods of teaching, and never criticise the very framework itself? Call this thing that goes on in the modern schoolroom schooling, if you like. Only don't call it education.

4. The Obstacle of Child Labor[1]
✦ Jacob A. Riis

In 1876 the New York legislature had enacted a so-called "wrongs to children" law. It regulated the hours a young person could work, prohibited night work, set the minimum age for factory employment at fourteen, and provided an inspection system to enforce the regulations. A number of other states passed similar legislation as the public gradually became convinced that education for all youth was a necessity in a democracy. Child labor was seen as a major obstacle in the achievement of such a goal.

Jacob Riis, a newspaper reporter who covered the immigrant neighborhoods of New York, vividly described the misery of the slums and the evils of child labor. His accounts did much to arouse the American people to the need for social reform. In the selection below, Riis advances the idea that childhood should be a time of training and development instead of a period of "profitless drudgery." He points out the need for enforcement of not only child labor laws but also for compulsory education legislation. ■

[1] Jacob A. Riis, *The Children of the Poor* (New York: Charles Scribner's Sons, 1892), pp. 92–93, 97, 113–114, 127–128.

Today we have compulsory education and a factory law prohibiting the employment of young children. All between eight and fourteen years old must go to school at least fourteen weeks in each year. None may labor in factories under the age of fourteen; not under sixteen unless able to read and write simple sentences in English. These are the barriers thrown up against the inroads of ignorance, poverty's threat. They are barriers of paper. We have the laws, but we do not enforce them.

By that I do not mean to say that we make no attempt to enforce them. We do. We catch a few hundred truants each year and send them to reformatories to herd with thieves and vagabonds worse than they, rather illogically, since there is no pretence that there would have been room for them in the schools had they wanted to go there. We set half a dozen factory inspectors to canvass more than twice as many thousand workshops and to catechise the children they find there. Some are turned out and go back the next day to that or some other shop. The great mass that are under age lie and stay. And their lies go on record as evidence that we are advancing, and that child-labor is getting to be a thing of the past. That the horrible cruelty of a former day [still exists]; that the children have better treatment and a better time of it in the shops — often a good enough time to make one feel that they are better off there learning habits of industry than running about the streets, so long as there is no way of *making* them attend school — I believe from what I have seen. That the law has had the effect of greatly diminishing the number of child-workers I do not believe. . . .

From among a hundred and forty hands on two big lofts in a Suffolk Street factory we picked seventeen boys and ten girls who were patently under fourteen years of age, but who all had certificates, sworn to by their parents, to the effect that they were sixteen. One of them whom we judged to be between nine and ten, and whose teeth confirmed our diagnosis — the second bicuspids in the lower jaw were just coming out — said that he had worked there "by the year." The boss, deeming his case hopeless, explained that he only "made sleeves and went for beer." Two of the smallest girls represented themselves as sisters, respectively sixteen and seventeen, but when we came to inquire which was the oldest, it turned out that she was the sixteen-year one. . . .

To send the boys to school and see that they stay there until they have learned enough to at least vote intelligently when they grow up, is the [obligation] of the state — celebrated in theory but neglected in practice. If it did its duty much would have been gained, but even then the real kernel of this question of child labor would remain untouched. The trouble is not so much that the children have to work early as with the sort of work they have to do. It is, all of it, of a kind that leaves them, grown to manhood and womanhood, just where it found them, knowing no more, and therefore less, than when they began, and with the years that should have prepared them for life's work gone in hopeless and profitless drudgery. . . . Prohibition of child labor without compelling the attendance at school of the freed slaves is a mockery. The children are better off working than idling, any day. The physical objections to the one alternative are vastly outweighed by the moral iniquities of the other.

I have tried to set forth the facts. They carry their own lesson. The then State Superintendent of Education, Andrew Draper, read it aright when, in his report for 1889, he said about the compulsory education law:

"It does not go far enough and is without an executor. It is barren of results. . . . It may be safely said that no system will be effectual in bringing the unfortunate children of the streets into the schools which at least does not definitely fix the age within which children must attend the schools, which does not determine the period of the year within which all must be there, which does not determine the method for gathering all needed information, which does not provide especial schools for incorrigible cases, which does not punish people charged with the care of children for neglecting their education, and which does not provide the machinery and officials for executing the system."

5. Americanization of the Immigrant[1]

✤ A. R. Dugmore

New immigrants to the United States between 1885 and 1915 numbered thirty-five million. Tending to congregate in slum areas of the large urban centers and to retain their native languages and customs, these newcomers struck fear in the hearts of

[1] A. R. Dugmore, "New Citizens for the Republic," in *The World's Work*, V (November, 1902 to April, 1903), (New York: Doubleday, Page, and Co., 1902–1903), pp. 3323–3326.

many native Americans. Many agreed with the educational leader Ellwood Cubberley who said that the country had suffered a "serious case of racial indigestion." He described the recent immigrants as "largely illiterate, docile, . . . and wholly without Anglo-Saxon conceptions of righteousness, liberty, law, order, and public decency." Public schools, especially in the East, were called upon to integrate these foreigners into the American way of life. One such school that struggled to mold immigrants into citizens is described below. ■

At the corner of Catharine and Henry Streets in New York is a large white building that overlooks and dominates its neighborhood. Placed in the middle of a region of tawdry flat-houses and dirty streets, it stands out pre-eminent because of its solid cleanliness and unpretentiousness. It is the home of Public School No. 1. In it are centered all the hopes of the miserably poor polyglot population of the surrounding district — for its pupils the scene of their greatest interest and endeavor, and for their parents an earnest of the freedom they have come far and worked hard to attain.

The child of American parentage is the exception in this school. The pupils are of the different nationalities or races that have their separate quarters in the immediate neighborhood. If they were to be divided according to their parental nationality, there would be twenty-five or more groups. The majority of the pupils, however, are Swedes, Austrians, Greeks, Russians, English, Irish, Scotch, Welsh, Rumanians, Italians, Poles, Hungarians, Canadians, Armenians, Germans and Chinese. The Germans, Russians and Polish predominate, for there are a very large number of Jewish pupils. . . .

The interest in politics is only one of the evidences of a great desire to "get along in the world." Another is the fact that many of the boys are self-supporting. The number of boys working their way through can only be guessed. They are reluctant to tell anything about their home life or conditions. It is known, however, that about one hundred and twenty of the six hundred odd boys in the grammar department are self-supporting. A little Italian boy was late one morning and was asked for his excuse by the principal. After much questioning he told this story: His mother was dead, and his father, who worked on the railways, and consequently was away from home most of the time, could send him only enough money to pay the rent of the two small rooms in which he and a smaller brother and sister lived. To pay for their food and clothing he and his brother sold papers after school hours, making about $4 a week. The sister did the cooking and the housework. This particular morning she had been ill and unable to leave her bed, and it had taken him so long to care for her and attend to her work that he had been late. This was told quietly and quite as a matter of course. The boy was fourteen years old. He had no idea that his story seemed extraordinary. He had never thought of trying to get help of any kind. This earnestness is carried into all the school work. The boys, because of the sacrifices their schooling brings, realize more keenly how valuable it is to them. . . .

The school course is similar to that in all the other public schools. There is, however, one extra class called the "ungraded class." This class is divided into four subdivisions: those for (1) special discipline cases, (2) truants, (3) defective children — physically, mentally or morally, and that for (4) foreign-born children who do not speak English. The work done with these boys is perhaps the most valuable single service of the school. Here the entire stress of the teacher's task is given to remedy the individual defect. The children are taught only those things which the teacher believes are within the understanding of each individual. Sand and clay modeling, drawing lines with colored crayons, weaving with colored splints, cutting, pasting and using peg-boards are some of the occupations through which the minds are stimulated. Gradually, as they develop, tool and other work is given, and the results are remarkable. Their defect may be of eyesight, hearing, muscular control, speech, moral sense. Some are afflicted with paralysis or epilepsy. Whatever it is, all that can be done to better their condition and to make them self-supporting is being done by tactful teaching.

It is a large task that schools of this kind are doing, taking the raw, low-class foreign boys of many nationalities and molding them into self-supporting, self-respecting citizens of the republic. The amount of this work done by the public schools in New York is indicated by the figures of the immigration bureau, for of the great body of foreigners who come into this country, more than two-thirds come through the port of New York, beyond which most of them rarely get. The results shown by the public schools seem little short of marvelous. There are many things in which, as a rule, the public consider that the public schools fail, but the one thing that cannot be denied — and it is the greatest — is that these boys and girls of foreign parentage catch readily the simple American ideas of independence and individual work and, with them, social progress.

6. Civilizing the American Indian[1]
✣ Polingaysi Qoyawayma

> The desire for cultural unity, reflected in the attempt to Americanize the immigrant, was also apparent in the education provided the American Indian. The government saw its task as that of civilizing the first Americans. Indian children in the first years of school were expected to acquire a mastery of English and to learn the white man's way of living. In addition to day-schools close to the reservations, the government also set up boarding schools. Far removed from their original environments, young Indians were exposed to such amenities as beds, knives and forks, and showers. However, they were also taught to forget their past ways. Little sympathy was shown for the crisis in identity suffered by many pupils. The following selection is taken from an autobiography of a young Hopi girl; the time is the first decade of the twentieth century. ■

Since nothing had been said to excite her fear, Polingaysi went about her play unalarmed until a morning when her mother, whose voice was customarily low and calm, called out to her in agonized syllables.

"Polingaysi! Come! Come quickly!"

Frightened, Polingaysi gathered up the younger brother she had been pulling on her shoulder blanket and ran home with him. He gurgled with glee at the bouncing ride she gave him and cried when their mother ran to meet them and snatched him from Polingaysi roughly, saying, "Lie down behind that roll of bedding, Polingaysi. I will hide you with a sheep pelt. Hurry."

"Why?" Polingaysi asked in childish bewilderment.

[1] Polingaysi Qoyawayma (as told to Vada F. Carlson), *No Turning Back* (Albuquerque: The University of New Mexico Press, 1964), pp. 17–18, 20, 24–26. © The University of New Mexico Press, 1964. Reprinted by permission.

"Do as you're told!" her mother snapped. "*Bahana*[2] is catching children this morning, for the school. Sister is hiding at grandmother's house."

"Catching children!" What a fearful-sounding phrase. It made Polingaysi think of the older boys catching rabbits in snares. Without argument she darted across the room and flattened herself behind the rolled-up sheep pelts and blankets. Her mother covered her and returned to the doorway.

Polingaysi could hear her sick brother whimpering on his pallet beside the fireplace, then she heard a strange voice, speaking a language she did not understand. When the mother made no answer, another man began talking, this time in not very good Hopi.

"He says, tell you we are going to take your children to school. Where are they?"

"That sick boy is all I have, except for the babies," Polingaysi's mother lied. "He is too sick to go away from home."

There was more talk in the foreign language, then the interpreter said, in Hopi: "*Bahana* says the boy doesn't look sick. We'll take him. Come!"

Polingaysi's sick brother wept aloud, but he struggled to his feet and went with the men.

Almost smothered by the time her mother removed the heavy pelt, Polingaysi began at once to beg her mother not to let the men catch her.

"If they take you, they take you," her mother said, her usually gentle voice harsh in her angry helplessness. "What can we do? The *Bahana* does not care how we feel toward our children. They think they know everything and we know nothing. They think only of themselves and what they want. I don't know what they are going to do to our children, down there in that big house. It is not the Hopi way of caring for children, this tearing them from their homes and their mothers. . . ."

We Want to Be Hopis

Polingaysi's father had known what the *Bahanas* were planning, but since he had no answers for the many questions he knew his people would ask, he had kept silent. Actually, he did not know what

---

[2] **Bahana:** the white man.

"school" meant, and he had no inkling of what it would do for his people.

In spite of his pleasant association with the white missionary, Voth, and the red-faced, white-bristled government man at the school, Polingaysi's small Hopi father was a member of the conservative branch of the Hopi village and as eager as they to retain the ancient culture of his people. It was the so-called progressive group that had consented to adoption of white man's ways.

"When a Hopi becomes a white man," the conservatives said, meaning, of course, when the Indian is willing to take on an overlay of white culture, "he no longer has a face. We want to be Hopis, not white men. We want our children to learn Hopi ways and live by them."

But the white authorities had persuaded Lololoma, chief of the Bear Clan, to sanction their plans for his people. He had, as his people said, "taken the pencil." By making his mark with it, he committed the children of Oraibi to attendance at the new government school. He had given his promise that they would attend. . . .

They'll Tell You What to Do

[Two days later] it seemed to Polingaysi that all the children except herself had gone to school. She was lonely. None of her games held her interest. The simple, ordinary pursuits had lost their tang. Her thoughts were down below, at the school. . . .

At noon, when the children came out of the schoolhouse again, she was playing beside a nearby boulder. Two of her friends saw her and came running to her. Shy as a little desert animal, she hid from them at first. Though she could no longer endure being left in the backwash of all this excitement, she knew the enormity of her action. No one forced her to do this thing. She had come down the trail of her own free will. If she went into that schoolhouse, it would be because she desired to do so. Her mother would be very angry with her.

When she yielded to her desire to be with her friends and to savor the new experience at the cost of losing her freedom, the other girls took her hands, and between them, pulling back only slightly, she went to the schoolhouse.

A bell rang. The children lined up and marched past the kitchen where each was given a saucer of syrup, a piece of hardtack, and a tin cup of water. After they had eaten, the bell rang again and they lined up to march into the schoolhouse. The white man with the red face and the white whiskers stood beside the door, hairy hands on his hips. Polingaysi tried to sidle past him, but he stopped her. Her heart pounded like a Hopi drum as he said something to a Hopi girl, several years older.

"He says to take you and clean you up," the older girl said, taking Polingaysi's hand and leading her away. There was a big tub in the room to which Polingaysi was taken. The older girl poured water into it, instructing Polingaysi to undress. She helped her into the tub, soaped her generously, scrubbed her from head to toes, then rinsed and dried her body. As Polingaysi had hoped, the girl then gave her one of the ticking dresses and rolled her blanket dress, tying it with the woven sash.

"Now, go to school," she said when Polingaysi had struggled into the strange garment. "They'll tell you what to do."

The teacher must have been waiting for her. As she hesitated at the door, he came over, took her by the arm, and walked her rapidly to a desk where two other little girls were sitting. He shoved her in beside them and pushed a pencil and a piece of paper in front of her. He was a thin, sour-faced young man with cold, unsympathetic eyes. She could not understand what he said to her before he turned away.

One of the other girls whispered to her, "Make marks like the ones he makes."

The marks the teacher made on the blackboard spelled "cat," but Polingaysi did not know it. She copied them as best she could, filling her paper on both sides.

No Turning Back

Climbing the trail with the other children after school, she began to have misgivings. What would her mother say? She had no doubt wondered where Polingaysi had gone and worried about her. On the mesa once more, Polingaysi took a roundabout way home, dragging her bare feet to prolong the painful moment of confession. Her older sister reached home long before she did.

When Polingaysi stepped into the doorway, four pairs of eyes met hers: her sick brother's, sad and reproachful; her older sister's wide with excitement; her mother's sorrowful; and the baby brother's, warm and loving.

Her mother spoke.

"Who took you to school? I looked everywhere for you. The *Bahana* has not been in the village all day long."

Polingaysi hung her head, the rolled blanket dress clutched to her bosom.

"I took myself."

"So! You self-willed, naughty girl! You have taken a step in the wrong direction. A step away from your Hopi people. You have brought grief to us. To me, to your father, and to your grandparents. Now, you must continue to go to school each day. You have brought this thing upon yourself, and there is no turning back."

X. Educational Reform

Congested living conditions, unsafe factories, child labor, long working hours, and "boss" control of city government were among the many social ills confronting the nation in the early 1900's. Mass production became more widespread and urban life grew more complex. Criticisms of inadequate schooling were frequently heard in the first decade of the twentieth century. In response, proposals were developed for broadening the program and function of the school. New pedagogical principles were applied to classrooms, and experiments in progressive education were initiated. Schools to preserve agrarianism were founded. Vocational education and vocational guidance were fostered. Secondary education was redefined by influential commissions. The efficiency movement applied business practices to the schools. Teacher organizations developed. Educational reforms slowly got under way. ■

1. My Pedagogic Creed[1]

✦ John Dewey

The nation needed more than criticism of its traditional schools. There was need for a new conception of education and schooling that would both conserve the sense of community which had characterized the agrarian era and advance democratic values in the emerging urban centers. John Dewey was one of those who spoke out on this need. His childhood in rural New England and his work with Jane Addams in Chicago's Hull

[1] John Dewey, "My Pedagogic Creed," originally published as a pamphlet by E. L. Kellogg & Co., 1897. Reprinted in Reginald D. Archambault, ed., *John Dewey on Education: Selected Writings* (New York: The Modern Library, 1964), pp. 427–432, 437–439. © 1964, by Random House, Inc.

House had provided him with first-hand knowledge of the great changes taking place in American society at the turn of the century.

In 1897, when Dewey was a professor of philosophy, psychology, and education at the University of Chicago, he published a manifesto on education entitled "My Pedagogic Creed." During the Progressive Era (1900–1917), Dewey became known as a leader in "progressive education" much as Theodore Roosevelt and Woodrow Wilson became known as leaders in "political progressivism." ■

Article I — What Education Is

I Believe that . . .

— this educational process has two sides — one psychological and one sociological — and that neither can be subordinated to the other, or neglected, without evil results following. Of these two sides, the psychological is the basis. [The child's own instincts and powers furnish the material and give the starting-point for all education.] Save as the efforts of the educator connect with some activity which the child is carrying on of his own initiative independent of the educator, education becomes reduced to a pressure from without. It may, indeed, give certain external results, but cannot truly be called educative. Without insight into the psychological structure and activities of the individual, the educative process will, therefore, be haphazard and arbitrary. If it chances to coincide with the child's activity it will get a leverage; if it does not, it will result in friction, or disintegration, or arrest of the child nature.

— knowledge of social conditions, of the present state of civilization, is necessary in order properly to interpret the child's powers. The child has his own instincts and tendencies, but we do not know what these mean until we can translate them into their social equivalents. We must be able to carry them back into a social past and see them as the inheritance of previous race activities. We must also be able to project them into the future to see what their outcome and end will be. In the illustration just used, it is the ability to see in the child's babblings the promise and potency of a future social intercourse and conversation which enables one to deal in the proper way with that instinct.

— the psychological and social sides are organically related, and that education cannot be regarded as a compromise between the two, or a superimposition of one upon the other. We are told that the psychological definition of education is barren and formal — that it gives us only the idea of a development of all the mental powers without giving us any idea of the use to which these powers are put. On the other hand, it is urged that the social definition of education, as getting adjusted to civilization, makes of it a forced and external process, and results in subordinating the freedom of the individual to a preconceived social and political status.

— each of these objections is true when urged against one side isolated from the other. In order to know what a power really is we must know what its end, use, or function is, and this we cannot know save as we [view] the individual as active in social relationships. But, on the other hand, the only possible adjustment which we can give to the child under existing conditions is that which arises through putting him in complete possession of all his powers. With the advent of democracy and modern industrial conditions, it is impossible to foretell definitely just what civilization will be twenty years from now. Hence it is impossible to prepare the child for any precise set of conditions. To prepare him for the future life means to give him command of himself; it means so to train him that he will have the full and ready use of all his capacities; that his eye and ear and hand may be tools ready to command, that his judgment may be capable of grasping the conditions under which it has to work, and the executive forces be trained to act economically and efficiently. It is impossible to reach this sort of adjustment save as constant regard is had to the individual's own powers, tastes, and interests — that is, as education is continually converted into psychological terms.

In sum, I believe that the individual who is to be educated is a social individual, and that society is an organic union of individuals. [If we eliminate the social factor from the child we are left only with an abstraction; if we eliminate the individual factor from society, we are left only with an inert and lifeless mass.] Education, therefore, must begin with a psychological insight into the child's capacities, interests, and habits. It must be controlled at every point by reference to these same considerations. These powers, interests, and habits must be continually interpreted — we must know what they mean. They must be translated into terms of their social equivalents — into terms of what they are capable of in the way of social service.

Article II — What the School Is

I Believe that

— the school is primarily a social institution. Education being a social process, the school is simply that form of community life in which all those agencies are concentrated that will be most effective in bringing the child to share in the inherited resources of the race, and to use his own powers for social ends.

— education, therefore, is a process of living and not a preparation for future living.

— the school must represent present life — life as real and vital to the child as that which he carries on in the home, in the neighborhood, or on the playground....

Article V — The School and Social Progress

I Believe that

— education is the fundamental method of social progress and reform.

— all reforms which rest simply upon the enactment of law, or the threatening of certain penalties, or upon changes in mechanical or outward arrangements, are transitory and futile.

— education is a regulation of the process of coming to share in the social consciousness; and that the adjustment of individual activity on the basis of this social consciousness is the only sure method of social reconstruction.

— this conception has due regard for both the individualistic and socialistic ideals. It is duly individual because it recognizes the formation of a certain character as the only genuine basis of right living. It is socialistic because it recognizes that this right character is not to be formed by merely individual precept, example, or exhortation, but rather by the influence of a certain form of institutional or community life upon the individual, and that the social organism through the school, as its organ, may determine ethical results.

— in the ideal school we have the reconciliation of the individualistic and the institutional ideals.

— the community's duty to education is, therefore, its paramount moral duty. By law and punishment, by social agitation and discussion, society can regulate and form itself in a more or less haphazard and chance way. But through education society can formulate its own purposes, can organize its own means and resources, and thus shape itself with definiteness and economy in the direction in which it wishes to move. *understanding the child and treating him as an individual*

2. Schools to Conserve Agrarianism[1]
✤ William Starr Myers

> In the early 1900's many Americans both feared and rejected the city. Some educators united with groups of private citizens to establish schools which would preserve the agrarian way of life for urban children and youth. Such a school is described in the selection below. However, as the growth of industry and population caused an outward extension of city boundaries, country day schools became urbanized. They ceased to enroll poor boys from the city and many of them became private schools for upper class youth. ■

American Ideal — Rural, fresh air type Protnt.

"Back to the country" is the cry of the advocates of one of our sanest philanthropic movements. To free thousands of our best citizens from the unwholesome and harmful influences of crowded houses, poor light, and bad air, and to restore them to the open fields, a freedom from unnatural restraints, and the blessings of God's sunshine, are objects worthy of the best efforts of the American people.

The average city resident of comfortable means is accustomed to think that such a movement is merely a charity designed to help the poorer and more unfortunate elements of our population, but as a matter of fact it is of vital interest to every man, woman, and child that lives in a large city. Unhealthful conditions of life do not affect merely the inmates of small houses on alleys and back streets, but spread, through inevitable contact, to the handsome establishments of the more favored neighborhoods; sooner or later the whole city is affected.

---

[1] William Starr Myers, "Country Schools for City Boys," *U.S. Bureau of Education Bulletin*, No. 9 (Washington, D.C.: Government Printing Office, 1912), pp. 7, 11, 17, 18, 20, 21.

Realizing this fact, philanthropists have made an effort to find some means by which our boys who live in the city may spend at least the day in the country, and at the same time have the advantages of an education in the best schools. Some of our people of means, those who can afford the money necessary for an experiment, have hit upon a plan which has solved the problem, it is believed, and that is the plan of founding "country day schools for city boys." And girls, too, are going to be included among those who share the benefits of this movement.

Up to fifteen years ago the only two possible things for the city family, if a healthful outdoor life was desired for the children, were to live at a country home six months of the year and each day send the children in town to school, or else to break all home ties for a large part of the year by sending the boys and girls away to boarding school. A group of men and women of intelligence and enterprise in Baltimore had the vision to see and the faith to act, and the Gilman Country School for Boys, founded in 1897, is the result. . . .

Here is a new and thoroughly equipped building, which has accommodations for 60 boarders and 150 day pupils. The grounds consist of 70 acres in woodland, lawns, and athletic fields, and the large field now in use is one of the finest in the state. All water used in the school is drawn from a sealed well, driven more than 250 feet through solid rock. The yield is more than 40 gallons a minute, and is pronounced by the state board [of] health to be absolutely pure. The total capital invested in this new plant is more than $300,000, of which $225,000 has been put into the building and the grading of grounds. Mr. Frank Woodworth Pine is the present head master. . . .

Intellectual and Physical Exercise

The Gilman School now has a faculty of fifteen and a student body of 157. It provides a continuous and systematic course of instruction for boys from the time they are about ten until they are prepared to enter college. The exercises begin at 9 o'clock, and at 5:30 the day scholars return home to their parents, their minds trained by the best educational methods, their lungs filled with fresh air, and their bodies tired from healthy play. . . .

The ages of the boys usually vary from eight years to 19 or 20. By taking charge of the pupils when very young a firm foundation in the elements of learning is laid, upon which later may be built the firm structure of scholarship that is needed for the more advanced work in the college or university.

In fact it is worthy of note that *thoroughness* has been taken as the ideal for all the educational work of the schools under discussion. They have no desire to be merely "hothouses" for the nurture or forcing of delicate and tender human plants, but manly and healthful places, where the boy shall "stand upon his own feet without fear or favor." The effort is made to classify boys according to their proficiency in each subject and not according to their general standing. . . .

The following is a typical daily schedule:

Daily Schedule

9: a.m.	Roll call; prayers; announcements.
9:15 to 11:15 a.m.	Recitation and study.
11:15 to 11:30 a.m.	Recess, with bread and milk.
11:30 a.m. to 1:30 p.m.	Recitation and study.
1:30 p.m.	Dinner.
2:15 p.m.	Change to athletic clothes.
2:30 to 4 p.m.	Athletics.
4 to 4:30 p.m.	Bath and change to regular clothes.
4:30 to 5:30 p.m.	Study.
5:30 to 6 p.m.	Detention.

During the fall and spring terms the period for athletics is extended from 4 to 4:15, and each of the following periods is delayed a quarter of an hour. . . .

[The day opens with a religious service and Bible readings or moral and ethical instruction. Among the school patrons are Protestant and Catholic, Jew and Gentile, but all are able and willing to join in the practice of a broadly tolerant religion that is worthy of the American ideal. . . .]

Special Features

The Gilman school has for little boys of about eight or ten years an "open-air school" under the charge of a special teacher (a woman). It occupies a small, plain, wooden building, built up on three sides without windows, and the fourth side, with southern exposure, entirely open to the fresh air. Here are desks and necessary school furniture, and, wrapped up warmly, the children study and recite as in an ordinary schoolroom. So far no special difficulty has been experienced, even in the changeable climate of a Baltimore winter, and, as in the case of like experiments in public schools, the results for sick and delicate children have been most successful. . . .

In conclusion, it should be repeated that the country schools offer the advantages of boarding schools without the necessary separation from the parents. The best influences of a home are never supplied by a boarding school; and no teacher or any other person can show the loving care and affection or "insure the softening and refining influences which a mother, of all people, can best give." The right sort of a father should and does have a better influence on his son than any schoolmaster, and "if the master gets a stronger hold on the boy the father suffers in seeing his son more at ease in the companionship and preferring the society of another man to his own." Furthermore, the boarding school boy, when at home on his vacation, might be inclined to spend his time in a round of excitement and festivities, which would tend to pervert his idea of what a home is and how it should be enjoyed.

Finally, the school that keeps a boy in the open, with plenty of fresh air and room for healthful play and away from the streets, the matinées, and moving-picture shows, or perhaps from really harmful diversions, needs no further excuse for its being. The great problem is, how the advantages may be extended to the enormous mass of our public-school children, girls as well as boys. If school boards in country districts can consolidate schools for the purposes of efficiency and arrange for the transportation of children from widely scattered districts to a central school, why can not the method be reversed in the case of the city children? This means the arrangement of such matters as transportation, the noonday lunch, and supervision of athletics and play. It also means the formation of a public opinion necessary for inaugurating the movement and carrying it through.

3. Vocational Education and Vocational Guidance[1]
✤ William C. Redfield

One of the major educational responses to the cry for reform was the development of vocational guidance and instruction. Traditionally the vocational training of youth in agrarian Amer-

[1] "What Vocational Education and Vocational Guidance Mean to the Future of the Country," by William C. Redfield in *Proceedings of the National Society for the Promotion of Industrial Education*, Bulletin No. 18 (1913), pp. 83–84, 86–87.

ica had been performed by the family. But with the coming of urbanization, jobs proliferated rapidly and became highly specialized. Parents could no longer teach the required skills children needed to learn. Youth were left to drift from one "dead-end" job to another, or to idly roam the city streets.

In 1907 leaders in business, labor, politics, and education organized the National Society for the Promotion of Industrial Education in order to solve the growing problem of introducing youth into the world of work. The organization criticized the classical education provided in the public schools and urged the development of an education that would meet the cultural and occupational needs of the adolescent in an industrial environment. The following selection is extracted from a speech made by William Redfield, the Society's president. Redfield, who also served as Secretary of Commerce under President Woodrow Wilson, points out the desperate need of both boys and girls for vocational training. In 1917 President Wilson signed into law the Smith-Hughes vocational education bill which had been fostered by the National Society for the Promotion of Industrial Education. ■

I wonder if it will seem to you strange that I see no humor in the awful problem of industrial education. I have spent thirty years of my life in factories and I have been very poor. I know perfectly well what it means to go out into the great city of New York unable to do anything definite, after a high school education. I had no lack of books, there were many volumes in my father's library. I read Froude's History of England and Grote's History of Greece, and others when a cashier in a dry-goods store, in the intervals of making change. I had read Gibbon's Rome and I believe every standard history. I had translated much of Homer and read the whole first half of Virgil, but I had not been taught practically how to do anything.

It is a trying thing to face the city of New York alone, poor and untrained, no matter how much taught.

But What Can You Do?

Not long ago there came into my business office at different times two young women applying for work. I said to them, "What can you do?" I knew what they had been taught. I knew they could enter a drawing-room; I knew they had that fine quality called style, both of language and of dress; that they would shine at a reception and honor a home. I said to them, "What can you do," for poverty had come to the door and the nose of the wolf was inside the front window. They said to me "Nothing."

The struggle for self-support and self-respect of these fine young women would have convinced the most sceptical of the need for vocational training. . . .

In a club of which I was once president we had 800 boys from off the streets of the city. I doubt if any one of those boys had at any time in his life been taught to do anything. They had been to the grammar school. That was as far as they could go because father was poor, or mother was ill, and they must work, and they must earn something and they must earn it right away. But, they had been taught to do nothing. There was no place then where they could be taught at fourteen years of age to do anything. Most of the boys are that way in the big towns. Not only some, but most of them are so placed to a greater or less degree.

What did we do with these boys? I remember one fellow who had been taught nothing in the world, who drove a grocer's cart and got three dollars a week. He was not a great help to his father. But bye and bye we got into our little club in a modest way some industrial education. We got a good blacksmith to come at night without pay; we got a good carpenter to come, and we got a good electrician to come at night for nothing, and to teach these boys we also got a shoemaker to come in there as instructor. At the end of three years the grocer's boy was an electrician earning twenty odd dollars a week and was all through driving a cart. I remember very vividly that one night the shoe boys were working at cobbling and a little chap came in from the snowy street with his toes sticking out of his shoes. One of the boys at the table, himself only fifteen, looked around and said, "Here, youse, take off them shoes." The little boy took them off, not knowing what was to happen; and the fifteen-year-old shoemaker took that pair of shoes, cleaned them, oiled them, sewed a good honest patch on the shoe, and said, "Here, now, get along with your dry feet." There wasn't much manners, but the boy had learned to take pride in the capacity to do something. What those boys needed was a practical training to keep the wolf from the door; not for culture just then and there.

4. Secondary Education Redefined[1]
✤ National Education Association

Criticism of college-dominated high schools and recognition of society's pressing social ills moved the National Education Association (NEA) to support a massive reform of secondary education. A commission, comprised primarily of administrators and professors, was appointed in 1913 to outline a radically new role for the public high school. Its report five years later called for a comprehensive reorganization of secondary education centered around seven main principles: 1. Health; 2. Command of Fundamental Processes; 3. Worthy Home-Membership; 4. Vocation; 5. Civic Education; 6. Worthy Use of Leisure; and 7. Ethical Character. Each of these principles grew out of a major social problem then confronting urban America. Each principle stated an objective of education in relation to those problems. ■

Changes in the secondary-school population. — In the past 25 years there have been marked changes in the secondary-school population of the United States. The number of pupils has increased, according to federal returns, from one for every 210 of the total population in 1889–90 . . . to one for every 73 of the estimated total population in 1914–15. The character of the secondary-school population has been modified by the entrance of large numbers of pupils of widely varying capacities, aptitudes, social heredity, and destinies in life. Further, the broadening of the scope of secondary education has brought to the school many pupils who do not complete the full course but leave at various stages of advancement. The needs of these pupils cannot be neglected, nor can we expect in the near future that all pupils will be able to complete the secondary school as full-time students.

At present only about one-third of the pupils who enter the first year of the elementary school reach the four-year high school, and only about one in nine is graduated. . . . These facts can no longer be safely ignored. . . .

---

[1] National Education Association, "Cardinal Principles of Secondary Education: A Report of the Commission on the Reorganization of Secondary Education," *U.S. Bureau of Education Bulletin*, No. 35 (Washington, D.C.: Government Printing Office, 1918), pp. 8–9, 11–15.

Educational Reform

The Goal of Education in a Democracy

Education in the United States should be guided by a clear conception of the meaning of democracy. It is the ideal of democracy that the individual and society may find fulfillment each in the other. Democracy sanctions neither the exploitation of the individual by society, nor the disregard of the interests of society by the individual. More explicitly —

> The purpose of democracy is so to organize society that each member may develop his personality primarily through activities designed for the well-being of his fellow members and of society as a whole.

This idea demands that human activities be placed upon a high level of efficiency; that to this efficiency be added an appreciation of the significance of these activities and loyalty to the best ideals involved; and that the individual choose that vocation and those forms of social service in which his personality may develop and become most effective. For the achievement of these ends democracy must place chief reliance upon education.

> Consequently, education in a democracy, both within and without the school, should develop in each individual the knowledge, interests, ideals, habits, and powers whereby he will find his place and use that place to shape both himself and society toward ever nobler ends....

The Principal Aims of Education

... This commission favors such reorganization that secondary education may be defined as applying to all pupils of approximately twelve to eighteen years of age.

1. *Health.* Health needs cannot be neglected during the period of secondary education without serious danger to the individual and the race. The secondary school should therefore provide health instruction, inculcate health habits, organize an effective program of physical activities, regard health needs in planning work and play, and co-operate with home and community in safe-guarding and promoting health interests....

2. *Command of Fundamental Processes.* Much of the energy of the elementary school is properly devoted to teaching certain fundamental processes, such as reading, writing, arithmetical computations, and the elements of oral and written expression. The facility that a child of twelve or fourteen may acquire in the use of these tools is

not sufficient for the needs of modern life. This is particularly true of the mother tongue. Proficiency in many of these processes may be increased more effectively by their application to new material. . . .

3. *Worthy Home-Membership.* Worthy home-membership as an objective calls for the development of those qualities that make the individual a worthy member of a family, both contributing to and deriving benefit from that membership.

This objective applies to both boys and girls. The social studies should deal with the home as a fundamental social institution and clarify its relation to the wider interests outside. Literature should interpret and idealize the human elements that go to make the home. Music and art should result in more beautiful homes and in greater joy therein. The co-educational school with a faculty of men and women should, in its organization and its activities, exemplify wholesome relations between boys and girls and men and women. . . .

In the education of every high-school girl, the household arts should have a prominent place because of their importance to the girl herself and to others whose welfare will be directly in her keeping. The attention now devoted to this phase of education is inadequate, and especially so for girls preparing for occupations not related to the household arts and for girls planning for higher institutions. The majority of girls who enter wage-earning occupations directly from the high school remain in them for only a few years, after which home making becomes their lifelong occupation. For them the high-school period offers the only assured opportunity to prepare for that lifelong occupation. . . .

In the education of boys, some opportunity should be found to give them a basis for the intelligent appreciation of the value of the well-appointed home and of the labor and skill required to maintain such a home, to the end that they may co-operate more effectively. For instance, they should understand the essentials of food values, of sanitation, and of household budgets.

4. *Vocation.* Vocational education should equip the individual to secure a livelihood for himself and those dependent on him, to serve society well through his vocation, to maintain the right relationships toward his fellow workers and society, and, as far as possible, to find in that vocation his own best development.

This ideal demands that the pupil explore his own capacities and aptitudes, and make a survey of the world's work, to the end that he may select his vocation wisely. Hence, an effective program of vocational guidance in the secondary school is essential. . . .

5. *Civic Education.* Civic education should develop in the individual those qualities whereby he will act well his part as a member of neighborhood, town or city, state, and nation, and give him a basis for understanding international problems. . . .

The comprehension of the ideals of American democracy and loyalty to them should be a prominent aim of civic education. The pupil should feel that he will be responsible, in co-operation with others, for keeping the nation true to the best inherited conceptions of democracy, and he should also realize that democracy itself is an ideal to be wrought out by his own and succeeding generations.

Civic education should consider other nations also. As a people we should try to understand their aspirations and ideals that we may deal more sympathetically and intelligently with the immigrant coming to our shores, and have a basis for a wiser and more sympathetic approach to international problems. . . .

6. *Worthy Use of Leisure.* Education should equip the individual to secure from his leisure the re-creation of body, mind, and spirit, and the enrichment and enlargement of his personality.

This objective calls for the ability to utilize the common means of enjoyment, such as music, art, literature, drama, and social intercourse, together with the fostering in each individual of one or more special avocational interests. . . .

7. *Ethical Character.* In a democratic society ethical character becomes [foremost] among the objectives of the secondary school. Among the means for developing ethical character may be mentioned the wise selection of content and methods of instruction in all subjects of study, the social contacts of pupils with one another and with their teachers, the opportunities afforded by the organization and administration of the school for the development on the part of pupils of the sense of personal responsibility and initiative, and, above all, the spirit of service and the principles of true democracy which should permeate the entire school — principal, teachers, and pupils.

5. Bureaucratizing American Schools

As criticism of the economic inefficiency and academic irrelevancy of the public schools mounted, many thought the solution lay in a school administration that would apply business methods to the operation of the schools. Dollars saved became a yardstick for measuring a superintendent's effectiveness. During the first third of the twentieth century, Ellwood P. Cubberley and Frank Spaulding became nationally recognized leaders in developing concepts of schools based on the factory model. Believing that schools should be, above all, smooth-running, economically efficient enterprises, they translated business methods into education. ■

A. THE SCHOOL AS FACTORY[1]

✤ *Ellwood P. Cubberley*

Wholly within the past decade one of the most significant movements in all of our educational history has arisen.... The movement is as yet only in its infancy, but so important is it in terms of the future of administrative service that it bids fair to change, in the course of time, the whole character of school administration. The numerous surveys of city school systems which have been made within the past five years, the frequent discussions of the question of standards in educational meetings, and the labors of many workers in attempting to evolve tentative standards for measurement and units of accomplishment, are all manifestations of this new movement. The movement indicates the growth not only of a professional consciousness as to the need of some quantitative units of measurement, but also, to a limited extent, of a public demand for a more intelligent accounting by school officers for the money expended for public education.

Meaning of the Movement

The significance of this new movement is large, for it means nothing less than the ultimate changing of school administration from guesswork to scientific accuracy; the elimination of favoritism and politics completely from the work; the ending forever of the day when a book-publishing company or a personal or political enemy of the superintendent can secure his removal, without regard to the efficiency

---

[1] Ellwood P. Cubberley, *Public School Administration* (Boston: Houghton Mifflin Company, 1916), pp. 325–327, 338. © by Ellwood P. Cubberley. Reprinted by permission.

of the school system he has built up; the substitution of professional experts for the old and successful practitioners; and the changing of school supervision from a temporary or a political job, for which little or no technical preparation need be made, to that of a highly skilled piece of professional social engineering. . . .

The Scientific Purpose

The scientific purpose of the movement has been to create some standards of measurement and units of accomplishment which may be applied to school systems, to individual schools or classes, or to pupils, to determine the efficiency of the work being done, and of substituting these for that personal opinion which has, in the past, constituted almost the only standard of measurement of educational procedure. The efficiency or inefficiency of teachers, principals, and superintendent, and of courses of instruction, have for long been measured by such personal standards, in which the opinions of laymen have often been of quite as much value as the opinions of school men. The importance of the work done in the schools and the value of their output have also been subject to the same standards of personal opinion. The school, too, and not the world outside, has framed the specifications for the training of its graduates, and these have been based wholly on personal opinions as to needs held by schoolmasters. When laymen on school boards have broken in, and have dismissed teachers and superintendents or altered courses of study, the intrusion has naturally been resented without anyone being able really to prove that such an intrusion was unjustified.

In other words, the school, the most important undertaking of any community, has stood isolated in the community, unable to prove that what it was doing was the best possible, and unable to speak to the community of its accomplishments in a language which the community could easily understand. Instead, we have asked the community to accept on faith our statements that what we are doing is of very great importance, and that we are doing it very well. The result has been an isolation of the school which has defeated some of its best efforts. . . .

Every manufacturing establishment that turns out a standard product or series of products of any kind maintains a force of efficiency experts to study methods of procedure and to measure and test the output of its works. Such men ultimately bring the manufacturing establishment large returns, by introducing improvements in processes and procedure, and in training the workmen to produce a larger and a better output. Our schools are, in a sense, factories in which the raw products (children) are to be shaped and fashioned into products to meet the various demands of life. The specifications for manufacturing come from the demands of twentieth-century civilization, and it is the business of the school to build its pupils according to the specifications laid down. This demands good tools, specialized machinery, continuous measurement of production to see if it is according to specifications, the elimination of waste in manufacture, and a large variety in the output.

B. MANUFACTURING CITIZENSHIP[2]

✤ *Ellwood P. Cubberley*

Education . . . must make good the continual losses which a nation suffers, and it must enable it to move forward continuously. In the first place, our yearly losses are large, and call for heavy replacements. We are a nation of something over 125 million people today. Of this number approximately fourteen millions are children not yet of school age, 26 millions are children between the ages of five and fifteen, another eleven millions are youths between the ages of fifteen and twenty, and nineteen millions are men and women who have passed fifty years of age and whose great usefulness is past. Over thirty millions of young people are enrolled in some kind of school or college, public or private.

Our total losses by deaths each year are approximately one and three-quarter millions. Of these, almost a half million are children who have not lived long enough to enter the public schools; approximately a hundred thousand are children of school age; and almost a million and a quarter are men and women over twenty, who have presumably passed through our schools and received the training and knowledge which the schools can give, and large numbers of whom

---

[2] Ellwood P. Cubberley, *An Introduction to the Study of Education and to Teaching* (Boston: Houghton Mifflin Company, 1933), pp. 43–45. © by Ellwood P. Cubberley. Reprinted by permission.

have also attained that very important maturity of judgment and experience that comes with age and service.

These losses are comparable, in the industrial world, to the parts discarded due to imperfections and not usable in the manufacture of the finished product, and to the wearing-out and breaking-down of pieces of valuable machinery which have been bought and paid for. These discarded parts and worn-out machines have to be replaced with new parts and pieces of machinery of equivalent type, merely to maintain output and keep the factory running on an equal scale of efficiency. Every well-managed business counts these replacements as important items in the cost of manufacturing any article, be it hats or shoes, plows or hoes, washing machines or typewriters, books or newspapers, automobiles or steam engines, or electric light and power or telephone service. The greater the perfection demanded of parts and the greater the rapidity of wear-out of the machinery, the larger must be the replacement item in estimating the costs of conducting the business and manufacturing an output.

The education of a people is not any exception to this fundamental business law. The public schools are the chief factories of American citizenship, and the citizenship manufactured represents the machinery with which our national life is carried on. The losses of units in the process of manufacture, and the wear-out of these units when completed, calls for continual replacements merely to retain the level of intelligence, character, culture, morality, decency, idealism, and business and governmental efficiency to which we had before attained. This calls for the continuous training of the children of all the people in our schools, that we may pass on to the coming citizenry the accumulated knowledge and experience and training of the past. This is merely the preparation of the new generation to take the place of the older members of our citizenship as they retire from active work and die. Unless this replacement is provided for in full, the quality of the citizenship and the general intelligence of the people surely will decline. A large proportion — just how large we cannot say — of our more than three billion dollars of expenditure per year, for the education of the 30 millions of young people, is merely an expenditure for units lost during the process of manufacture, and for replacement, depreciation, or obsolescence of completed units, as these terms are spoken of and calculated in the business world. It is the economic cost of merely holding on to the civilization to which we have in the course of centuries attained.

C. THE SCHOOL BOARD AS MANAGEMENT[3]

✤ Ellwood P. Cubberley

That such an intelligent service may be rendered by citizens requires the selection of men and women of the right type for school board membership. In many respects membership on a school board calls for a higher and more intelligent type of community service than is called for on any other kind of local board. The persons best fitted for such service are men who have been successful in their business or their profession, who have learned to seek and act upon expert advice, and who are not afraid to spend money when that is the thing to do. Those least well fitted are politicians, inexperienced young men, unsuccessful men, ignorant men, petty business men, and old men. Women are often classed as desirable for district school boards and undesirable for city boards, because they are usually most interested in the detailed work of the schools as it relates to teachers and children, and usually least interested in the larger business and financial problems of school control. The crank, the hobby-rider, and the extremist — either men or women — should never be put on a board of education. The call is for business experience and grasp, ability to act rather than talk, self-confidence, courage, practice in selecting experts and relying on them for advice, tact and perseverance in getting things done, and ability to withstand pressure when upholding an adopted policy. The advantages of a small and well-selected board come out strongly here. . . .

In addition to a willingness to render service, the position calls for some technical knowledge as to what the schools ought to do and be, and what are the best means for reaching the desired ends. It also calls for an acquaintance with executive relationship such as few men, outside of those used to managing large business undertakings, ordinarily possess. It would be well if all school board members, on taking office, would first inform themselves as to their proper work and duties by reading carefully some good textbook on public school administration — one that will give them a clear statement of the fundamental principles underlying the proper organization and administration of our public schools.

[3] Ellwood P. Cubberley, *An Introduction to the Study of Education and to Teaching* (Boston: Houghton Mifflin Company, 1933), pp. 99–101. © by Ellwood P. Cubberley. Reprinted by permission.

D. EDUCATION MEASURED BY THE DOLLAR[4]

♣ F. E. Spaulding

As we recall the familiar stock examples of scientific management that come to us from the material industries — such as the moving of pig iron, the laying of brick, and the cutting of metals — as we recall the multitude of stop watch observations and experiments, the innumerable, accurate measurements and comparisons of processes and results, out of which after many years these examples have grown, we may be pardoned if we feel a momentary doubt of the applicability to the educational industry of any management worthy to be characterized as scientific. But when we learn of the marvelous results achieved in some material industries through the elimination of waste motions that were not detectable by the unaided eye and the stop watch, but which yielded to analysis made possible only through motion pictures, we are somewhat reassured; for we are impressed with the fact that great improvements, if not perfect efficiency, may arise from observations and measurements that are relatively crude. Scientific management is a method, characterized by its spirit quite as much as by its accuracy.

The essentials of this method are:
1. The measurement and comparison of comparable results.
2. The analysis and comparison of the conditions under which given results are secured — especially of the means and time employed in securing given results.
3. The consistent adoption and use of those means that justify themselves most fully by their results, abandoning those that fail so to justify themselves. The progressive improvement of a school system demands that these essentials of scientific management be applied incessantly.

Let us waste no time over the obvious but fruitless objection that the ultimate and real products of a school system — those products that are registered in the minds and hearts of the children that go out from the schools — are immeasurable, and hence incomparable. There are [indirect] products in abundance that are measurable —

---

[4] F. E. Spaulding, "The Application of the Principles of Scientific Management," in *Journal of Proceedings and Addresses of the National Education Association* (July 5–11, 1913), pp. 260, 265.

products that every school system seeks to turn out because of the well-founded knowledge or belief that through these the desired ultimate products are achieved. Neither will we take any time to enumerate exhaustively those school products that can be measured and that are worth measuring; to describe suitable units of measurement, and their application; and to enlarge upon the improvements that may be effected in any school system through such measurements and the procedure that the results suggest. . . .

Academic discussion of educational values is as futile as it is fascinating. Which is more valuable, a course in Latin or a course in the machine shop? Which is more valuable, an acre of land or a loaf of bread? There are, there can be, no permanent, no absolute and universal answers to such questions as these; but there are, and there must be, temporary, relative, and local assignments of value to everything, material or spiritual, that man desires. So while we educational practitioners have been waiting on the educational theorists for an evaluation of the various subjects of actual or possible school curricula, we have been determining for our own schools definitely and minutely the relative values of every such subject. And we have done this, for the most part, without knowing it! The school administrator simply cannot avoid assigning educational values every time he determines the expenditure of a dollar.

It may give us a shock — but it will be a wholesome one — to confront ourselves with the relative values that we have thus unconsciously assigned to various subjects. . . . It has been determined, wisely or unwisely, thoughtlessly or intelligently, that in that school [previously cited] 5.9 pupil-recitations in Greek are of the same value as 23.8 pupil-recitations in French; that 12 pupil-recitations in science are equivalent in value to 19.2 pupil-recitations in English; and that it takes 41.7 pupil-recitations in vocal music to equal the value of 13.9 pupil-recitations in art.

Thus confronted, do we feel like denying the equivalency of these values — we cannot deny our responsibility for fixing them as they are? That is a wholesome feeling, if it leads to a wiser assignment of values in [the] future. Greater wisdom in these assignments will come, not by reference to any supposedly fixed and inherent values in these subjects themselves, but from a study of local conditions and needs. I know nothing about the absolute value of a recitation in Greek as compared with a recitation in French or in English. I am convinced, however, by very concrete and quite local considerations, that when the obligations of the present year expire, we ought to purchase no more Greek instruction at the rate of 5.9 pupil-recitations for a dollar. The price must go down, or we shall invest in something else.

6. Should Teachers Affiliate with Organized Labor?[1]
✤ Harry A. Overstreet and David Snedden

> With the increasing bureaucracy of school organization, especially in large cities such as Chicago, New York, Philadelphia, Cleveland, and St. Louis, teachers began to feel that they occupied positions as laborers rather than as professionals. So they began to call for the National Education Association — founded in 1857 — to deal with such problems as teachers' salaries, tenure, and class size. Some urban teachers felt the NEA was too slow in these matters and too dominated by school administrators. They decided that an organization other than the NEA was needed. In 1916 the American Federation of Teachers was formed. Immediately a storm of protest arose against teachers affiliating with labor. The following debate reflects the conflict which continued for decades. Harry Overstreet of the College of the City of New York took the affirmative position in support of the AFT and David Snedden of Teachers' College, Columbia University, took the negative position. ■

A. THE AFFIRMATIVE

... "Should teachers affiliate with organized labor?" My own immediate reaction is: "Why not?" We teachers are laborers. We belong to the "working class." Certainly we shall not be accused of being capitalists. We are not employers who give [wages] and receive the profits which wage workers are able to earn. Now as hired workers, it does not seem a strange nor reprehensible thing to me that we should establish a cordial, co-operative relation with others who likewise are hired workers. For obviously there are certain respects in which our outlook and our needs are identical, respects in which we

---
[1] Harry A. Overstreet and David Snedden, "Should Teachers Affiliate with Organized Labor?" *The Survey* (March 13, 1920), pp. 736–737.

may naturally and with profit consult with each other to the end of mutual enlightenment and support.

And yet that is not the whole story. For when we declare that we are workers, some persons make a reservation: "Yes," they say: "You are indeed workers, but of a very special kind. Most workers work for their own interests. They are a 'class' in the community. You teachers work for the public interest. Hence, when, in any sense, you cease to represent the public, you demean yourselves, you degrade your profession."

For the Public Good

That, it seems to me, touches the very heart of this problem. The glory of the schools is that they have, in theory at least, served the public interest. Now when a number of teachers appear who say: "We are going to affiliate with labor," there comes to us the horrifying thought that the schools are to lose their fine universality and become instruments of partisan or class interests.

Is that true? Does affiliation with labor mean affiliation with a class? If it does, then I for one will have none of it; and I believe that practically everyone else who is associated with this movement will have none of it. . . .

I suppose that one of the most public-minded men that ever lived was Jesus of Nazareth. When he died he belonged to an insignificant minority of a few hundred. Would one say that a man who cast in his fortunes with Jesus of Nazareth and his small band of followers was joining a "class"? Or would one not rather say that in joining a body of people who had transcended "class" interest, who were working for the interest of a finer humanity, he was indeed acting in the spirit of the public good? . . .

Now if that is true; if the service of the public is to be found not in the undiscriminating service of the numerical aggregate, but in co-operation with that group whose *intent* is public, I ask you, ladies and gentlemen, where, in the long history of the world, do we find more continuously, more heroically, more effectively an intent for the bettering of human conditions than in the labor movement? . . .

For Mutual Support

In a very real sense, the teachers can help labor. They can help with their understanding of history, of economics, of politics, of science. They can bring to the labor struggle intellectual balance and penetration; they can help to give to those struggles a direction that is unfalteringly social. Labor hitherto has stumbled along in all sorts of confusions and blindness. Why? Because the laborers, in their pressing need, have had to work out their own salvation, while we teachers, with trained intelligence to contribute, have sat superciliously[2] apart and thanked God that we were not as they. . . .

But labor likewise can help the teacher. The teacher's position today is not an enviable one. It has not been enviable for many years. In the first place financially. The teachers notoriously have been among the lowest paid workers in the land. They have been willing to endure this condition in return for certain apparent advantages — social position, joy in their work, a sense of real service to the community. But the laborer is worthy of his hire; and when a group of laborers for years have not been able to convince the public that their hire should approximate more nearly to their worth, it either means that there is something wrong with the group or with the public. Some of us have come at last to believe that the trouble has been with the teacher group and not with the public. The public is an indeterminate mass swayed this way and that by the prevailing agencies of publicity. . . . Teachers, with their exaggerated "class consciousness," have organized their teachers' councils, their high school associations, their professors' associations and what not. But the sound of them — to the public — has been as of a stone dropped into the ocean. What the teachers need is a great body of organized citizenry who sympathize with their services and their needs and who will make their cause their own. I say organized advisedly; for the vague sympathy of unorganized citizenry counts for little.

For Industrial Democracy

I now come to the most significant matter of all. Labor's fight for many years has been simply for a decent wage and for humanly tolerable working conditions — a materialistic fight, it has been called. Its fight has already passed beyond that stage. It is now fighting for the great spiritual thing we call "industrial democracy." What is industrial democracy? It is that condition in which the worker is first of all a free man in his craft, in which he is no longer the mere "commodity," the mere usable slave of his employers. In the second place, it is that condition in которой, as a free citizen of his craft, he has

---

[2] **superciliously:** proudly and disdainfully.

his citizen's voice in the organization of his craft work. It is for industrial citizenship that the worker is now fighting — and winning in his fight.

Is the teacher today a free man in his craft? Is he a citizen with full rights of participation in the organization of the work of his craft? Thanks to the labor movement, a common manual laborer may not, in most cases, be dismissed save as his dismissal is approved by his peers. Not so a teacher. A principal, a superintendent, a board of education, a board of trustees — in these still resides the right, with a sheer arbitrariness that is often revolting, to wreck a teacher's career. Shall not the teacher have the workingman's right to a review of his case by his peers?

Again, thanks to the labor movement, the common workingman is beginning to participate in the councils of business and production. Is the teacher? For the most part, he is told what is to be done. The orders come from above. And woe to the teacher who is not pliant to the will of the petty autocracies that rule many of our schools! . . .

Industrial democracy is the great spiritual need of the workingman. It is the great spiritual need of the teacher. Shall they not, then, strike hands in a great comradeship of common interest — an interest not partisan, and not degrading; an interest, rather, which is as deeply valid as human nature, as profoundly inevitable as the ongoing of fundamental democracy.

B. THE NEGATIVE

. . . The central objection that I have to raise against any collective affiliation of teachers with the American Federation of Labor is the age-old objection to the affiliation of public school teachers in any collective capacity with partisan organizations of any description whatever.

Your first question I know will be this: Does the American Federation of Labor, or does organized labor altogether, today represent a partisan movement? . . .

Now, it is the essence of any partisan group that it believes it is in large measure the embodiment of sound social policies and right ideals. It could not be a wholesome movement if that were not the case. Most members of the Republican Party can conscientiously appeal for support on the ground that the Republican policies are the best for the country at large. Most members of the Catholic church conscientiously believe that their Christianity is the best of existing types. I do not doubt for a moment that most members of organized labor honestly believe that all labor should be within their general organization. The real test of partisanship obviously is found in what the non-members of an organization believe and feel regarding it. It is not the membership of a partisan group as a rule that determines its partisanship; it is the beliefs, fears and contrary views of those outside. By these tests can anyone here claim that the American Federation of Labor does not stand in the minds of more than a majority of Americans today as a distinctly partisan organization? It is easy for us to imagine how citizens outside of organized labor, and certainly as honest and well informed as any within it, would view the proposal that their public school teachers, policemen, firemen or soldiers should ally themselves with the federation. They would certainly have as much grounds for complaint as they would have if these bodies of public servants for the sake of particular ends should deliberately undertake to affiliate themselves with a particular political party, religious sect, or reform movement that treads on vested interests. American public life, and I suspect the life of any good democracy, is to a large extent made up of parties, each one developing its own methods that are sanctioned as long as they evolve no methods excluded by the essentials of fair play. The greatness of America consists in its ability to tolerate great partisan differences without resort to force.

Professional Independence

But it is essential to this group order that those servants who minister to our common needs shall not themselves be partisans where such partisanship would involve impairment of their usefulness. Individual teachers may be members of political parties, churches and even economic organizations as they see fit; but collectively the experiences of our three hundred years of history convinces us that they, like other public servants, including soldiers, must not participate collectively in partisan activities. . . .

There is always a temptation confronting weak and unorganized human beings to place themselves under the protection of the powerful, usually without any clear conception of the cost that that may finally entail. . . .

Teachers should not for a moment imagine that they can procure help from any organization of a partisan nature without giving up something substantial in return. I do not in the least blame the federation for wanting to procure the adherence of thousands of teachers to their standards. It desires to enlist farmers, the clerks, the mail carriers, and many other kinds of workers. It wants all the proselytes it can get, of course, as does the Methodist church, the Republican Party, and the Anti-Saloon League. The federation wants members now because it knows that not always will its position be as strong and almost uncontested as at present.

I am confident that when teachers clearly perceive what it would cost them, their profession, and the public to trade their professional independence to organized labor for its support in salary and other movements for betterment, the profession as a whole will repudiate the tentative engagements already made by its more short-sighted leaders. Teachers should form more compact organizations than they now have, unions indeed, if it seems desirable; but unless these organizations retain complete powers of independent action they will ultimately defeat even the purposes of the teachers themselves.

XI. Debate over the Curriculum

The development of educational reforms did not end debates over American education. Each national crisis — such as the Great Depression of the 1930's, World War II, the cold war, the Russian launching of Sputnik I in 1957, the problems of the culturally disadvantaged during the 1960's — revived the debates as to the nature of an appropriate education for American youth. The question of what constitutes an adequate education continued to be an issue into the 1970's. ■

1. Schools Must Reconstruct America[1]
✦ George S. Counts

In a study made in 1929, George Counts reported that 90 per cent of the nation's school board members came from the business sector of the local community. Counts believed that the weakness of the free enterprise economic system was clearly revealed during the Great Depression. He argued, as had John Dewey and Jane Addams before him, that schools should serve all classes of society. Counts contended that moneyed interests exercised too much control over American education. In the essay which follows, Counts — a professor at Teachers' College, Columbia University — calls upon educators to exercise their responsibility in using the schools to build a new American society. ■

Like all simple and unsophisticated peoples we Americans have a sublime faith in education. Faced with any difficult problem of life we set our minds at rest sooner or later by the appeal to the school. We are convinced that education is the one unfailing remedy for

[1] © by George S. Counts. Reprinted from *Dare the School Build a New Social Order?* by George S. Counts, pp. 3, 4–5, 27–34, 35–37. By permission of The John Day Company, Inc., publisher.

every ill to which man is subject, whether it be vice, crime, war, poverty, riches, injustice, racketeering, political corruption, race hatred, class conflict, or just plain original sin. We even speak glibly and often about the general reconstruction of society through the school. We cling to this faith in spite of the fact that the very period in which our troubles have multiplied so rapidly has witnessed an unprecedented expansion of organized education. This would seem to suggest that our schools, instead of directing the course of change, are themselves driven by the very forces that are transforming the rest of the social order. . . .

That the existing school is leading the way to a better social order is a thesis which few informed persons would care to defend. Except as it is forced to fight for its own life during times of depression, its course is too serene and untroubled. Only in the rarest of instances does it wage war on behalf of principle or ideal. Almost everywhere it is in the grip of conservative forces and is serving the cause of perpetuating ideas and institutions suited to an age that is gone. . . .

Teacher Power

If we may . . . assume that the child will be imposed upon in some fashion by the various elements in his environment, the real question is not whether imposition will take place, but rather from what source it will come. If we were to answer this question in terms of the past, there could, I think, be but one answer: on all genuinely crucial matters the school follows the wishes of the groups or classes that actually rule society; on minor matters the school is sometimes allowed a certain measure of freedom. But the future may be unlike the past. Or perhaps I should say that teachers, if they could increase sufficiently their stock of courage, intelligence, and vision, might become a social force of some magnitude. About this eventuality, I am not over [optimistic], but a society lacking leadership as ours does, might even accept the guidance of teachers. Through powerful organizations they might at least reach the public conscience and come to exercise a larger measure of control over the schools than hitherto. They would then have to assume some responsibility for the more fundamental forms of imposition which, according to my argument, cannot be avoided.

That the teachers should deliberately reach for power and then make the most of their conquest is my firm conviction. To the extent that they are permitted to fashion the curriculum and the procedures of the school they will definitely and positively influence the social attitudes, ideals, and behavior of the coming generation. In doing this they should resort to no subterfuge or false modesty. They should say neither that they are merely teaching the truth nor that they are unwilling to wield power in their own right. The first position is false and the second is a confession of incompetence. It is my observation that the men and women who have affected the course of human events are those who have not hesitated to use the power that has come to them. Representing as they do, not the interests of the moment or of any special class, but rather the common and abiding interests of the people, teachers are under heavy social obligation to protect and further those interests. In this they occupy a relatively unique position in society. Also since the profession should embrace scientists and scholars of the highest rank, as well as teachers working at all levels of the educational system, it has at its disposal, as no other group, the knowledge and wisdom of the ages. It is scarcely thinkable that these men and women would ever act as selfishly or bungle as badly as have the so-called "practical" men of our generation — the politicians, the financiers, the industrialists. If all of these facts are taken into account, instead of shunning power, the profession should rather seek power and then strive to use that power fully and wisely and in the interests of the great masses of the people.

The point should be emphasized that teachers possess no magic secret to power. While their work should give them a certain moral advantage, they must expect to encounter the usual obstacles blocking the road to leadership. They should not be deceived by the pious humbug with which public men commonly flatter the members of the profession. To expect ruling groups or classes to give precedence to teachers on important matters, because of age or sex or sentiment, is to refuse to face realities. It was one of the proverbs of the agrarian order that a spring never rises higher than its source. So the power that teachers exercise in the schools can be no greater than the power they wield in society. Moreover, while organization is necessary, teachers should not think of their problem primarily in terms of organizing and presenting a united front to the world, the flesh, and the devil. In order to be effective they must throw off completely the slave psychology that has dominated the mind of the pedagogue more or less since the days of ancient Greece. They must be prepared to stand on their own feet and win for their ideas the support of the masses of the people. Education as a force for social regeneration must march hand in hand with the living and creative forces of the social order. In their own lives teachers must bridge the gap between school and society and play some part in the fashioning of those great common purposes which should bind the two together.

An Age of Revolution

This brings us to the question of the kind of imposition in which teachers should engage, if they had the power. Our obligations, I think grow out of the social situation. We live in troublous times; we live in an age of profound change; we live in an age of revolution. Indeed it is highly doubtful whether man ever lived in a more eventful period than the present. Today we are witnessing the rise of a civilization quite without precedent in human history — a civilization founded on science, technology, and machinery, possessing the most extraordinary power, and rapidly making of the entire world a single great society. Because of forces already released, whether in the field of economics, politics, morals, religion, or art, the old molds are being broken. And the peoples of the earth are everywhere seething with strange ideas and passions. If life were peaceful and quiet and undisturbed by great issues, we might with some show of wisdom center our attention on the nature of the child. But with the world as it is, we cannot afford for a single instant to remove our eyes from the social scene or shift our attention from the peculiar needs of the age. . . .

Consider the present condition of the nation. Who among us, if he had not been reared amid our institutions, could believe his eyes as he surveys the economic situation, or his ears as he listens to solemn [discourses] by our financial and political leaders on the cause and cure of the depression! Here is a society that manifests the most extraordinary contradictions: a mastery over the forces of nature, surpassing the wildest dreams of antiquity, is accompanied by extreme material insecurity; dire poverty walks hand in hand with the most extravagant living the world has ever known; an abundance of goods of all kinds is coupled with privation, misery, and even starvation; an excess of production is seriously offered as the underlying cause of severe physical suffering; breakfastless children march to school past bankrupt shops laden with rich foods gathered from the ends of the earth; strong men by the million walk the streets in a futile search for employment and with the exhaustion of hope enter the ranks of the damned; great captains of industry close factories without warning and dismiss the workmen by whose labors they have amassed huge fortunes through the years; automatic machinery increasingly displaces men and threatens society with a growing contingent of the permanently unemployed; racketeers and gangsters with the connivance of public officials fasten themselves on the channels of trade and exact toll at the end of the machine gun; economic parasitism, either within or without the law, is so prevalent that the tradition of honest labor is showing signs of decay. . . .

An Age of Promise

The point should be emphasized, however, that the present situation is also freighted with hope and promise. The age is pregnant with possibilities. There lies within our grasp the most humane, the most beautiful, the most majestic civilization ever fashioned by any people. This much at least we know today. We shall probably know more tomorrow. At last men have achieved such a mastery over the forces of nature that wage slavery can follow chattel slavery and take its place among the relics of the past. No longer are there grounds for the contention that the finer fruits of human culture must be nurtured upon the toil and watered by the tears of the masses. The limits to achievement set by nature have been so extended that we are today bound merely by our ideals, by our power of self-discipline, by our ability to devise social arrangements suited to an industrial age. If we are to place any credence whatsoever in the word of our engineers, the full utilization of modern technology at its present level of development should enable us to produce several times as much goods as were ever produced at the very peak of prosperity, and with the working day, the working year, and the working life reduced by half. We hold within our hands the power to usher in an age of plenty, to make secure the lives of all, and to banish poverty forever from the land. The only cause for doubt or pessimism lies in the question of our ability to rise to the stature of the times in which we live.

Our generation has the good or the ill fortune to live in an age when great decisions must be made. The American people, like most of the other peoples of the earth, have come to the parting of the ways; they can no longer trust entirely the inspiration which came to them when the republic was young; they must decide afresh what they are to do with their talents. Favored above all other nations with the resources of nature and the material instrumentalities of civilization, they stand confused and irresolute before the future. They seem to lack the moral quality necessary to quicken, discipline, and give direction to their matchless energies. In a recent paper Professor Dewey has, in my judgment, correctly diagnosed our troubles: "the schools, like the nation," he says, "are in need of a central purpose which will create new enthusiasm and devotion, and which will unify and guide all intellectual plans."

This suggests, as we have already observed, that the educational problem is not wholly intellectual in nature. Our progressive schools therefore cannot rest content with giving children an opportunity to study contemporary society in all of its aspects. This of course must be done, but I am convinced that they should go much farther. If the schools are to be really effective, they must become centers for the building, and not merely for the contemplation, of our civilization. This does not mean that we should endeavor to promote particular reforms through the educational system. We should, however, give to our children a vision of the possibilities which lie ahead and endeavor to enlist their loyalties and enthusiasms in the realization of the vision. Also our social institutions and practices, all of them, should be critically examined in the light of such a vision.

2. Schools Must Adapt to Change[1]

✤ Harold Benjamin

The debate over school curriculum intensified in the 1930's. The basic issue, argued especially between professors in the academic disciplines and professors of education, often centered around a "subject-centered" curriculum versus a "child-centered" curriculum. Harold Benjamin rejected both. Instead, he called upon the schools to provide educational experiences relevant to a changing social order. In his book, The Saber-Tooth Curriculum, *Benjamin (writing under a pseudonym) describes an imaginary caveman, "New-Fist," who developed the first systematic education. His curriculum, which was finally accepted by even the conservative tribe members, consisted of (1) fish-grabbing-with-the-bare-hands; (2) woolly-horse-clubbing; and (3) saber-*

[1] From *The Saber-Tooth Curriculum* by J. Abner Peddiwell, pp. 33–44. Copyright 1939 by McGraw-Hill, Inc. Used by permission of McGraw-Hill Book Company.

tooth-tiger-scaring-with-fire. This curriculum made good sense for many years. But conditions of life changed. And the old curriculum persisted. ■

... In due time everybody who was anybody in the community knew that the heart of good education lay in the three subjects of fish-grabbing, horse-clubbing, and tiger-scaring. New-Fist and his contemporaries grew old and were gathered by the Great Mystery to the Land of the Sunset far down the creek. Other men followed their educational ways more and more, until at last all the children of the tribe were practiced systematically in the three fundamentals. Thus the tribe prospered and was happy in the possession of adequate meat, skins, and security.

It is to be supposed that all would have gone well forever with this good educational system if conditions of life in that community had remained forever the same. But conditions changed, and life which had once been so safe and happy in the cave-realm valley became insecure and disturbing.

A new ice age was approaching in that part of the world. A great glacier came down from the neighboring mountain range to the north. Year after year it crept closer and closer to the headwaters of the creek which ran through the tribe's valley, until at length it reached the stream and began to melt into the water. Dirt and gravel which the glacier had collected on its long journey were dropped into the creek. The water grew muddy. What had once been a crystal-clear stream in which one could see easily to the bottom was now a milky stream into which one could not see at all.

At once the life of the community was changed in one very important respect. It was no longer possible to catch fish with the bare hands. The fish could not be seen in the muddy water. For some years, moreover, the fish in this creek had been getting more timid, agile, and intelligent. The stupid, clumsy, brave fish, of which originally there had been a great many, had been caught with the bare hands for fish generation after fish generation, until only fish of superior intelligence and agility were left. These smart fish, hiding in the muddy water under the newly deposited glacial boulders, eluded the hands of the most expertly trained fish-grabbers. Those tribesmen who had studied advanced fish-grabbing in the secondary school could do no better than their less well-educated fellows who had taken only an elementary course in the subject, and even the university graduates with majors in ichthyology[2] were baffled by the problem. No matter how good a man's fish-grabbing education had been, he could not grab fish when he could not find fish to grab.

The melting waters of the approaching ice sheet also made the country wetter. The ground became marshy far back from the banks of the creek. The stupid woolly horses, standing only five or six hands high and running on four-toed front feet and three-toed hind feet, although admirable objects for clubbing, had one dangerous characteristic. They were ambitious. They all wanted to learn to run on their middle toes. They all had visions of becoming powerful and aggressive animals instead of little and timid ones. They dreamed of a far-distant day when some of their descendants would be sixteen hands high, weigh more than half a ton, and be able to pitch their would-be riders into the dirt. They knew they could never attain these goals in a wet, marshy country, so they all went east to the dry, open plains, far from the paleolithic hunting grounds. Their places were taken by little antelopes who came down with the ice sheet and were so shy and speedy and had so keen a scent for danger that no one could approach them closely enough to club them.

The best trained horse-clubbers of the tribe went out day after day and employed the most efficient techniques taught in the schools, but day after day they returned empty-handed. A horse-clubbing education of the highest type could get no results when there were no horses to club.

Finally, to complete the disruption of paleolithic life and education, the new dampness in the air gave the saber-tooth tigers pneumonia, a disease to which these animals were peculiarly susceptible and to which most of them succumbed. A few moth-eaten specimens crept south to the desert, it is true, but they were pitifully few and weak representatives of a once numerous and powerful race.

So there were no more tigers to scare in the paleolithic community, and the best tiger-scaring techniques became only academic exercises, good in themselves, perhaps, but not necessary for tribal security. Yet this danger to the people was lost only to be replaced by another and even greater danger, for with the advancing ice sheet came ferocious glacial bears which were not afraid of fire, which walked the trails by day as well as by night, and which could not be driven away by the

---

[2] ichthyology: the study of fish.

most advanced methods developed in the tiger-scaring courses of the schools.

The community was now in a very difficult situation. There was no fish or meat for food, no hides for clothing, and no security from the hairy death that walked the trails day and night. Adjustment to this difficulty had to be made at once if the tribe was not to become extinct.

The New Inventions

Fortunately for the tribe, however, there were men in it of the old New-Fist breed, men who had the ability to do and the daring to think. One of them stood by the muddy stream, his stomach contracting with hunger pains, longing for some way to get a fish to eat. Again and again he had tried the old fish-grabbing technique that day, hoping desperately that at last it might work, but now in black despair he finally rejected all that he had learned in the schools and looked about him for some new way to get fish from that stream. There were stout but slender vines hanging from trees along the bank. He pulled them down and began to fasten them together more or less aimlessly. As he worked, the vision of what he might do to satisfy his hunger and that of his crying children back in the cave grew clearer. His black despair lightened a little. He worked more rapidly and intelligently. At last he had it — a net, a crude seine. He called a companion and explained the device. The two men took the net into the water, into pool after pool, and in one hour they caught more fish — intelligent fish in muddy water — than the whole tribe could have caught in a day under the best fish-grabbing conditions.

Another intelligent member of the tribe wandered hungrily through the woods where once the stupid little horses had abounded but where now only the elusive antelope could be seen. He had tried the horse-clubbing technique on the antelope until he was fully convinced of its futility. He knew that one would starve who relied on school learning to get him meat in those woods. Thus it was that he too, like the fish-net inventor, was finally impelled by hunger to new ways. He bent a strong, springy young tree over an antelope trail, hung a noosed vine therefrom, and fastened the whole device in so ingenious a fashion that the passing animal would release a trigger and be snared neatly when the tree jerked upright. By setting a line of these snares, he was able in one night to secure more meat and skins than a dozen horse-clubbers in the old days had secured in a week.

A third tribesman, determined to meet the problem of the ferocious bears, also forgot what he had been taught in school and began to think in direct and radical fashion. Finally, as a result of this thinking, he dug a deep pit in a bear trail, covered it with branches in such a way that a bear would walk out on it unsuspectingly, fall through to the bottom, and remain trapped until the tribesmen could come up and dispatch him with sticks and stones at their leisure. The inventor showed his friends how to dig and camouflage other pits until all the trails around the community were furnished with them. Thus the tribe had even more security than before and in addition had the great additional store of meat and skins which they secured from the captured bears.

As the knowledge of these new inventions spread, all the members of the tribe were engaged in familiarizing themselves with the new ways of living. Men worked hard at making fish nets, setting antelope snares, and digging bear pits. The tribe was busy and prosperous.

Fundamentals, Not Fads and Frills

There were a few thoughtful men who asked questions as they worked. Some of them even criticized the schools.

"These new activities of net-making and operating, snare-setting, and pit-digging are indispensable to modern existence," they said. "Why can't they be taught in school?"

The safe and sober majority had a quick reply to this naive question. "School!" they snorted derisively. "You aren't in school now. You are out here in the dirt working to preserve the life and happiness of the tribe. What have these practical activities got to do with schools? You're not saying lessons now. You'd better forget your lessons and your academic ideals of fish-grabbing, horse-clubbing, and tiger-scaring if you want to eat, keep warm, and have some measure of security from sudden death."

The radicals persisted a little in their questioning. "Fishnet-making and using, antelope-snare construction and operation, and bear-catching and killing," they pointed out, "require intelligence and skills — things we claim to develop in schools. They are also activities we need to know. Why can't the schools teach them?"

But most of the tribe, and particularly the wise old men who controlled the school, smiled indulgently at this suggestion. "That wouldn't be *education*," they said gently.

"But why wouldn't it be?" asked the radicals.

"Because it would be mere training," explained the old men patiently. "With all the intricate details of fish-grabbing, horse-clubbing, and tiger-scaring — the standard cultural subjects — the school curriculum is too crowded now. We can't add these fads and frills of net-making, antelope-snaring, and — of all things — bear-killing. Why, at the very thought, the body of the great New-Fist, founder of our paleolithic educational system, would turn over in its [grave]. What we need to do is to give our young people a more thorough grounding in the fundamentals. Even the graduates of the secondary schools don't know the art of fish-grabbing in any complete sense nowadays, they swing their horse clubs awkwardly too, and as for the old science of tiger-scaring — well, even the teachers seem to lack the real flair for the subject which we oldsters got in our teens and never forgot."

"But, damn it," exploded one of the radicals, "how can any person with good sense be interested in such useless activities? What is the point of trying to catch fish with the bare hands when it just can't be done any more? How can a boy learn to club horses when there are no horses left to club? And why in hell should children try to scare tigers with fire when the tigers are dead and gone?"

"Don't be foolish," said the wise old men, smiling most kindly smiles. "We don't teach fish-grabbing to grab fish; we teach it to develop a generalized agility which can never be developed by mere training. We don't teach horse-clubbing to club horses; we teach it to develop a generalized strength in the learner which he can never get from so prosaic and specialized a thing as antelope-snare-setting. We don't teach tiger-scaring to scare tigers; we teach it for the purpose of giving that noble courage which carries over into all the affairs of life and which can never come from so base an activity as bear-killing."

All the radicals were silenced by this statement, all except the one who was most radical of all. He felt abashed, it is true, but he was so radical that he made one last protest.

"But — but anyway," he suggested, "you will have to admit that times have changed. Couldn't you please *try* these other more up-to-date activities? Maybe they have *some* educational value after all?"

Even the man's fellow radicals felt that this was going a little too far.

The wise old men were indignant. Their kindly smiles faded. "If you had any education yourself," they said severely, "you would know that the essence of true education is timelessness. It is something that endures through changing conditions like a solid rock standing squarely and firmly in the middle of a raging torrent. You must know that there are some eternal verities, and the saber-tooth curriculum is one of them!"

3. Schools Must Foster National Survival[1]
✤ Hyman Rickover

Critics of progressive education received their greatest support from the launching of Sputnik I, the Russian space satellite, in 1957. This great scientific accomplishment led many Americans to believe that the United States had lost its leadership as a world power. Critics were quick to blame the public schools and especially any advocates of a child-centered education. They argued that Russian pupils had been given a more rigorous intellectual diet — hence, their country's scientific superiority. Admiral Hyman Rickover, developer of the nuclear submarine, charged that inadequate instruction in science, math, and other subjects had weakened America's capacity for survival. Pressure was applied to the public schools to produce a new breed of American, able to effectively combat Soviet communism. ■

MEET THE PRESS

Moderator: NED BROOKS
Panel: ERNEST K. LINDLEY, *Newsweek Magazine*
           JAMES RESTON, *The New York Times*
           CHALMERS ROBERTS, *The Washington Post*
           LAWRENCE E. SPIVAK, *Regular Panel Member*

MR. BROOKS: Welcome once again to MEET THE PRESS. Our guest today is Vice Admiral Hyman Rickover, widely recognized as the father of the atomic Navy. His achievement in applying atomic energy to submarine propulsion is ranked as one of the greatest scientific contributions of our time. In 1958 Congress voted him a special

[1] MEET THE PRESS, Volume 4, No. 4 (Sunday, January 24, 1960), pp. 3–11. © 1960, by the National Broadcasting Company, Inc. Reprinted by permission.

gold medal. Last year he was assigned by President Eisenhower to accompany Vice President Nixon on his visit to the Soviet Union.

Admiral Rickover has aroused nationwide interest in his crusade for fundamental changes in our educational system. He believes that education holds the key to our survival. He has become one of the sharpest critics of the school system at all levels. He has made a deep impression on the country by his brilliance and his refusal to be diverted when he considers the goal important.

Admiral Rickover is making his first appearance today on a panel interview program.

Still Behind the Russians

Mr. Spivak: Admiral, some of your critics are saying "Admiral Rickover is a great engineer. Why doesn't he stick to engineering and leave education to the educators?" Will you tell us why you have taken so much of your valuable time to attack our educational system?

Admiral Rickover: You remember what Clemenceau said about war — it was too important to leave to the [generals]. The educators are public servants. As such they have every right to be criticized by any citizen in a democracy. When you cannot criticize your public servants, then you have the Russian system. Therefore, if we cannot criticize, we do not have democratic education.

Mr. Spivak: About two years ago in an article for *This Week* magazine you wrote: "As a people we have been caught napping, but the launching of Sputnik may well do for education what Pearl Harbor did for industry and the military." Would you say that the hope you expressed two years ago has been fulfilled?

Admiral Rickover: No, sir, it has not. There is some little activity going on; there is some lip service being given to better education, but it is by fits and starts. Our people do not yet recognize how far we are falling behind.

Mr. Spivak: Arthur Flemming, Secretary of Health, Education and Welfare, who certainly is in a position to know, or ought to be in a position to know, says "I do not agree with those who say we are behind Europe and Russia in education. Taking the educational system as a whole, we have the best there is anywhere at the present time." Upon what do you base your judgment?

Admiral Rickover: If that is the case, why then is he asking for more money for education — if we already have the best educational system in the world? I base my estimate on the fact that the United States Office of Education has published examinations which are asked of about 1.6 million Russians at the age of seventeen, in mathematics, in physics, in chemistry, in history, in foreign languages and so on. Very few of our high school graduates can pass that examination. When our children can pass an examination as severe as that — and that examination is not as severe as children in Western Europe can pass — then I will be satisfied with our school system.

Mr. Reston: Is our trouble that we are lacking brains, or that we are not using the brains we have?

Admiral Rickover: We have plenty of brains in this country. We simply are not using them. The children in our schools are wasting their time on many subjects which have nothing to do with education whatsoever. Of course, this makes many jobs for guidance counsellors, athletic coaches, school administrators and so on, but it does not add to education. . . .

Mr. Roberts: Starting with the fact that this country is in favor of general free public education for everybody, and recognizing that we don't all have the same amount of brains — you are the only one in the room who could do anything about this submarine; none of the rest of us could — is your quarrel with the total nature of our system, or only that it doesn't pull out of it the relatively small percentage of our people who can do these extraordinarily skillful jobs that seem to be needed to be done in this competition with the Communists?

Admiral Rickover: My objection is to the total system. I believe that many, many more of our youngsters can be trained to be good scientists, good engineers, good administrators, good musicians and good artists if we simply make the try. The United States Office of Education claims officially that 60 per cent of our youngsters cannot be trained in the way I would wish. I think that many can. We simply are not trying hard enough. We give up too soon. This is my basic complaint against our education system. . . .

The Need for Standards

Mr. Spivak: What major steps would you take? If you were a dictator of education, today, if you could change the system. What would be your first step; what would you go about doing?

Admiral Rickover: The first thing I would do is set up a standard, as I said before. You cannot get anywhere unless you have standards. For example, when we went to nuclear power in the Navy, we had to set up new standards for the welding of stainless steel and many other types of standards. We found unless we had those standards the shipyards and the factories could not do a good job. This is true everywhere in life. So, first, is the standard. Second, I would get better teachers. Third, I would knock off some of the administrators who are really running our schools. For example, in one state, 60 per cent of the public school principals are ex-athletic coaches. People of that type should not be running our schools. In fact, the voice of education is not the voice of the teachers; it is the voice of the administrators. The teachers never get to talk. I get many letters from teachers who tell me about conditions in the schools, and they say, "Please don't use my name; I am afraid."

Mr. Spivak: You talk about standards, but we have standards, here. I mean a boy has to get certain grades; he has to pass certain subjects in order to get through Harvard or Yale or any college, so we do have standards. What do you mean by standards? You would set your own standards?

Admiral Rickover: I am talking mostly about the grammar schools and the high schools. The high school diploma in this country has very little meaning because the requirements are so different in various parts of the country. It merely means in general that the child has sat in school for four years. It does not have anywhere near the same meaning that it has in Western Europe. . . .

The Role of Parents

Mr. Reston: What about the responsibility of the home in all this?

Admiral Rickover: I believe that if the parents did their job, we could have much better educated children. It has been found out after considerable research that how children do in school, not only here but even in Russia, is based on the influence of the home. If the home is a place where there are simply good surroundings, where the children simply get good clothes and lots of entertainment and there is no intellectual discussion in the home, that has quite an effect on the children. You will find many studies show that the parents are the greatest influence in how well their children do. Until and unless the parents recognize that if they decide to bring children forth into this world, they have a deep responsibility to look out for their posterity. Until they decide that, until they understand that that is their most important function in life, we will not have better schools. Today the parents are mostly satisfied with having a good time, and with looking out for things that are not concerned with the intellect of their children.

Mr. Reston: What do you do about the kids that come out of good homes and where there is agitation for standards of excellence in the family, intellectually, and who go to good universities, and then they use this excellence in very secondary endeavors, whereas in Russia, which you are always quoting, they direct their brains to the place where the state needs those brains the most. What do you do about this problem?

Admiral Rickover: We can do the same thing here without state compulsion, if our values were not such that we gave material possession such a high place in our scheme of things — if we were taught now that this is really an affluent society where everybody really has enough to get along on, that there are many other things in life besides possessions, filling our homes with new things. Every day the nursery rhymes on TV and radio urge us to buy new things. If we would learn that these things are thrown in the ashcan in a couple of years but what you put in a child's mind stays there forever, if we realize that the intellectual life, the life of the mind, is just as important as getting money and material things, I believe many of these youngsters would go on to do intellectual endeavors.

Mr. Reston: What you are talking about now is the whole philosophy of the country?

Admiral Rickover: Yes, sir.

Mr. Reston: The sense of values of the country, not the educational system? Is this the heart of the problem?

Admiral Rickover: The education of our country is a part of the sum total. You can't divorce the educational system from the country, nor can you divorce the responsibility of all the people from our educational troubles. You can't blame one group of society. It is our collective fault.

Developing Each Child's Potential

Mr. Roberts: I'd like to ask you about one proposal you have made specifically, if I understand it correctly, and that is the idea of doing something more for the so-called bright kids in our schools, who, if I understand your criticism and that of others, have been often lost by making schools the lowest common denominator. The bright kid is lost in the mass. Am I right that you want to have a separate school system for the brighter kids, or how would you pull that boy or girl up above the level of the mass of the kids?

ADMIRAL RICKOVER: I believe that every child in this country no matter where he comes from, what the financial status of his parents is, what his social status is, should have an equal opportunity to develop himself to the maximum. I would give federal aid to education as is necessary to accomplish this. I would not stop any youngster who is brilliant, I would not have him held back by anyone else. I would let each child proceed at his maximum. I would not have separate schools, necessarily. You could have it in separate parts of the same school, but I would group children, after about ten or eleven years of age, in accordance with their abilities, so that every child in every school is working as hard as he can. If you put the bright youngster in with the dullard, the bright one becomes lazy and becomes troublesome. The dullard becomes dissatisfied because he reaches an inferiority complex. So I would separate them so that each one is doing the best he can.

MR. ROBERTS: Are you in favor of a strictly limited kind of education? You have criticized so-called frills or trivia in education. Do you think we ought to get rid of all sports that we have in our school system, high school football and that sort of thing, and stick to the classroom? Is that what you are talking about?

ADMIRAL RICKOVER: I would stick to the classroom with the exception of physical education. Physical education is essential, but many of the organized sports are done more for the entertainment of the parents than it is for the children themselves. It also is done to a great extent to make jobs for various people. The school is not the place for this. The school is tax supported. There is a distinction between training and education. Education can be done best in the school. Training should be done by the home, by the church and by the community. And when we try in a 180-day school year, five hours a day, to do everything in a school, we accomplish nothing well. I would use the school to train the intellect. . . .

MR. SPIVAK: Admiral, do you think we are in a life and death struggle with the Soviet Union?

ADMIRAL RICKOVER: Why, of course, we are.

MR. SPIVAK: And do you think education or military defense is more important in that life and death struggle at the present time?

ADMIRAL RICKOVER: Education is more important because military developments are transitory. They change every year or so, but education is permanent. Unless we have a thoroughly educated citizenry, we will not be able to solve either our military problems or the many other problems that are facing this country. This is why I consider education of far greater importance than anything there is in this country, any problem we have.

4. Schools Must Prepare for the Future[1]
♣ Jerome S. Bruner

"What to teach, and to what end?" This question was actively debated by educators in the early 1960's. Subject areas were re-examined. Scholars were called upon to reconstruct the content of their separate fields. Primary stress was placed on developing concepts and principles, rather than on amassing isolated bits of knowledge.

In 1959 the National Academy of Sciences sponsored a conference of leading scholars and educators to consider new educational approaches. Jerome Bruner, psychology professor at Harvard, served as its chairman. His book, The Process of Education, *is the result of the conference. The passage below is taken from his chapter entitled "The Importance of Structure."* ■

The first object of any act of learning, over and beyond the pleasure it may give, is that it should serve us in the future. Learning should not only take us somewhere; it should allow us later to go further more easily. There are two ways in which learning serves the future. One is through its specific applicability to tasks that are highly similar to those we originally learned to perform. Psychologists refer to this phenomenon as specific transfer of training; perhaps it should be called the extension of habits or associations. Its utility appears to be limited in the main to what we usually speak of as skills. Having learned how to hammer nails, we are better able later to learn how to hammer tacks or chip wood. Learning in school undoubtedly creates skills of a kind that transfers to activities encountered later, either in school or after. A second way in which earlier learning renders later performance more efficient is through what is conveniently called

[1] Reprinted by permission of the publishers from Jerome S. Bruner, *The Process of Education* (Cambridge, Mass.: Harvard University Press, 1960), pp. 17, 19–20. Copyright, 1960, by the President and Fellows of Harvard College.

nonspecific transfer or, more accurately, the transfer of principles and attitudes. In essence, it consists of learning initially not a skill but a general idea, which can then be used as a basis for recognizing subsequent problems as special cases of the idea originally mastered. This type of transfer is at the heart of the educational process — the continual broadening and deepening of knowledge in terms of basic and general ideas. . . .

The experience of the past several years has taught at least one important lesson about the design of a curriculum that is true to the underlying structure of its subject matter. It is that the best minds in any particular discipline must be put to work on the task. The decision as to what should be taught in American history to elementary school children or what should be taught in arithmetic is a decision that can best be reached with the aid of those with a high degree of vision and competence in each of these fields. To decide that the elementary ideas of algebra depend upon the fundamentals of the commutative, distributive, and associative laws, one must be a mathematician in a position to appreciate and understand the fundamentals of mathematics. Whether schoolchildren require an understanding of Frederick Jackson Turner's ideas about the role of the frontier in American history before they can sort out the facts and trends of American history — this again is a decision that requires the help of the scholar who has a deep understanding of the American past. Only by the use of our best minds in devising curricula will we bring the fruits of scholarship and wisdom to the student just beginning his studies.

The question will be raised, "How enlist the aid of our most able scholars and scientists in designing curricula for primary and secondary schools?" The answer has already been given, at least in part. The School Mathematics Study Group, the University of Illinois mathematics projects, the Physical Science Study Committee, and the Biological Sciences Curriculum Study have indeed been enlisting the aid of eminent men in their various fields, doing so by means of summer projects, supplemented in part by year-long leaves of absence for certain key people involved. They have been aided in these projects by outstanding elementary and secondary school teachers and, for special purposes, by professional writers, film makers, designers, and others required in such a complex enterprise.

There is at least one major matter that is left unsettled even by a large-scale revision of curricula in the direction indicated. Mastery of the fundamental ideas of a field involves not only the grasping of general principles, but also the development of an attitude toward learning and inquiry, toward guessing and hunches, toward the possibility of solving problems on one's own.... To instill such attitudes by teaching requires something more than the mere presentation of fundamental ideas. Just what it takes to bring off such teaching is something on which a great deal of research is needed, but it would seem that an important ingredient is a sense of excitement about discovery — discovery of regularities of previously unrecognized relations and similarities between ideas, with a resulting sense of self-confidence in one's abilities.

XII. Striving for Equal Opportunity

Though legally free, the American Negro in the twentieth century experienced discrimination and continuing segregation. Many educators have recognized the effect of compulsory separation of the races on limiting the aspirations of black children and youth. In 1954, the United States Supreme Court looked at the accumulating scholarly evidence of the baleful effects of a policy of "separate but equal" and ruled segregation in the public schools to be unconstitutional. Following the decision, the struggle for desegregation took place in many Southern communities. In recent years the battleground has shifted to Northern cities where questions of neighborhood schools, largely segregated because of segregated housing patterns, were heatedly disputed. The ubiquitous yellow school bus became for many a hated symbol as busing was used as a means of dismantling racially segregated schools. At the same time, a growing number of black parents sought control of their neighborhood schools, demanding the introduction of black studies and the employment of more black teachers and administrators. By the 1970's equal educational opportunity was still an unachieved goal. ■

1. Perpetuating the Inequity

A racially separate educational system had been firmly entrenched in the South by 1900. Northern cities in the early 1900's experienced an unprecedented influx of migrants from the rural South. In the decade between 1910–1920 about one-half million Negroes migrated north of the Mason-Dixon line. Seeking jobs and education, these black freedmen soon encountered another type of discrimination — less formal but usually just as prohibitive. This type of discrimination resulted from de facto segregation — schools segregated in fact, though not by law. The two selections, the first by a Negro principal and the second by a white principal, point out the effects of such practices. ■

A. LIMITED ASPIRATIONS[1]

♣ William L. Bulkley

Some one has remarked that, if a boy in the city of New York wants to learn a trade he must commit a crime, meaning by this that he would be sent to one of the reformatories where manual training forms an important part of the school curriculum. It may not be so bad as this, but this much is certain, the boy, whether white or black, finds it no easy task to learn a trade. For the white boy, however, this difficulty is counterbalanced, at least to some extent, by the many opportunities offered in business. The colored boy, on the other hand, runs sheer up against a stone wall here. As an illustration of the difficulties that confront a colored boy I may cite one case. I received a communication the other day from an electric company (possibly all other male principals received the same) stating that they could use some bright, clean, industrious boys in their business, starting them at so much a week and aiding them to learn the business. I suspected that they did not comprehend colored boys under the generic term "boys," but thought to try. So I wrote asking if they would give employment to a colored boy who could answer to the qualifications stated. The next mail brought the expected reply that no colored boy, however promising, was wanted. I heaved a sigh and went on.

The saddest thing that faces me in my work is the small opportunity for a colored boy or girl to find proper employment. A boy comes to my office and asks for his working papers. He may be well up in the school, possibly with graduation only a few months off. I question him somewhat as follows: "Well, my boy, you want to go to work, do you? What are you going to do?" "I am going to be a doorboy, sir." "Well, you will get $2.50 or $3 a week, but after a while that will not be enough; what then?" After a moment's pause he will reply: "I should like to be an office boy." "Well, what next?" A moment's silence, and, "I should try to get a position as bell-boy." "Well, then, what next?" A rather contemplative mood, and then, "I

[1] William Bulkley, "The Industrial Condition of the Negro in New York City," in *The Annals of the American Academy of Political and Social Science*, XXVII (January-June, 1906), pp. 592–593.

should like to climb to the position of head bell-boy." He has now arrived at the top; farther than this he sees no hope. He must face the bald fact that he must enter business as a boy and wind up as a boy.

A bright boy came to me one day for his working papers. I was sorry to see him want to leave school, but he had no father, and his poor mother had the hardest sort of job to earn enough over the wash-tub to pay the rent for their two rooms and to buy their meager food and clothing. The boy earned what little he could by odd jobs in the afternoon, Saturdays and holidays. Still, I felt that if I could get him to stay till he could finish he might chance to find something better; but that would mean at least three years more of school. In reply to my urgent request that he try to battle through, with sad face he said: "I am old enough now to help mother; she needs me. And again, there is nothing better for a colored boy to do if he finishes the course." The reply pierced my heart like a white-hot bolt. I shall remember that scene till my dying day. All the monster evils of prejudice passed before me in procession like the hideous creatures of an Inferno, and I thought of the millions of hopes that have been blighted . . . , all because the iron heel of this base, hell-borne caste is upon the neck of every boy, of every girl who chanced to be born black.

B. SEPARATION IN EFFECT[2]

✤ E. George Payne

Previous to the Civil War education for the Negro was provided only in scattered schools in the North, when 1.7 per cent of the Negro population of school age attended school; so that we may say that sixty-odd years ago Negro education in the United States, as a whole, was near the zero point. Therefore, the development of Negro education to its present state [in 1928] has taken place in the past sixty-five years. . . .

It may be noted here that legally segregation of the Negro population of Negro children in schools is not recognized in the Northern

---

[2] E. George Payne, "Negroes in the Public Elementary Schools of the North," in *The Annals of the American Academy of Political and Social Science*, CXXXX (November, 1928), pp. 224, 226–228.

states. Segregation, however, is no less a matter of fact, as indicated by a typical case, namely New Jersey.

Segregation of School Children

There will be found in New Jersey types of schools varying from those completely mixed, with Negro teachers placed without strict regard to the preponderance of Negro pupils, in the northern part of the state, to types in which segregation is carried to the point of dividing a building so that white and Negro children are completely separated, with white teachers for the white and Negro teachers for the Negro students, and a heavy wire screen dividing the playground; a white principal of the entire school and a Negro assistant whose duties are concerned wholly with the Negro part. In Trenton, while there is no segregation in principle, there is separation in effect, with every possible advantage of this separation generously emphasized and developed. It is evident that the desire of the school board has been in the direction of separation, and they have been willing to pay handsomely for it. Theoretically the racial make-up of the neighborhood has determined the complexion of the school for the district. But it so happens that there are no neighborhoods in which only Negroes live, although there are many small ones in which they predominate. The schools of these areas have come to be set aside as Negro schools, and Negro teachers and principals provided....

The situation in New Jersey is by no means atypical, and represents in general the method of bringing about segregation artificially in cases where natural means do not turn the trick.... It may, therefore, be said that the various factors leading to segregation do not allow the Negro to be exposed to the same educational or cultural situations to which the whites are exposed in the North. Moreover, the special treatment is not lost in its effect. It serves to create an attitude of mind in both the whites and the Negroes that enforces totally different educational effects. The most vicious case of distinction is that in which the Negroes and whites are separated by rooms and a wire screen on the playground, always with the general recognition of distinctive white superiority. The effect of such distinction, whether in the extreme or moderate form, is to make an understanding or common culture impossible. The Negro is almost as much out of the picture of American civilization as he would be in the native haunts of Africa. We cannot face the problem of the Negro in America without a distinct consciousness of this fact.

2. Rejecting the Doctrine of Innate Inferiority[1]
✤ Charles H. Thompson

The racist doctrine of white superiority is often called into play to account for the generally lower academic achievement of black students. White prejudice made it difficult for black fathers to get other than low paying and uncertain jobs and contributed to unequal family and educational opportunities for black children. However, this was not considered by leading scholars during the first half of the twentieth century as a primary factor contributing to the lower academic achievement of blacks. Nor were the cultural biases inherent in intelligence tests viewed as a reason for the difference in average test scores between whites and blacks.

By 1950 Allison Davis, a black social scientist, had begun to call attention to the white cultural bias built into widely used tests. During the years that followed, the majority of educators looked for environmental reasons to account for differences between black and white students. However, as early as 1928, a black scholar had challenged (without success) the doctrine of white academic superiority. At the time, test data were being used to support the theory of "white supremacy." ■

A... series of studies is represented by school survey reports made by special survey staffs, and investigations made by local authorities in city and state school systems. We have chosen ... as a basis for the appraisal of the educational achievement of Negro children, one of the typical but more extensive of the school surveys.

The Virginia Education Commission and Virginia Survey Staff present in two volumes the results of a survey of the public school system of the state of Virginia as represented by eighteen typical rural counties and nine selected cities. This survey was conducted under the direction of the late Professor Alexander J. Inglis of Harvard University, during the school year 1918–1919. It is unique in three respects: first, the factor of racial comparison is incidental; second, it summarizes the *direct* educational achievement of Negro children

---

[1] Charles H. Thompson, "The Educational Achievements of Negro Children," in *The Annals of the American Academy of Political and Social Science*, Vol. CXXXX, (November, 1928), pp. 205, 207–208.

under "*normal*," I should say typical, school conditions; third, it involves a much larger number of subjects than one usually finds in studies involving racial comparisons.

The comparative results presented ... give the scores for the following subjects ... : READING — ... 3768 white pupils (city), 1029 Negro pupils (city), 3038 white pupils (rural), and 1000 Negro pupils (rural); ARITHMETIC — ... 2557 white pupils (city), 372 Negro pupils (city), 5021 white pupils (rural), and 770 Negro pupils (rural); HANDWRITING — ... Number of pupils not given; SPELLING — ... Number of pupils not given. ...

Environment, Not Race

It will be seen that the efficiency of the city whites is the highest, that of the city Negroes and the rural whites coming next with a negligible difference between them, and that of the rural Negroes coming last. If the reader will compare the rank order of the school efficiencies of these groups with their respective educational achievements, as shown in [the table here], he will note that in general, the

Educational Efficiency of City Negroes, Rural Whites, and Rural Negroes in Terms of the City Whites ...

Racial and School Groups in Terms of City Whites	Tests			Handwriting
	Addition	Spelling	Reading	
City whites	100.0	100.0	100.0	100.0
City Negroes	85.8	82.3	81.9	97.1
Rural whites	80.7	75.3	82.4	85.5
Rural Negroes	77.8	73.1	80.1	93.5

correspondence is perfect. It should be pointed out here that the rural Negroes in the light of their very poor educational facilities, show a higher degree of educational achievement than do the rural whites. The observation should be made that although the rural whites have a school system equal in efficiency to that of the city Negroes, they do not equal them in educational achievement. This situation is due undoubtedly to some environmental difference other than school opportunity not measured by the school efficiency index. If, however, one were to follow the logic of the proponents of the hypothesis of inherent racial mental inferiority, he would necessarily have to conclude that rural whites are inherently mentally inferior to city Negroes. This interpretation is usually made where the inferiority is found in Negro achievement. It, of course, is unwarranted in either case except we can prove conclusively that the environments were comparable.

A critical examination of the facts presented in this study shows that when Negroes are given equal environmental and school opportunities their educational achievements are equal to or better than that of the whites. (*In fact, it is surprising to note that Negroes achieve as much as they do in consideration of the poor environmental and school opportunities they are afforded.*) In other words, the educational achievement of Negro children, as with white children, is, in the main, a direct function of their environmental and school opportunities, rather than a function of some special inherent difference in mental ability.

Conclusion

A critical appraisal of the facts with reference to the educational achievements of Negro children forces one to conclude:
1. That the doctrine of an inherent mental inferiority of the Negro is a myth unfounded by the most logical interpretation of the scientific facts on the subject produced to date.
2. That the mental and scholastic achievements of Negro children, as with white children, are, in the main, a direct function of their environmental and school opportunities rather than a function of some inherent difference in mental ability.
3. That a philosophy of education based upon the current unwarranted interpretations of achievement differences between white and Negro children, as due to inherent racial mental inferiority of the Negro, is not only UNJUST, but a little short of disastrous, especially in view of the many other disabilities the Negro has to undergo in this country.

3. Outlawing the Inequity[1]
✦ Brown v. Board of Education of Topeka

Plessy v. Ferguson (1896) — the Supreme Court decision that said segregation was legal so long as facilities for both races were

[1] *Brown v. Board of Education of Topeka*, 347 U.S. 483 (1954), excerpts.

equal — governed court rulings for sixty years. Despite this policy of "separate but equal," most schools for blacks were not equal to those for whites. In the 1930's, most Southern states were spending about one-third as much per black pupil as per white child. Negroes had long protested the inequity. But whenever relief was granted by the courts it was on the basis of unequal treatment, not on the argument that the system itself was illegal. As late as 1951 twenty-one states either compelled or permitted the separate education of the races.

Finally in 1952 a series of cases came before the Supreme Court dealing with the heart of the problem: is equal educational opportunity possible in a dual school system? One of these cases, Brown v. Board of Education, involved an eight-year-old Negro girl who was required to attend the segregated school 21 blocks from her home when there was a white school only five blocks away. In May, 1954, the Supreme Court handed down one of the most important rulings of the century. In a unanimous decision it declared: "Separate educational facilities are inherently unequal." Segregated schooling was at last unconstitutional. ■

Mr. Chief Justice Warren delivered the opinion of the Court. . . .

In approaching this problem, we cannot turn the clock back to 1868 when the [Fourteenth] Amendment was adopted, or even to 1896 when *Plessy v. Ferguson* was written. We must consider public education in the light of its full development and its present place in American life throughout the nation. Only in this way can it be determined if segregation in public schools deprives these plaintiffs of the equal protection of the laws.

Today, education is perhaps the most important function of state and local governments. Compulsory school attendance laws and the great expenditures for education both demonstrate our recognition of the importance of education to our democratic society. It is required in the performance of our most basic public responsibilities, even service in the armed forces. It is the very foundation of good citizenship. Today it is a principal instrument in awakening the child to cultural values, in preparing him for later professional training, and in helping him to adjust normally to his environment. In these days, it is doubtful that any child may reasonably be expected to succeed in life if he is denied the opportunity of an education. Such an opportunity, where the state has undertaken to provide it, is a right which must be made available to all on equal terms.

A Feeling of Inferiority

We come then to the question presented: Does segregation of children in public schools solely on the basis of race, even though the physical facilities and other "tangible" factors may be equal, deprive the children of the minority group of equal educational opportunities? We believe that it does.

In *Sweatt v. Painter*, . . . in finding that a segregated law school for Negroes could not provide them equal educational opportunities, this Court relied in large part on "those qualities which are incapable of objective measurement but which make for greatness in a law school." In *McLaurin v. Oklahoma State Regents*, . . . the Court, in requiring that a Negro admitted to a white graduate school be treated like all other students, again resorted to intangible considerations: ". . . his ability to study, to engage in discussions and exchange views with other students, and, in general, to learn his profession." Such considerations apply with added force to children in grade and high schools. To separate them from others of similar age and qualifications solely because of their race generates a feeling of inferiority as to their status in the community that may affect their hearts and minds in a way unlikely ever to be undone. The effect of this separation on their educational opportunities was well stated by a finding in the Kansas case by a court which nevertheless felt compelled to rule against the Negro plaintiffs:

> Segregation of white and colored children in public schools has a detrimental effect upon the colored children. The impact is greater when it has the sanction of the law; for the policy of separating the races is usually interpreted as denoting the inferiority of the Negro group. A sense of inferiority affects the motivation of a child to learn. Segregation with the sanction of law, therefore, has a tendency to [retard] the educational and mental development of Negro children and to deprive them of some of the benefits they would receive in a racially integrated school system.

Whatever may have been the extent of psychological knowledge at the time of *Plessy v. Ferguson*, this finding is amply supported by modern authority. Any language in *Plessy v. Ferguson* contrary to this finding is rejected.

We conclude that in the field of public education the doctrine of "separate but equal" has no place. Separate educational facilities are inherently unequal. Therefore, we hold that the plaintiffs and others similarly situated for whom the actions have been brought are, by reason of the segregation complained of, deprived of the equal protection of the laws guaranteed by the Fourteenth Amendment....

4. The Battle of Little Rock[1]
✤ Daisy Bates

> *The Brown decision spread gloom among the advocates of white supremacy. Segregationist leaders bitterly attacked the ruling, but Southern moderates called for reason to prevail. By 1956 nine of the seventeen states which had enforced dual school systems had begun at least token integration. Greatest progress was achieved in the border states where the Negro population was relatively smaller than further south. Meanwhile, in the Deep South, opposition to desegregation was hardening.*
>
> *In Little Rock, Arkansas, a major clash erupted in 1957 when the school board made plans to admit nine Negroes to the formerly all-white high school. State Governor Orval Faubus announced his opposition to "forcible integration." Attempts to enroll the black students resulted in open defiance by angry crowds. Finally President Eisenhower ordered federal troops to restore order and to protect the rights of the nine students. Daisy Bates, one of the NAACP leaders in the struggle, describes these historic events in her book,* The Long Shadow of Little Rock, *from which the following passage is excerpted.* ■

Around 6 P.M., the long line of trucks, jeeps, and staff cars entered the heart of the city to the wailing sound of sirens and the dramatic flashing of lights from the police cars escorting the caravan to Central High School. The "Battle of Little Rock" was on.

Some of the citizens watching the arrival of the troops cried with relief. Others cursed the federal government for "invading our city." One got the impression that the "Solid South" was no longer solid....

[Next morning], reporters were asking the nine how they felt, and the children, tense and excited, found it difficult to be articulate about the significance of the troops' mission. Half an hour crawled by. Jeff, standing at the window, called out, "The Army's here! They're here!"

Jeeps were rolling down Twenty-eighth Street. Two passed our

---

[1] Daisy Bates, *The Long Shadow of Little Rock* (New York: David McKay Co., 1962), pp. 100–101, 103–106. © by Daisy Bates. Reprinted by permission.

house and parked at the end of the block, while two remained at the other end of the block. Paratroopers quickly jumped out and stood across the width of the street at each end of the block — those at the western end standing at attention facing west, and those at the eastern end facing east.

An Army station wagon stopped in front of our house. While photographers, perched precariously on the tops of cars and rooftops, went into action, the paratrooper in charge of the detail leaped out of the station wagon and started up our driveway. As he approached, I heard Minnijean say gleefully, "Oh, look at them, they're so — soldierly! It gives you goose pimples to look at them!" And then she added solemnly, "For the first time in my life, I feel like an American citizen."

The officer was at the door, and as I opened it, he saluted and said, his voice ringing through the sudden quiet of the living-room where a number of friends and parents of the nine had gathered to witness this moment in history: "Mrs. Bates, we're ready for the children. We will return them to your home at three-thirty o'clock."

I watched them follow him down the sidewalk. Another paratrooper held open the door of the station wagon, and they got in. Turning back into the room, my eyes none too dry, I saw the parents with tears of happiness in their eyes as they watched the group drive off.

Entering the "Never-Never Land"

Tense and dramatic events were taking place in and around the school while the Negro pupils were being transported by the troops of the 101st Airborne from my home to Central High.

Major General Edwin A. Walker, operation commander, was explaining to the student body, in the school auditorium, the duties and responsibilities of his troops.

". . . You have nothing to fear from my soldiers and no one will interfere with your coming, going, or your peaceful pursuit of your studies. However, I would be less than honest if I failed to tell you that I intend to use all means necessary to prevent any interference with the execution of your school board's plan . . ."

A block from the school, a small group of hard-core segregationists ignored Major James Meyers' orders to disperse peacefully and return to their homes. The major repeated the command when the surly, angry crowd refused to disperse. He was forced to radio for additional help. About thirty soldiers answered the emergency call "on the double," wearing steel helmets, carrying bayonet fixed rifles, their gas masks in readiness, and "walkie-talkies" slung over their shoulders.

The soldiers lowered their rifles and moved slowly and deliberately into the crowd. The mob quickly gave way, shouting insults at the troops in the process. In a matter of minutes the streets, which for days had been littered with hate-filled mobs, cigarette butts, half-eaten sandwiches, and used flash bulbs, were strangely quiet.

At 9:22 A.M. the nine Negro pupils marched solemnly through the doors of Central High School, surrounded by twenty-two [Airborne troops] soldiers. An Army helicopter circled overhead. Around the massive brick schoolhouse 350 paratroopers stood grimly at attention. Scores of reporters, photographers, and TV cameramen made a mad dash for telephones, typewriters, and TV studios, and within minutes a world that had been holding its breath learned that the nine pupils, protected by the might of the United States military, had finally entered the "never-never land."

When classes ended that afternoon, the troops escorted the pupils to my home. Here we held the first of many conferences that were to take place during the hectic months ahead.

I looked into the face of each child, from the frail, ninety-pound Thelma Mothershed with a cardiac condition, to the well-built, sturdy Ernest Green, oldest of them all. They sat around the room, subdued and reflective — and understandably so. Too much had happened to them in these frenzied weeks to be otherwise.

I asked if they had a rough day. Not especially, they said. Some of the white pupils were friendly and had even invited them to lunch. Some were indifferent, and only a few showed open hostility.

Minnijean Brown reported that she had been invited by her classmates to join the glee club.

"Then why the long faces?" I wanted to know.

"Well," Ernest spoke up, "you don't expect us to be jumping for joy, do you?"

Someone said, "But Ernest, we *are* in Central, and that shouldn't make us feel sad exactly."

"Sure we're in Central," Ernest shot back, somewhat impatiently. "But how did we get in? We got in, finally, because we were protected by paratroops. Some victory!" he said sarcastically.

"Are you sorry," someone asked him, "that the President sent the troops?"

"No," said Ernest. "I'm only sorry it had to be that way."

5. Neighborhoods and Schools[1]
✦ Peggy Streit

The 1954 Brown decision said nothing about de facto segregation. In the North poverty and discrimination often confined the Negro to limited areas of large cities. As a result, neighborhood schools were predominantly black or predominantly white. In the late 1950's, civil rights groups called attention to increasingly inadequate Negro schools — overcrowded conditions, a higher proportion of inexperienced teachers, outdated facilities, irrelevant courses of study, and low standards of pupil performance. Local school boards introduced various techniques to reduce racial imbalance. These included the rezoning of school districts, pairing of white and black schools, open enrollment, employment of more minority teachers, and busing. Response to such changes in the North was not always favorable, as the description below illustrates. ■

"The way I see it, it's like this," said the taxi driver. "If I had kids of school age I'd join P.A.T. [Parents and Taxpayers]. And I'd keep the kids out of school just as long as we white people didn't get our rights. Now don't get me wrong. I ain't got nothing against colored people. If they want good schools, they ought to have good schools. But they ought to go to schools in *their* neighborhood — just like white kids ought to go to school in *their* neighborhood."

The taxi stopped at a red light. The traffic on Van Wyck Boulevard rumbled by the drab, squat commercial buildings — a bar, a hardware store, a beauty parlor, a real-estate office advertising a six-room two-story, one-family house for $15,000. . . .

Leaving behind the pounding commercial traffic, the taxi turned off abruptly into a more tranquil world of narrow residential streets lined by modest homes — house after identical house, like rows of ditto marks. But they shared the sedate dignity of a clean, orderly neighborhood, their aging, ungracious architecture softened by the sycamore trees.

---

[1] Peggy Streit, "Why They Fight for P.A.T.," *New York Times Magazine*, September 20, 1964, pp. 20–21. © 1964 by The New York Times Company. Reprinted by permission.

"Like I was saying," continued the taxi driver, "you buy a house because you want your kid to go to a school nearby and the church is just around the corner. And then, here comes the government or school board and what do they say? They say, 'Mister, you can't send your kid to school near you. You got to bus him to school in a Negro neighborhood, 20 blocks away, that's been — what do they call it — *paired* with a white school because of racial imbalance.' Now I ask you, is that right? And I say to you, no — that ain't right. We're losing our freedoms in this country. Next thing you know, they'll be telling you where to go to church."

The taxi slowed to a halt outside the home of P.A.T. official June Reynolds. . . .

"Now," said Mrs. Reynolds, "what would you like to know about our group?" . . .

Size? "There are about 2,700 of us," she replied, "with 300 hard-core members doing most of the work — the executive board, the telephone girls who call about P.A.T. meetings and poll members, and the block captains who ring doorbells for new members."

Membership? "Mostly parents with elementary-school kids, of course, but some people without children. This is a moral issue, too, not just an educational one."

Purpose? "To protect our children, preserve our neighborhood-school system, and keep our children from being bused into strange districts."

Activities? "Well, we organize protests against pairing and busing, and we've been urging members to write to their newspapers and councilmen. Things like that."

The racial issue? She paused irresolutely. "The racial issue doesn't have anything to do with what we want," she said. "We believe in open enrollment. If Negroes want to go to white schools where there's room, they should be allowed to. And we believe in the improvement of Negro schools. It's not true what people say — that we don't like Negroes and we don't want them in our schools. If they live in our neighborhood they have a right here. But nobody has a right to send our children *away* from our neighborhood."

The telephone jangled again and she turned her young, earnest face back to business. "Membership meeting this evening," she said to the caller with urgency. "Try to make it. This is a battle we're fighting, and without your support we'll lose it. Yes, everybody will be there. . . ."

XIII. Separation of Church and State

The proper relationship between church and state continued to be a controversial question for Americans in the twentieth century. The Supreme Court in 1925 determined that a state could not require parents to send their children to public schools; the parent was free to send his child to private or parochial schools which meet state requirements. But large issues on separation of church and state remained. What about such religious instruction as Bible reading or prayer in the public schools? What kind of financial aid, if any, were parochial schools entitled to receive? ■

1. The Legality of Private Schools[1]
✤ Pierce v. Society of Sisters

> In 1922 the state of Oregon passed a compulsory education law requiring all normal children who were between eight and sixteen years of age and had not completed the eighth grade to attend the public schools. A parochial school corporation challenged the law, claiming that parents had the right to choose schools where their children would receive appropriate moral and religious training. The Supreme Court in 1925 agreed. The Oregon act, said the Court, interfered with the "liberty of parents and guardians to direct the upbringing and education of children under their control." Private religious schools which meet state requirements were judged to be legal alternatives to public schools. ■

MR. JUSTICE MCREYNOLDS delivered the opinion of the Court. . . .
The challenged act, effective September 1, 1926, requires every parent, guardian, or other person having control or charge or custody of a child between eight and sixteen years to send him "to a public school for the period of time a public school shall be held during the

[1] *Pierce v. Society of Sisters*, 268 U.S. 510 (1925), excerpts.

current year" in the district where the child resides; and failure to do so is declared a misdemeanor. There are exemptions — not specially important here — for children who are not normal, or who have completed the eighth grade, or whose parents or private teachers reside at considerable distances from any public school, or who hold special permits from the county superintendent. The manifest purpose is to compel general attendance at public schools by normal children, between eight and sixteen, who have not completed the eighth grade. And without doubt enforcement of the statute would seriously impair, perhaps destroy, the profitable features of appellees' business, and greatly diminish the value of their property.

Appellee the Society of Sisters is an Oregon corporation, organized in 1880, with power to care for orphans, educate and instruct the youth, establish and maintain academies or schools, and acquire necessary real and personal property. It has long devoted its property and effort to the secular and religious education and care of the children, and has acquired the valuable good will of many parents and guardians. It conducts interdependent primary and high schools and junior colleges, and maintains orphanages for the custody and control of children between eight and sixteen. In its primary schools many children between those ages are taught the subjects usually pursued in Oregon public schools during the first eight years. Systematic religious instruction and moral training according to the tenets of the Roman Catholic Church are also regularly provided. All courses of study, both temporal and religious, contemplate continuity of training under appellee's charge; the primary schools are essential to the system and the most profitable. It owns valuable buildings, especially constructed and equipped for school purposes. The business is remunerative, — the annual income from primary schools exceeds $30,000, — and the successful conduct of this requires long-time contracts with teachers and parents. The Compulsory Education Act of 1922 has already caused the withdrawal from its schools of children who would otherwise continue, and their income has steadily declined. The appellants, public officers, have proclaimed their purpose strictly to enforce the statute.

After setting out the above facts, the Society's bill alleges that the enactment conflicts with the right of parents to choose schools where their children will receive appropriate mental and religious training, the right of the child to influence the parents' choice of a school, the right of schools and teachers therein to engage in a useful business or profession, and is accordingly repugnant to the Constitution and void. And, further, that unless enforcement of the measure is enjoined, the corporation's business and property will suffer irreparable injury. . . .

No question is raised concerning the power of the state reasonably to regulate all schools, to inspect, supervise, and examine them, their teachers and pupils; to require that all children of proper age attend some school, that teachers shall be of good moral character and patriotic disposition, that certain studies plainly essential to good citizenship must be taught, and that nothing be taught which is manifestly [harmful] to the public welfare.

The inevitable practical result of enforcing the act under consideration would be destruction of appellees' primary schools, and perhaps all other private primary schools for normal children within the state of Oregon. Appellees are engaged in a kind of undertaking not inherently harmful, but long regarded as useful and meritorious. Certainly there is nothing in the present records to indicate that they have failed to discharge their obligations to patrons, students, or the state. And there are no peculiar circumstances or present emergencies which demand extraordinary measures relative to primary education.

. . . We think it entirely plain that the Act of 1922 unreasonably interferes with the liberty of parents and guardians to direct the upbringing and education of children under their control. As often heretofore pointed out, rights guaranteed by the Constitution may not be abridged by legislation which has no reasonable relation to some purpose within the competency of the state. The fundamental theory of liberty upon which all governments in this Union repose excludes any general power of the state to standardize its children by forcing them to accept instruction from public teachers only. The child is not the mere creature of the state; those who nurture him and direct his destiny have the right, coupled with the high duty, to recognize and prepare him for additional obligations. . . .

2. Compulsory Prayer Illegal[1]
✣ *Engel v. Vitale*

The state of New York adopted a short non-denominational prayer for use in its public schools. Written by the State Board

[1] *Engel v. Vitale*, 370 U.S. 421 (1962), excerpts.

of Regents, the prayer stated: "Almighty God, we acknowledge our dependence upon Thee, and we beg Thy blessings upon us, our parents, our teachers and our Country." According to law, the prayer was to be recited by each class at the beginning of every school day. State officials promoted the prayer as part of the "Moral and Spiritual Training in the Schools." The practice was challenged in the courts by parents of ten children of New Hyde Park, New York, on the grounds that it violated the Establishment of Religion Clause of the Constitution. In 1962 the Supreme Court declared compulsory prayer in the public schools illegal. ■

MR. JUSTICE BLACK delivered the opinion of the Court. . . .

Shortly after the practice of reciting the Regent's prayer was adopted by the [Union Free] School District, the parents of ten pupils brought this action in a New York state court insisting that use of this official prayer in the public schools was contrary to the beliefs, religions, or religious practices of both themselves and their children. Among other things, these parents challenged the constitutionality of both the state law authorizing the School District to direct the use of prayer in public schools and the School District's regulation ordering the recitation of this particular prayer on the ground that these actions of official governmental agencies violate that part of the First Amendment of the federal Constitution which commands that "Congress shall make no law respecting an establishment of religion" — a command which was "made applicable to the state of New York by the Fourteenth Amendment of the said Constitution. . . ."

We think that by using its public school system to encourage recitation of the Regents' prayer, the state of New York has adopted a practice wholly inconsistent with the Establishment Clause. There can, of course, be no doubt that New York's program of daily classroom invocation of God's blessings as prescribed in the Regents' prayer is a religious activity. It is a solemn avowal of divine faith and supplication for the blessings of the Almighty. The nature of such a prayer has always been religious. . . .

The petitioners contend among other things that the state laws requiring or permitting use of the Regents' prayer must be struck down as a violation of the Establishment Clause because that prayer was composed by governmental officials as a part of a governmental program to further religious beliefs. For this reason, petitioners argue, the state's use of the Regents' prayer in its public school system breaches the constitutional wall of separation between church and state....

There can be no doubt that New York's state prayer program officially establishes the religious beliefs embodied in the Regents' prayer. The respondents' argument to the contrary, which is largely based upon the contention that the Regents' prayer is "non-denominational" and the fact that the program, as modified and approved by state courts, does not require all pupils to recite the prayer but permits those who wish to do so to remain silent or be excused from the room, ignores the essential nature of the program's constitutional defects. Neither the fact that the prayer may be denominationally neutral nor the fact that its observance on the part of the students is voluntary can serve to free it from the limitations of the Establishment Clause....

No Hostility Toward Religion

It has been argued that to apply the Constitution in such a way as to prohibit state laws respecting an establishment of religious services in public schools is to indicate a hostility toward religion or toward prayer. Nothing, of course, could be more wrong. The history of man is inseparable from the history of religion. And perhaps it is not too much to say that since the beginning of that history many people have devoutly believed that "More things are wrought by prayer than this world dreams of." It was doubtless largely due to men who believed this that there grew up a sentiment that caused men to leave the cross-currents of officially established state religions and religious persecution in Europe and come to this country filled with the hope that they could find a place in which they could pray when they pleased to the God of their faith in the language they chose. And there were men of this same faith in the power of prayer who led the fight for adoption of our Constitution and also for our Bill of Rights with the very guarantees of religious freedom that forbid the sort of governmental activity which New York has attempted here. These men knew that the First Amendment, which tried to put an end to governmental control of religion and of prayer, was not written to destroy either. They knew rather that it was written to quiet well-justified fears which nearly all of them felt arising out of an awareness that governments of the past had shackled men's tongues to make them speak only the religious thoughts that government wanted them to speak and to pray only to the God that government wanted them to pray to. It is neither sacrilegious nor antireligious to say that each separate government in this country should stay out of the business of writing or sanctioning official prayers and leave that purely religious function to the people themselves and to those the people choose to look to for religious guidance....

3. Compulsory Bible Reading Illegal[1]
✤ *Abington v. Schempp*

No other modern Supreme Court case save Brown v. Board of Education *stirred deeper emotions than* Abington v. Schempp. *In compliance with a Pennsylvania state law, the Abington High School began each day with the reading of ten Bible verses over the public address system. Following this, students recited the Lord's Prayer. The Schempp family, members of the Unitarian church, objected that these practices violated their religious beliefs. This stormy issue came before the Supreme Court in 1963. In its decision the Court distinguished between studying the Bible as literature or history and reading it as a devotional exercise. The latter, said the Court, was a violation of the First Amendment. Bible reading in the public schools was ruled unconstitutional.* ■

Mr. Justice Clark delivered the opinion of the Court....

It is true that religion has been closely identified with our history and government. As we said in *Engel v. Vitale*, ... "The history of man is inseparable from the history of religion. And ... since the beginning of that history many people have devoutly believed that 'More things are wrought by prayer than this world dreams of.'" In *Zorach v. Clauson*, ... we gave specific recognition to the proposition that 'We are a religious people whose institutions presuppose a Supreme Being." The fact that the Founding Fathers believed devotedly that there was a God and that the unalienable rights of man

[1] *School District of Abington v. Schempp*, 374 U.S. 203 (1963), excerpts.

were rooted in Him is clearly evidenced in their writings, from the Mayflower Compact to the Constitution itself. . . .

Freedom of Worship

This is not to say, however, that religion has been so identified with our history and government that religious freedom is not likewise as strongly imbedded in our public and private life. Nothing but the most telling of personal experiences in religious persecution suffered by our forebears . . . could have planted our belief in liberty of religious opinion any more deeply in our heritage. It is true that this liberty frequently was not realized by the colonists, but this is readily accountable by their close ties to the Mother Country. However, the views of Madison and Jefferson, preceded by Roger Williams, came to be incorporated not only in the federal Constitution but likewise in those of most of our states. This freedom to worship was indispensable in a country whose people came from the four quarters of the earth and brought with them a diversity of religious opinion. Today authorities list 83 separate religious bodies, each with membership exceeding 50,000, existing among our people, as well as innumerable smaller groups. . . .

The wholesome "neutrality" of which this Court's [case speaks] thus stems from a recognition of the teachings of history that powerful sects or groups might bring about a fusion of governmental and religious functions or a concert or dependency of one upon the other to the end that official support of the state or federal government would be placed behind the tenets of one or of all orthodoxies. This the Establishment Clause prohibits. And a further reason for neutrality is found in the Free Exercise Clause, which recognizes the value of religious training, teaching and observance and, more particularly, the right of every person to freely choose his own course with reference thereto, free of any compulsion from the state. This the Free Exercise Clause guarantees. . . .

Strict Neutrality

Applying the Establishment Clause principles . . . we find that the [state is] requiring the selection and reading at the opening of the school day of verses from the Holy Bible and the recitation of the Lord's Prayer by the students in unison. These exercises are prescribed as part of the curricular activities of students who are required by law to attend school. They are held in the school buildings under the supervision and with the participation of teachers employed in those schools.... The trial court ... has found that such an opening exercise is a religious ceremony and was intended by the state to be so. We agree with the trial court's finding as to the religious character of the exercises. Given that finding, the exercises and the law requiring them are in violation of the Establishment Clause.

... The state contends ... that the program is an effort to extend its benefits to all public school children without regard to their religious belief. Included within its secular purposes, it says, are the promotion of moral values, the contradiction to the materialistic trends of our times, the perpetuation of our institutions, and the teaching of literature.... [I]t is no defense to urge that the religious practices here may be relatively minor encroachments on the First Amendment. The breach of neutrality that is today a trickling stream may all too soon become a raging torrent and, in the words of Madison, "it is proper to take alarm at the first experiment on our liberties...."

Strict Neutrality

It is insisted that unless these religious exercises are permitted a "religion of secularism" is established in the schools. We agree of course that the state may not establish a "religion of secularism" in the sense of affirmatively opposing or showing hostility to religion, thus "preferring those who believe in no religion over those who do believe...." We do not agree, however, that this decision in any sense has that effect. In addition, it might well be said that one's education is not complete without a study of comparative religion or the history of religion and its relationship to the advancement of civilization. It certainly may be said that the Bible is worthy of study for its literary and historic qualities. Nothing we have said here indicates that such study of the Bible or of religion, when presented objectively as part of a secular program of education, may not be effected consistently with the First Amendment. But the exercises here do not fall into those categories. They are religious exercises, required by the [state] in violation of the command of the First Amendment that the government maintain strict neutrality, neither aiding nor opposing religion....

The place of religion in our society is an exalted one, achieved through a long tradition of reliance on the home, the church and the [protected] citadel of the individual heart and mind. We have come to recognize through bitter experience that it is not within the power of government to invade that citadel, whether its purpose or effect be to aid or oppose, to advance or retard. In the relationship between man and religion, the state is firmly committed to a position of neutrality. Though the application of that rule requires interpretation of a delicate sort, the rule itself is clearly and concisely stated in the words of the First Amendment. . . .

4. Financial Aid and the Parochial School[1]
✣ Lemon v. Kurtzman

A large majority of the nation's private schools in the 1970's were Roman Catholic. Since the Pierce decision in 1925, courts and lawmakers have grappled with the question of what should be the proper relation between state and religious schools. Does the principle of separation of church and state imply that the state has no financial responsibility towards parochial schools? In 1947 the Supreme Court ruled that a state could provide free bus transportation to students in both public and private schools. Based on this "child-benefit" theory — that the student and not the school received the aid — numerous states passed laws providing for some type of indirect aid to financially-pinched private schools. A 1968 Pennsylvania law provided state aid for parochial teachers' salaries, textbooks for "secular" subjects, and other instructional materials. In 1971, the Supreme Court ruled the law unconstitutional. In the decision which follows, the Court declared that "the cumulative impact of the entire relationship arising under the statutes . . . involves excessive entanglement between government and religion." ■

MR. CHIEF JUSTICE BURGER delivered the opinion of the Court. . . .

The Pennsylvania Nonpublic Elementary and Secondary Education Act was passed in 1968 in response to a crisis that the Pennsylvania legislature found existed in the state's nonpublic schools due to rapidly rising costs. The statute affirmatively reflects the legislative conclusion that the state's educational goals could appropriately be

[1] *Lemon v. Kurtzman,* 403 U.S. 602 (1971), excerpts.

fulfilled by government support of "those purely secular educational objectives achieved through nonpublic education. . . ."

The statute authorizes appellee state Superintendent of Public Instruction to "purchase" specified "secular educational services" from nonpublic schools. Under the "contracts" authorized by the statute, the state directly reimburses nonpublic schools solely for their actual expenditures for teachers' salaries, textbooks, and instructional materials. A school seeking reimbursement must maintain prescribed accounting procedures that identify the "separate" cost of the "secular educational service." These accounts are subject to state audit. The funds for this program were originally derived from a new tax on horse and harness racing, but the Act is now financed by a portion of the state tax on cigarettes.

There are several significant statutory restrictions on state aid. Reimbursement is limited to courses "presented in the curricula of the public schools." It is further limited "solely" to courses in the following "secular" subjects: mathematics, modern foreign languages, physical science, and physical education. Textbooks and instructional materials included in the program must be approved by the state Superintendent of Public Instruction. Finally, the statute prohibits reimbursement for any course that contains "any subject matter expressing religious teaching, or the morals or forms of worship of any sect."

The Act went into effect on July 1, 1968, and the first reimbursement payments to schools were made on September 2, 1969. It appears that some $5 million has been expended annually under the Act. The state has now entered into contracts with some 1,181 nonpublic elementary and secondary schools with a student population of some 535,215 pupils — more than 20 per cent of the total number of students in the state. More than 96 per cent of these pupils attend church-related schools, and most of these schools are affiliated with the Roman Catholic Church.

Appellants brought this action in the District Court to challenge the constitutionality of the Pennsylvania statute. The organizational plaintiffs-appellants are associations of persons resident in Pennsylvania declaring belief in the separation of church and state; individual plaintiffs-appellants are citizens and taxpayers of Pennsylvania. Plaintiff Lemon, in addition to being a citizen and a taxpayer, is a parent of a child attending public school in Pennsylvania. In addition, Lemon alleges that he purchased a ticket at a race track and thus had paid the specific tax that supports the expenditures under the Act. Appellees are state officials who have the responsibility for administering the Act. In addition seven church-related schools are defendants-appellees. . . .

The Opaque Language of the First Amendment

In *Everson v. Board of Education,* . . . this Court upheld a state statute that reimbursed the parents of parochial school children for bus transportation expenses. There Mr. Justice Black, writing for the majority, suggested that the decision carried to "the verge" of forbidden territory under the Religion Clauses. . . . Candor compels acknowledgment, moreover, that we can only dimly perceive the lines of demarcation in this extraordinarily sensitive area of constitutional law.

The language of the Religion Clauses of the First Amendment is at best opaque, particularly when compared with other portions of the Amendment. Its authors did not simply prohibit the establishment of a state church or a state religion, an area history shows they regarded as very important and fraught with great dangers. Instead they commanded that there should be "no law *respecting* an establishment of religion. . . ."

In the absence of precisely stated constitutional prohibitions, we must draw lines with reference to the three main evils against which the Establishment Clause was intended to afford protection: "sponsorship, financial support, and active involvement of the sovereign in religious activity. . . ."

Every analysis in this area must begin with consideration of the cumulative criteria developed by the Court over many years. Three such tests may be gleaned from our cases. First, the statute must have a secular legislative purpose; second, its principal or primary effect must be one that neither advances nor inhibits religion, . . . finally, the statute must not foster "an excessive government entanglement with religion. . . ."

Inquiry into the legislative purposes of the Pennsylvania and Rhode Island statutes[2] affords no basis for a conclusion that the legislative intent was to advance religion. On the contrary, the statutes themselves clearly state that they are intended to enhance the quality of the secular education in all schools covered by the compulsory at-

---

[2] The Rhode Island law provided salary supplements for teachers of secular subjects in private schools.

tendance laws. There is no reason to believe the legislatures meant anything else. A state always has a legitimate concern for maintaining minimum standards in all schools it allows to operate. . . .

In *Allen* [1968] the Court acknowledged that secular and religious teachings were not necessarily so intertwined that secular textbooks furnished to students by the state were in fact instrumental in the teaching of religion. . . . The legislatures of Rhode Island and Pennsylvania have concluded that secular and religious education are identifiable and separable. In the abstract we have no quarrel with this conclusion.

The two legislatures, however, have also recognized that church-related elementary and secondary schools have a significant religious mission and that a substantial portion of their activities is religiously oriented. They have therefore sought to create statutory restrictions designed to guarantee the separation between secular and religious educational functions and to ensure that state financial aid supports only the former. All these . . . are precautions taken in . . . recognition that these programs approached, even if they did not intrude upon the forbidden areas under the Religion Clauses. We . . . conclude that the cumulative impact of the entire relationship arising under the statutes in each state involves excessive entanglement between government and religion. . . .

Absolute Separation Impossible

Our prior holdings do not call for total separation between church and state; total separation is not possible in an absolute sense. Some relationship between government and religious organizations is inevitable. . . . Fire inspections, building and zoning regulations, and state requirements under compulsory school attendance laws are examples of necessary and permissible contacts. . . . Judicial [warnings] against entanglement must recognize that the line of separation, far from being a "wall," is a blurred, indistinct and variable barrier depending on all the circumstances of a particular relationship. . . .

Finally, nothing we have said can be construed to disparage the role of church-related elementary and secondary schools in our national life. Their contribution has been and is enormous. Nor do we ignore their economic plight in a period of rising costs and expanding need. Taxpayers generally have been spared vast sums by the maintenance of these educational institutions by religious organizations, largely by the gifts of faithful adherents.

The merit and benefits of these schools, however, are not the isssue before us in these cases. The sole question is whether state aid to these schools can be squared with the dictates of the Religion Clauses. Under our system the choice has been made that government is to be entirely excluded from the area of religious instruction and churches excluded from the affairs of government. The Constitution decrees that religion must be a private matter for the individual, the family, and the institutions of private choice, and that while some involvement and entanglement is inevitable, lines must be drawn. . . .

XIV. Continuing Criticism

With the urbanization of America, the position of youth in relation to adults has undergone radical change. The young in the agrarian era spent most of their time in the presence of adults at work in the family. Hence, the adult culture constituted the environment for youth. But with the decline of the family in modern America, and with compulsory school attendance until at least age sixteen, the young now spend most of their time in a youth culture. Much as factories created a labor class of workers at the turn of the century, the schools have created a youth class.

As an agency of adult values the school became an object of criticism by many young people and sympathetic teachers. During the decade of the 1960's, open conflict erupted between youth and the educational establishment. Especially was this true on college and university campuses. But the conflict and criticism also found their way to the high schools. Hence, there emerged a new body of literature calling for educational reform, relevance, involvement, and even "deschooling." Formal education came under fire from a group of young teachers who advocated what they believed was more humanistically-oriented, personalized, and relevant education. Sometimes termed the compassionate critics, they supported student criticisms of schools through their descriptions of the inadequate schools in which they taught. ■

1. The Grim Reality of Ghetto Schools[1]
✧ Jonathan Kozol

Jonathan Kozol taught in the Boston public schools until he was fired. Controversy arose over his use of a poem by Langston Hughes in his fourth-grade classroom. The poem, "Ballad of the Landlord," is free of profanity and obsenity; it concerns the con-

---
[1] Jonathan Kozol, *Death at an Early Age* (Boston: Houghton Mifflin Company, 1967), pp. 185–187, 190–191. Reprinted by permission.

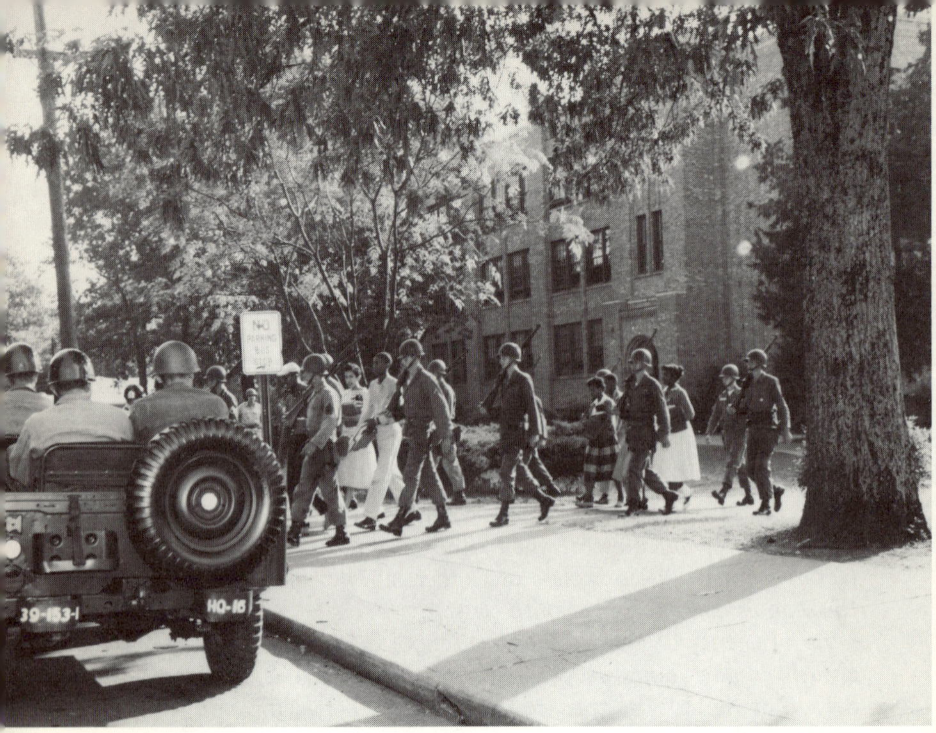
39-153-1
HQ-16

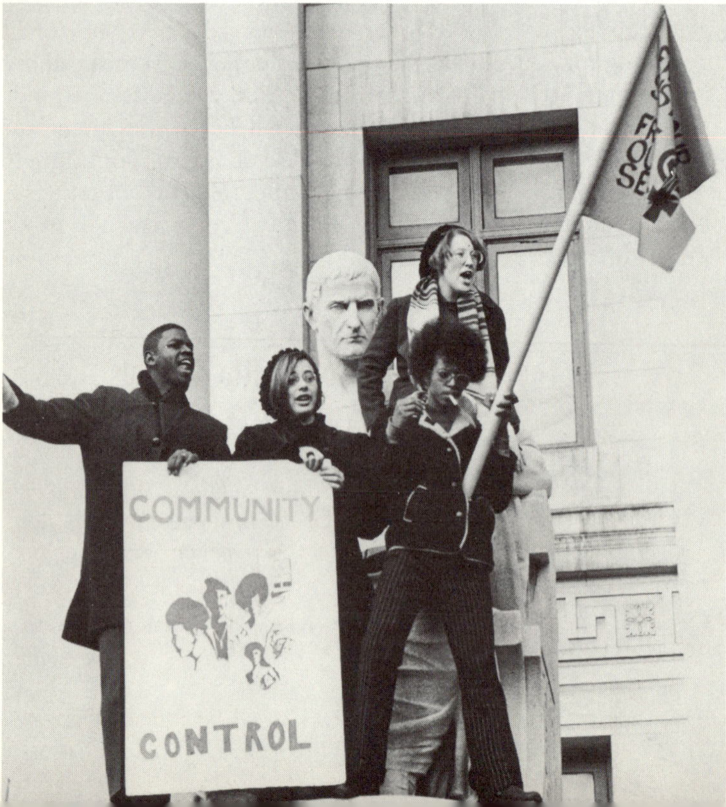
COMMUNITY
CONTROL

School desegregation efforts were often met with strong resistance, as in Little Rock, Arkansas, in the fall of 1957 (opposite page, above). Army troops were finally called in to restore order and to protect the nine black students who enrolled in the formerly all-white high school. By the late 1960's, some blacks, especially in the North, had lost faith in integration as a means of achieving equal educational opportunities. New demands were voiced for community control of black neighborhood schools and for the introduction of black studies into the curriculum. Whites too expressed discontent with American education. High school students in increasing numbers demanded a voice in the policy-making decisions of school life. Dissatisfaction with the curriculum was also widespread. The "open classroom" gained acceptance, particularly at the elementary level, as an attempt to create more meaningful and enjoyable environments for learning.

flict between a black tenant and a white landlord. Kozol's book, Death at an Early Age, *vividly describes the inadequacy of the ghetto school and the human consequences of a rigid and unsympathetic school program.* ■

Perhaps a reader would like to know what it is like to go into a new classroom in the same way that I did and to see before you suddenly, and in terms you cannot avoid recognizing, the dreadful consequences of a year's wastage of real lives.

You walk into a narrow and old wood-smelling classroom and you see before you 35 curious, cautious and untrusting children, aged eight to thirteen, of whom about two-thirds are Negro. Three of the children are designated to you as special students. Thirty per cent of the class is reading at the Second Grade level in a year and in a month in which they should be reading at the height of Fourth Grade performance or at the beginning of the Fifth. Seven children out of the class are up to par. Ten substitutes or teacher changes. Or twelve changes. Or eight. Or eleven. Nobody seems to know how many teachers they have had. Seven of their lifetime records are missing: symptomatic and emblematic at once of the chaos that has been with them all year long. Many more lives than just seven have already been wasted but the seven missing records become an embittering symbol of the lives behind them which, equally, have been lost or mislaid. (You have to spend the first three nights staying up until dawn trying to reconstruct these records out of notes and scraps.) On the first math test you give, the class average comes out to 36. The children tell you with embarrassment that it has been like that since fall.

You check around the classroom. Of forty desks, five have tops with no hinges. You lift a desk-top to fetch a paper and you find that the top has fallen off. There are three windows. One cannot be opened. A sign on it written in the messy scribble of a hurried teacher or some custodial person warns you: DO NOT UNLOCK THIS WINDOW IT IS BROKEN. The general look of the room is as of a bleak-light photograph of a mental hospital. Above the one poor blackboard, gray rather than really black, and hard to write on, hangs from one tack, lopsided, a motto attributed to Benjamin Franklin: "*Well begun is half done.*" Everything, or almost everything like that, seems a mockery of itself.

"Not for Fourth Grade"

Into this grim scenario, drawing on your own pleasures and memories, you do what you can to bring some kind of life. You bring in some cheerful and colorful paintings by Joan Miro and Paul Klee. While the paintings by Miro do not arouse much interest, the ones by Klee become an instantaneous success. One picture in particular, a watercolor titled "Bird Garden," catches the fascination of the entire class. You slip it out of the book and tack it up on the wall beside the doorway and it creates a traffic jam every time the children have to file in or file out. You discuss with your students some of the reasons why Klee may have painted the way he did and you talk about the things that can be accomplished in a painting which could not be accomplished in a photograph. None of this seems to be above the children's heads. Despite this, you are advised flatly by the Art Teacher that your naïveté has gotten the best of you and that the children cannot possibly appreciate this. Klee is too difficult. Children will not enjoy it. You are unable to escape the idea that the Art Teacher means herself instead.

For poetry, in place of the recommended memory gems, going back again into your own college days, you make up your mind to introduce a poem of William Butler Yeats. It is about a lake isle called Innisfree, about birds that have the funny name of "linnets" and about a "bee-loud glade." The children do not all go crazy about it but a number of them seem to like it as much as you do and you tell them how once, three years before, you were living in England and you helped a man in the country to make his home from wattles and clay. The children become intrigued. They pay good attention and many of them grow more curious about the poem than they appeared at first. Here again, however, you are advised by older teachers that you are making a mistake: Yeats is too difficult for children. They can't enjoy it, won't appreciate it, wouldn't like it. You are aiming way above their heads. . .* Another idea comes to mind and you decide to try out an easy and rather well-known and not very complicated poem of Robert Frost. The poem is called "Stopping By Woods on a Snowy Evening." This time, your supervisor happens to drop in from the School Department. He looks over the mimeograph, agrees with you that it's a nice poem, then points out to you — tolerantly, but strictly — that you have made another mistake. "Stop-

---

* Ellipsis in original source.

ping By Woods" is scheduled for Sixth Grade. It is not "a Fourth Grade poem," and it is not to be read or looked at during the Fourth Grade. Bewildered as you are by what appears to be a kind of idiocy, you still feel reproved and criticized and muted and set back and you feel that you have been caught in the commission of a serious mistake....

Of all of the poems of Langston Hughes that I read to my Fourth Graders, the one that the children liked most was a poem that has the title "Ballad of the Landlord." ... This poem may not satisfy the taste of every critic, and I am not making any claims to immortality for a poem just because I happen to like it a great deal. But the reason this poem did have so much value and meaning for me and, I believe, for many of my students, is that it not only seems moving in an obvious and immediate human way but that it *finds* its emotion in something ordinary. It is a poem which really does allow both heroism and pathos to poor people, sees strength in awkwardness and attributes to a poor person standing on the stoop of his slum house every bit as much significance as William Wordsworth saw in daffodils, waterfalls and clouds. At the request of the children later on I mimeographed that poem and, although nobody in the classroom was asked to do this, several of the children took it home and memorized it on their own. I did not assign it for memory, because I do not think that memorizing a poem has any special value. Some of the children just came in and asked if they could recite it. Before long, almost every child in the room had asked to have a turn.

2. Revolt Reaches the High School[1]
✤ Michael Marqusee

Criticism of American education by the late 1960's was coming from the students themselves. Beginning on the college campus, the protests soon filtered down to the high school. Both black and white students expressed their hostility to school and society. In the following selection from The High School Revolu-

---

[1] From *High School Revolutionaries*, by Marc Libarle and Tom Seligson, pp. 13–14, 19–20. Copyright © by Marc Libarle and Tom Seligson. Reprinted by permission of Random House, Inc.

tionaries, *a white high-school youth from a wealthy suburban community protests a school system "directed toward limitation, demoralization, and . . . manipulation."* ■

The Scarsdale community can be described as an upper middle-class community. With the average income over $25,000 and a virtually all-white population, Scarsdale is the ideally insulated town, excluding the poor and the black. It is a community of family units in which the father usually commutes to New York City while the mother stays home to tend the children who attend, for the most part, one of the highly-rated Scarsdale public schools. The jobs that the men in Scarsdale commute to are almost all either in one of the professions or in business. In this community, my friends and myself are all the children of desk-sitters. Our fathers work in a nine-to-five, tie-and-jacket world where the guiding principle is usually that of finding the easiest path to the most money.

Obviously, laborers of any kind and low-ranking desk-job holders find no place for themselves in Scarsdale. In fact, for most of us, the only working-class people we ever have contact with are the employees our parents hire to clean house, do the gardening, or repair the washing machines, heaters, cars, stoves, and swimming pools.

Scarsdale prides itself on its cultural and intellectual interests. There are many patrons of Lincoln Center, frequent theater-goers, and supposedly avid book-readers. Most of us live in large, one-family houses, among which there is little variety. The town has a calm, serene mood, with its quiet, uncrowded streets, and absence of night activity. There is a generally restrained and almost unfriendly attitude toward one's neighbors. The mothers of the town engage in various "wifely" activities: watching the kids, directing her staff, chatting on the phone, shopping, playing tennis, or maybe some occasional stuffing letters at a local political office.

Finally, in this catalogue of Scarsdale family elements, there are the children, and we are in many ways the center of family and community attention. Virtually all parents see their child's function within school as the attainment of high grades, or in other words, academic success and a better chance for admission to a highly-rated college. This is the goal and primary function of our high schools. . . .

I return to the subject of school because finally it is the center of all our activity and is the primary tool with which the young of

Scarsdale are molded into finished products. The word "process" has repeatedly cropped up here because it is indicative of the nature of existence in my community. Thus, Scarsdale High seeks to produce college graduates who are in turn directed into a field within the professional or business community. . . . We are subservient to all authority and our lives are controlled by that authority from the selection of our careers to the development of our values. This is a system which should be abhorrent to all who hold supposedly "human," "progressive" values, yet it is endorsed by almost all in the adult world, for they see it as a necessary preface to that wondrous goal — a career.

Humiliation in Regimentation

Choose anything you want but have a career — a definite, disciplined job or skill that involves a routine of work. In that routine is security, happiness, and normalcy. This is a standard defense of the school system. They preach that this process aids in our attainment of fulfillment. It gives us opportunities. [Bull]. This process, as I and my friends in affluent Scarsdale have discovered, is one of limitation and misdirection. Imagine spending your entire thinking life attending classes which have been planned by someone thirty years older than you who usually has little in common with you; having your daily schedule worked out by someone who probably has never seen you; sitting down in assigned desks at the signal of a bell and standing up again fifty minutes later at the same signal, only to move to another preplanned class and follow the same routine, all day, every day, in pursuit of a goal someone else has set for you and which, whether you believe in it or not, seems to offer as little excitement as the dreary schedule you now go through. This is the high school student, and that existence is one directed toward limitation, demoralization, and I repeat, manipulation. One of the weapons which the school uses in directing our course is a steady, subtle humiliation which starts the moment we learn in kindergarten that we must raise our hand (an absurd ritual) in order to get permission to go to the bathroom. It is continued in the hundreds of orderly lines we all form to move around elementary school, the disgrace we suffer when we make a wrong answer to an easy question, and the paranoia and tension that accompany the distribution of grades on all levels of education.

For a student, grades can become an obsessive force in life. All our activities in school revolve around our grades. However, few students actually believe they are an accurate measure of someone's intelligence or capabilities. Teachers often say they indicate a student's "performance." They picked the right word. Attaining high grades in school is usually just a matter of performing or acting out the role of dutiful student with a straight face. . . . The parents are almost all excessively concerned with their child's grades, and some will punish or reward their kids according to their quarterly standing. All of them encourage and even push their kids into working for a higher grade whether that means learning anything or not. Often, we find ourselves orienting everything toward creating a good impression the last few weeks of each marking period and then dropping it at the beginning of a new one until report-card time comes around again.

3. The Generation Gap

The St. Louis Globe-Democrat *in May, 1970, published an article by K. Ross Toole, professor of history at the University of Montana. Entitled "It's Time to Stop Apologizing to Youth," the article apparently hit a responsive chord with* Globe *readers, for the request for reprints was the greatest of any article ever published in the newspaper. In his article, part of which appears below, Dr. Toole criticizes irrational campus "rebels." "It's time to put these people in their places," declared Professor Toole. A group of students working for Canvass for Peace at Washington University saw the article, felt that it did not give a true picture of the views of the majority of college students, and wrote an open letter of reply to Dr. Toole.* ■

A. IT'S TIME TO STOP APOLOGIZING[1]

✤ K. Ross Toole

I am 49 years old. It took me many years and considerable anguish to get where I am — which isn't much of any place except exurbia. I was nurtured in a depression; I lost four years to war; I am invested

---

[1] K. Ross Toole, "It's Time to Stop Apologizing to Youth." Reprinted by permission of the author.

with sweat; I have had one coronary; I am a "liberal," square, and I am a professor. I am sick of the "younger generation," hippies, Yippies, militants, and nonsense.... I am sick of the total irrationality of the campus "Rebel," whose bearded visage, dirty hair, body odor, and "tactics" are childish but brutal, naive but dangerous, and the essence of arrogant tyranny — the tyranny of spoiled brats.

It's time to call a halt; time to live in an adult world where we belong and time to put these people in their places. We owe the "younger generation" what all "older generations" have owed younger generations — love, protection to a point, and respect when they deserve it. We do not owe them our souls, our privacy, our whole lives, and above all, we do not owe them immunity from our mistakes or their own.

Every generation makes mistakes, always has and always will. We have made our share. But my generation has made America the most affluent country on earth; it has tackled head-on a racial problem which no nation on earth in the history of mankind has dared to do. It has publicly declared war on poverty and it has gone to the moon; it has desegregated schools and abolished polio; it has presided over what is probably the greatest social and economic revolution in man's history.

It has begun these things, not finished them. It has declared itself, and committed itself, and taxed itself, and damn near run itself into the ground in the cause of social justice and reform.

Its mistakes are fewer than my father's generation — or his father's, or his. Its greatest mistake is not Vietnam; it is the abdication of its first responsibility; its pusillanimous[2] capitulation to its youth and its sick preoccupation with the problems, the mind, the psyche, the *raison d'être* of the young.

The best place to start is at home. But the most practical and effective place, right now, is our campuses. This does not mean a flood of angry edicts, a sudden clamp down, a "new" policy. It simply means that faculties should stop playing chicken, that demonstrators should be met not with police but with expulsions.

This is a country full of decent, worried people like myself. It is also a country full of people fed up with nonsense. We need (those of us over 30) — tax-ridden, harried, confused, weary, and beat-up — to reassert our hard-won prerogatives. It is our country, too. We have

[2] **pusillanimous:** cowardly.

fought for it, bled for it, dreamed for it, and we love it. It is time to reclaim it.

B. DEMOCRACY AND COMMUNICATION[3]

Dear Dr. Toole:

In your letter you raised a number of issues to which we would like to reply. The main point which we want to stress is that your generation and ours are not as radically opposed to each other as your letter implies. There are a great many points on which we can agree, and we feel that these points should be recognized.

First of all, we recognize the many accomplishments of your generation. We are pleased that you have tackled the racial problem in America, that your intelligence and ability have developed the technology to land men on the moon and enabled polio to become a disease of the past.

In examining our country today, however, we also recognize that all of our problems have not yet been solved. The racial problem is still in a state of confusion and upheaval and is far from over. Technology is needed to improve conditions in our polluted environment and to cure cancer and other diseases. Therefore, we are now saying, let us join together through our common concern for our country. Let us build on your accomplishments so that we can continue to solve our nation's problems.

We also contend that because of the progress that you have made in this country, because of the increased technology of the past several decades, because of the education which you have offered us, we are also capable of understanding the problems of our nation and have the willingness and ability to help solve them. Sure we're idealistic. But why not let our idealism work with you toward the common goal which we hold, international peace?

However, the commonality of our goals has often been obscured by our lack of communication with each other. Part of this communication problem has been the result of the many stereotypes which your generation has about ours and vice versa. You refer to irrational campus "rebels" who are bearded, dirty and smelly in their appearance and childish and naive in their actions. You describe youth as

[3] *Washington University Magazine*, Summer 1970, pp. 43–45. Reprinted by permission.

an enemy defined by the style of their dress and the length of their hair, and you assume that all youth who fit this description are involved with acts of violence. However, we insist that individuals must be judged according to their own merits, not by how they look or by what others do, but only by what they do themselves.

You could listen to a French peasant or an Indian national in native dress more readily, it seems, than to the youth of your own country. Only when Americans avoid stereotypes of each other and start communicating can we honestly work together to solve problems in our nation.

In your letter, you stated, "We (the older generation) do not owe them (the younger generation) our souls, our privacy, our whole lives, and above all, we do not owe them immunity from our mistakes, or their own." We could not agree more! Your generation owes ours nothing more than that which all human beings owe one another — respect for human dignity and the right of free expression. Our generation is now attempting to exercise its constitutional right to expression by speaking out against a war in Indochina and other problems in this country.

The entire philosophy which underlies our American government is that of participatory democracy. Does your notion of a participatory democracy include keeping our "generation in its place" and the idea that we must be put "back there when (we get) out of it?" We think that our place is in that world which you would deny us. We feel a burden of responsibility as citizens who are concerned about the state of our country and we feel a responsibility to express this concern and to act upon it.

Our means of expression have been those which are sanctioned by the Constitution of the United States and the tradition of democratic process. We are not naive enough to believe that all of our generation uses such means. However, we know that we speak for the vast majority of our colleagues. We recognize the value and importance of the basic American rights of petition, assembly, and free speech. Furthermore, we think that it is imperative for us to use these rights in our efforts to communicate our concerns to our Congressmen, whom we have democratically elected to be our spokesmen in formulating the policies of this country.

You say, Dr. Toole, that "society . . . is not a foreign thing we seek to impose on the young. We know it is far from perfect. We did not make it; we have only sought to change it." We concur with and endorse this point of view and are utilizing constitutional methods to bring about the very change that you call for.

We too are frightened by the number of students who are turning to violent methods in their attempt to be heard. This says to us, and we hope that it says to you, that there is a great need for more communication among the people of this country. Generally, people who turn to violence do so out of frustration.

In fact, our country was born as a result of brave and outspoken men who became frustrated with King George's refusal to listen to their ideas and demands for equal rights. We do not feel that these patriots were being "arrogant slobs," nor do we feel that we are being arrogant slobs in our efforts to exercise our constitutional rights which were insured for us by these men. Don't be like King George, Dr. Toole, please listen!

Again, we must agree with you when you say, "To the extent that we now rely on the police, mace, the National Guard, tear gas, steel fences and a wringing of hands, we will fail." Such methods only serve the violent ends which we are attempting at all costs to avoid. Your generation, Dr. Toole, uses these methods out of fear that the younger generation is threatening the American system of government by voicing ideas which are contrary to the policies of the current administration. At the same time, young people use these methods out of fear that they are not being listened to by the older generation.

Violence is always spawned by fear; when the fear can be dispelled, the violence will end. Ultimately, this dispelling of fear will break down the communication barrier which has been erected by violent methods and bring our generations closer together.

But fear has given birth to something worse than violence, which is the repression that both our generations inflict on each other. In offering solutions to the problems which you see in student participation on campuses, Dr. Toole, you advocate the indiscriminant application of rigid rules which are intended to repress the very freedom of speech which you contend the United States is fighting to preserve in Indochina.

To you the name of the game is "Authority and Repression." To us, it's "Democracy and Communication." Should students be denied the right to express their opinions and to participate in the activities of our government simply because they are students? This is what you seem to be advocating. You say, "The first obligation of the administration (of a university) is to lay down the rules early, clearly, and positively, and to attach to this statement the penalty for violation." However, it is not necessary for these rules to be repressive. They should be flexible enough to allow students the freedom to participate in the activities of their government even while they are engaged in the process of being educated at a university. To deny this is to deny students their constitutional rights.

You state, Dr. Toole, that your generation's greatest mistake is not Vietnam. This is a gross evasion of the issues, since your article was inspired by student concern about the war in Vietnam. Other people express themselves more articulately. They write letters and leaflets, talk to people in their communities, and hand out leaflets expressing their view. Others, their anger even more bitter, express their defiance and rage by demonstrating, sometimes peacefully, sometimes violently. But we challenge anyone who is disgusted and outraged by a burned ROTC building to try and imagine the extent and degree of horrifying destruction which we have wrought in Vietnam. What is your reaction to a bombed-out town, totally destroyed, in Vietnam or Cambodia or Laos? What is your reaction to 7,000 square miles of land defoliated in Vietnam? Don't Americans have any imagination? Please, Dr. Toole, now let's discuss the issues!

— Francene Turken, Linda Ray,
Sharon Dressler, Jay Judson,
Philip Shreffler

■ *The Student's Paperback Library*

Additional insights into the history of education in America are provided by the following paperbacks. Merle Curti, *The Social Ideas of American Educators*, treats the social and economic sources of American education from the Colonial Period through the Depression of the 1930's. For intellectual sources of American education see V.T. Thayer, *Formative Ideas in American Education*.

Bernard Bailyn, *Education in the Forming of American Society*, is an excellent account of the processes of socialization and education in colonial New England. Also helpful is Samuel Eliot Morison, *The Intellectual Life of Colonial New England*.

John Hardin Best (ed.), *Benjamin Franklin on Education*, shows the decline of religious-oriented education and the rise of practical secular-oriented education. The continuing conflict of values and theories about education, from the National Period to the present, is portrayed by Charles Burgess and Merle Borrowman in *What Doctrines to Embrace*.

The responses of educators and schools to post-Civil War industrialization and urbanization are illustrated by Raymond Callahan in *Education and the Cult of Efficiency*. *Transformation of the School* by Lawrence Cremin features the leaders, ideas, and social forces in the progressive education movement from 1876–1957.

The problem of religion in American education is treated by a number of authors in Theodore R. Sizer (ed.), *Religion and Public Education*. Sam Duker's *The Public Schools and Religion: The Legal Context*, and Herbert Kliebard's *Religion and Education in America*, present documentary accounts of the legal aspects of education.

Booker T. Washington, *Up From Slavery*, and Malcolm X, *The Autobiography of Malcolm X*, offer comparative and contrasting analyses of the education of the black American. Harry L. Miller and Marjorie B. Smiley, *Education in the Metropolis*, presents a useful compilation of essays on urban education. *School Reform Past and Present*, by Michael B. Katz, is useful for gaining perspective on the character of reform throughout American education. Interesting titles by the "compassionate critics" of the late 1960's include John Holt, *How Children Fail*, James Herndon, *The Way It Spozed to Be*, and Herbert Kohl, *Thirty-Six Children*. The high school protests of recent years are well documented in a collection of readings by Irving Hendrick and Reginald Jones (eds.), *Student Dissent in the Schools*. Probably the most important book to come out of this period is *Crisis in the Classroom* by Charles Silberman.

■ *Questions for Study and Discussion*

I. The Sacred Emphasis of Education

1. What was the main purpose of founding Harvard College? What did the founders mean by the phrase "to advance learning"? What meaning does this phrase have today?

2. Why were the education laws of 1642 and 1647 passed? What were the major provisions of each? What principles did they establish? If church and state were separate institutions, on what grounds could the civil government justify these laws?

3. What educational goals did the Puritans have for their children? Why did the Bible play such a large role in the educational process? According to the poem "Praise to God," what were the benefits of learning to read? Do you agree or disagree with the view that the New England colonists were not interested in fostering knowledge for its own sake? Why?

4. What values did the Puritans attempt to inculcate in their young? What role did parents play in the education of their children? What defense could be made in Cotton Mather's behalf to refute charges of excessive strictness?

II. The Conduct of Education

1. How did the attitudes of Jane Turell and John Barnard toward education differ? Despite this difference, both shared the same moral attitudes and values. What were they?

2. What were the major terms of the apprenticeship contract? Was either party in the contract favored? Would any of the terms be considered unfair today? How effective do you think such arrangements were in providing an adequate education for the apprentice? Why?

3. The view that education should be organized around subject matter, rather than student desire, is deeply rooted in the colonial tradition. Give examples from the readings to support this statement.

III. Education in the South

1. How did the three main types of education in the colonial South reflect the attitude of class distinction?

2. How did educational experiences on the Virginia plantation differ from those in the New England grammar school? What differences in values are apparent? What similarities were there?

3. What arguments were commonly given for not educating the Negro in the South? How does Thomas Bacon refute these arguments? Why did Bacon's views receive little support? What do you think would have been the results had slaveowners heeded Bacon's sermons?

IV. Defining a New American Education

1. How did Ben Franklin's educational philosophy differ from that of the Puritans? In what ways were they similar? What do you think Franklin's school in Philadelphia was like?

2. Why did Noah Webster think it was dangerous to send young Americans to Europe for their education? What benefits did he think would be derived from a strictly American education? How do you think Webster's *American Spelling Book* helped promote his educational goals for the new nation?

3. Although Jefferson's plan for schools in Virginia preceded Horace Mann's tenth annual report by 64 years, it could be argued that Jefferson's plan carried out Mann's principle that every child has the right to be educated. Give reasons to support or refute this statement.

V. Educational Provisions for the New America

1. Education in the 1830's and 1840's was becoming the great panacea for solving the nation's social needs. What supporting evidence can you find in the educational positions taken by advocates of the Sunday school movement? In the Indiana state constitution? By supporters of the public high school? By the workingmen's organizations? By the Society for the Reformation of Juvenile Delinquents?

2. Did the above groups view the purpose of education to be that of insuring national order and stability or insuring individual liberty? Give examples from the documents to support your answer.

3. What does the selection by Emma Willard reveal about prevalent attitudes about education for girls? What goals did Mrs. Willard have for female education? How did they differ from those outlined for boys in Boston's English Classical School?

VI. Christianizing the Common School

1. What values did the McGuffey readers promote? Give examples from the selections to support your answer. What influence do you think the readers had on students during the more than 80 years they were sold?

2. In the famous Cincinnati case of 1872, Judge Storer and Reverend Beecher based their arguments on two different interpretations of the Freedom of Religion Clause. What were these views? How did each interpretation relate to Bible reading in the public schools? Which is the more prevalent view today? Which do you accept?

VII. Character and Conduct of the Common School

1. What kind of teacher training did most common school teachers receive in the mid-nineteenth century? What does this tell you about the general quality of education?
2. In what ways were the educational experiences of John Barnard in the 1690's and Marshall Barber in the 1870's similar? How do you account for these likenesses?
3. What does the description of Domer's first teaching job tell you about the following: the attitude of the community towards the teacher; the teacher's relationship to the pupils; the characteristics of an "educated person"; the purpose of education?

VIII. Beginning of Black Education

1. What ingenuity did Douglass display in learning how to read and write? What did he mean by the statement that the pathway to freedom was in learning to read?
2. What does Elizabeth Rice's description tell you about the meaning of freedom for the ex-slave? About his attitude toward education? The problems involved in teaching a massive group of illiterate people?
3. Why did teachers such as Cornelius McBride encounter widespread hostility in the South? What does this selection tell you about the Negro's desire for education in the 1870's?
4. What kinds of educational experiences did Booker T. Washington think were essential for blacks? Why were his views later criticized by more militant blacks?

IX. Inadequate Schooling

1. In what way was the typical high school curriculum of the late nineteenth century a cause of the large school dropout problem?
2. What do the criticisms of public education by Rice and Bourne tell you about prevalent teaching techniques? Typical teacher training? Student attitudes about school? Common curriculum patterns?
3. Why were efforts to pass child labor laws so closely related to the movement for compulsory education? Why does Riis say the laws were difficult to enforce?
4. What added burden was placed on the public schools by the influx of immigrants in the early 1900's? What problems encountered by the immigrants did the schools attempt to deal with? How effective were the schools in "Americanizing" the immigrant?
5. According to Qoyawayma, what goals did the white man have in educating the American Indian in the early twentieth century? Which

of these goals, if any, did the Indians share? What conflicts occurred because of the government school?

X. Educational Reform

1. According to John Dewey's creed, what did he consider to be the major problems in education? What solutions did he offer? How did he view the role of education in society?

2. Why was the movement for country day schools begun? What did such schools propose to accomplish? How effective do you think they were? Why?

3. Compare the views of Dewey and Redfield on the implications of preparing a child for the future. Which position offered the best hope for solving the social problems of the day?

4. Why were the NEA's seven "Cardinal Principles" considered by many to represent a revolutionary change in educational goals?

5. How appropriate is the comparison of the school to a factory? What were the effects of such business conceptions of school administration? How do you think Dewey would have responded to Cubberley's plan for the schools? How does the desire of some teachers to affiliate with labor reflect changing attitudes of educators in light of the new business approaches to education?

XI. Debate over the Curriculum

1. What did Counts envision for a new society? According to Counts, why were teachers able to bring about this change? How were they to participate in social change?

2. Why did the "radicals" in the *Saber-Tooth Curriculum* encounter such opposition to their proposed new curriculum? How did the wise old men distinguish between "education" and "training"? What might the "glacier from the north" be representative of today?

3. What were Rickover's major criticisms of American education? What criteria did he use to evaluate American versus Russian education? What changes in American schools do you think were introduced as a result of Sputnik?

4. In what ways did Bruner say learning should serve the future? What part were scholars to play in changing the curriculum?

XII. Striving for Equal Opportunity

1. What evidence is there that segregated schools were not equal? What psychological effects did such a dual educational system have on black children, according to Bulkley and Payne?

2. What arguments did Thompson give to refute the theory of innate Negro inferiority? Are his data sound? Why were his ideas ignored for so many years?

3. What did Chief Justice Warren mean by the statement in *Brown v. Board of Education* that segregated educational facilities are "inherently unequal"? Do you agree or disagree?

4. Would it have been possible to integrate the Little Rock public schools without the aid of federal troops? What was the reaction of the black students after their first day at Central High School?

5. What is *de facto* segregation? How was it used in the North to maintain racial separation? What arguments did Mrs. Reynolds of the P.A.T. use to support neighborhood schools? Do you agree or disagree that the P.A.T. was not involved in a racial issue?

XIII. Separation of Church and State

1. What factors in the nineteenth century account for the establishment of parochial schools? On what basis did the Supreme Court rule such schools to be legal alternatives to public education?

2. How does the Supreme Court in *Engel* and in *Abington* refute the argument that to prohibit religious activities in the public schools is to "indicate a hostility toward religion"? How do the arguments of these two cases resemble those expressed in the 1870's by Henry Ward Beecher? Efforts have continued into the 1970's to reintroduce prayer and Bible reading in the public schools on a strictly voluntary basis. How do you think the Supreme Court would rule today on such practices?

3. On what basis did the Supreme Court rule against Pennsylvania's financial aid plan to parochial schools? What effect do you think the Court's decision will have on parochial education in the future?

XIV. Continuing Criticism

1. Why does Kozol say that the missing student records are symbolic of their entire educational experiences? What other criticisms does he make of the ghetto school in which he taught? Why did he find it so difficult to change the situation?

2. In what ways are the educational experiences described by Marqusee similar to those of the students in Kozol's school? What additional aspects of school life does Marqusee object to? What recommendations would you make to relieve the tension between high school students such as Marqusee and the older generation of parents and school personnel?

■ Acknowledgments

Thanks are extended to the following organizations and persons for making pictures available for reproduction: National Life Insurance Company, Montpelier, Vt., 8 (top); Addison Gallery of American Art, Phillips Andover Academy, 8 (bottom); New York Public Library, 9 (both); Yale Gallery, 47 (top); The Bettman Archive, 47 (middle and bottom), 123 (top and bottom); *The Anti-Slavery Almanac*, Widener Library, Harvard University, 102 (top); *Harper's Weekly*, 102 (middle); Library of Congress, 102 (bottom); Underwood & Underwood, 103; Culver Pictures, 123 (middle); COMPIX, United Press International, 216 (top); D. and A. Pellegrino/Black Star, 216 (bottom); Michael Abramson, © 1972, Photon West, 217 (top); Erich Hartmann/Magnum Photos, 217 (bottom).

■ Index

(*Note:* Excerpts from specific authors or sources are indicated by boldface numbers. Entries followed by *f* refer to footnotes; those followed by *p* to pictures.)

Abbott, Grace, 74f
Abington v. Schempp, **207–210**
Abolition movement, 43
Academies, 67; girls admitted to, 71
Accountability, 122
Addams, Jane, 120, 129, 168
Addison, Joseph, 34f
Administration of schools, 155–162
Agrarianism, schools to conserve, 145–148
American Federation of Labor, 165, 166
American Federation of Teachers, 162
American Indians. *See* Indians
Americanism, 81
Americanization of immigrants, 121, 133–136
American Spelling Book (Webster), 55
American Sunday School Union, 64
Anti-slavery movement. *See* Abolition movement
Apprenticeship, 4, 31–32, 33, 36–37, 49–50
Archambault, Reginald D., 141f
Arithmetic, 98, 126–127
Attendance at school, 45; compulsory, 46, 120–121, 131–133, 195, 202

Bachelor of Arts degree, 4, 12
Bacon, Thomas, **38–40**
Baltimore, Gilman Country School for Boys in, 146–148
Barber, Marshall, **97–100**
Barnard, Henry, 44
Barnard, John, **27–30**
Bates, Daisy, **197–199**
Beecher, Catherine, 71
Beecher, Henry Ward, **88–89**
Benjamin, Harold, **173–179**
Bethesda Orphan House (Georgia), 36–38
Bible, and colonial education, 3, 6, 9p, 16; read in public schools, 81, 86–88, 207–210; in McGuffey's readers, 83; study of, as literature, 209
Bigelow, John, 48f
Blacks, denial of education and political rights to, 7, 33, 42, 102p, 104; educated, in colonial times, 33; an argument for instruction of (slaves), 38–40; beginnings of education for, 43, 101–118, 102p; in Continental Army, 43; rising school enrollment of, 45; hostility to, 81; intimidation of, 106; state constitutional provisions for segregating, 106–108; during Reconstruction, 102p, 109–112; hostility toward teachers of, 112–115; and accommodation with white power, 102p, 115–118; colleges for, 103p, 117, 123p; struggle of, for equal opportunities, 121–122, 188–201, 216p; control of neighborhood schools by, 188,

216*p*; means of segregating, 190–191, 200; educational achievement of, 192–194; in a ghetto school, 218–220. *See also* Discrimination; Prejudice; Segregation; Slavery
Boston, Free Grammar School of (Boston Latin), 6, 28*f*; high school founded in, 67–71
Boston School Committee, 67–71
Bourne, Randolph S., **129–131**
Brackett, Anna C., 71*f*
Brooks, Ned, 179–180
Brown, Linda, 122
Brown v. Board of Education of Topeka, **194–197**
Bruner, Jerome S., **185–187**
Bulkley, William L., **189–190**
Bushnell, Horace, 48
Busing, as means of desegregation, 188; to public and private schools, 210, 212

Carlisle Industrial School, 45
Carlson, Vada F., 136*f*
Carter, James G., 90
Catechizing, 23
Censorship, colonial, 6
Certificate of merit, 9*p*
Cheever, Ezekiel, 6, 27, 28
Chicago, high school curriculum in, 124–125
"Child-benefit" theory, 210
Child labor laws, 120, 131–133
Christianity, colonial interpretation of, 2; and education, 2–3, 4, 9*p*, 10–22, 63, 81–89. *See also* Bible; Church; Protestantism; Religion; Roman Catholicism
Church, and colonial education, 2–3, 4, 10; and political rights, 10; colleges founded by, 63; and state, separation of, 81, 202–214. *See also* Religion
Cincinnati, Bible readings in schools of, 85–88
Cities, social ills of, 74–76; and social change, 120; schools in, 123*p*, 124–128, 129, 134–136, 218–220
Citizenship, manufacturing of, 157–158; industrial, 165
Civic education, 154
Class consciousness, 164
Classics, study of, in colonial period, 3
Clement, John Addison, 124*f*
Colleges, founding of, 3–4, 10–11; as chief goals of colonial schools, 6; church-related, 63; land grant, 63, 66; for blacks, 103*p*, 117; high school curriculum dominated by, 151, 221, 222
Colman, Benjamin, 25*f*, 26
Colonial period, 2–40
Commons, John R., 77*f*
Common schools, spread of, 42, 43–46, 48, 60–62, 63, 64, 121; political pressure for, 77–80; religious exercises in, 81–89; teachers for, 90–97; ideal and reality of, 90–100; curriculum of, 97–100. *See also* Public schools
Communication between generations, 225–228
Compulsory education laws, 15–17, 46, 120–121, 131–133, 195, 202
Connecticut, education laws in, 23
Constitution, U.S., Tenth Amendment, 65; Fourteenth Amendment, 106; Thirteenth Amendment, 106, 121; First

Amendment, 205, 206, 207, 209, 212–213, 214; Establishment of Religion Clause, 205, 206, 208, 209, 212; Free Exercise Clause, 208
Constitutions, state, education requirements in, 63, 65–67; segregation provisions in, 106–108, 122
Country day schools, 145–148
Counts, George S., **168–173**
Crèvecoeur, Hector, 48
Cubberley, Ellwood, 134, **155–159**
Curriculum, English Classical School, 69–70; House of Refuge, 76–77; common school, 97–100; for instruction of Negroes, 103*p*, 117–118; high school, 124–125; debate over, 168–187; restructuring of, 186

Dame schools, 6, 8*p*
Dartmouth College, 4
Davis, Allison, 192
Day, Nathan, **31–32**
Death at an Early Age (Kozol), 218
De facto segregation, 122, 188, 200
Delinquents, school for, 74–77
Democracy, education and, 152; ideals of, 154; industrial, 164–165; and communication, 225–228
Desegregation, struggle for, 188, 194–199, 216*p*
Dewey, John, 120, **141–145**, 168, 173
Discrimination, racial, 122, 188, 200; in colonial period, 6–7; in employment, 189–190. *See also* Segregation

Diversity, common schools to counteract, 43–44; reflected in schools, 85; ethnic, in cities, 120, 123*p*
Domer, D. S., **94–97**
Douglass, Frederick, **101–106**
Draper, Andrew, 133
Dropouts, 124
Dual school system, 101, 106, 107, 108, 122, 195
DuBois, W. E. B., 122
Dugmore, A. R., **133–136**

Educational reform, 58–60, 122, 140–167, 215, 217*p*
Education laws, early, 4–5, 10, 15–17, 46, 120–121, 131–133
Edwards, Jonathan, 2, 4, 42
Efficiency movement, 154–159
Eisenhower, Dwight D., 197
Engel v. Vitale, **204–207**
English High School (English Classical), Boston, 67–71
Environment, effect of, on Negro achievement, 192, 193–194
Equality of opportunity, 78; education for, 79–80, 102*p*; struggle for, 121–122, 188–201, 216*p*
Ethical character, 154
Everson v. Board of Education, 212
Evil, laws to eradicate, 5–6; equating black with, 7; to be overcome by education, 12–17; parental alertness to, 18

Farish, Hunter Dickenson, 34*f*
Faubus, Orval, 197
Fear, in colonial classroom, 23
Female Seminary (Troy, N.Y.), 72
Fithian, Philip, **34–36**
Flemming, Arthur, 180

Ford, Paul Leicester, 57f
Foreign education, disadvantages of, 55–57
Franklin, Benjamin, 4, **48–54**
Freedmen's Bureau, 101, 102p
Free Grammar School (Boston), 6, 28f
Friends. See Quakers

Garvey, Marcus, 122
Generation gap, 223–228
Georgia, Whitefield's orphanage in, 36–38
Ghetto school, 215–220
Gilman Country School for Boys (Baltimore), 146–148
Girls, education for, 25–26, 51, 71–74. See also Women
Goals of education, 152–154, 157, 221
Government, responsibility of, for universal education, 61; education traditionally a function of, 66. See also Church and state, separation of; States; Supreme Court
Grades, 222–223
Grammar schools, 6, 17, 23, 27, 59, 68
Guidance, vocational, 148–150, 153

Hamilton, Alexander, 43
Harvard College, 3, 4, 10–12, 27–32
Health needs of students, 152
Henry, Patrick, 4
High schools, 67–71, 120–121, 123p, 124–125, 129–131; criticisms by students of, 217p, 220–223
High School Revolutionaries (Libarle and Seligson), 220–221
History class, 99–100

Home, learning for membership in, 153; responsibility of, for educational standards, 182–183
Hopkins Grammar School Trustees, **23–25**
Hornbook, 8p
House of Refuge (New York), 74–77
Housing, segregated, 122
Hughes, Langston, 215, 220
Humanistic beliefs, 42
Humanitarians, 63

Ideal, and reality of learning, 25–30; and reality, in common school, 90–100; changing images of, 121
Illiteracy, reduction of, 45
Immigrants, Americanization of, 121, 123p, 133–136
Impersonalization of classroom, 129–130
Indiana constitution, **65–67**
Indian Removal Act, 45
Indians, political freedoms and education denied to, 42; schools for, 45, 136–140; Christianizing and educating of, 66; "civilizing" of, 136–140
Industrial democracy, 164–165
Industrial education, 149–150. See also Vocational education
Inglis, Alexander J., 192
Integration, instituted and rescinded, 101, 106, 107, 108; token, in South, 197, 216p; in Little Rock, 197–199, 216p; in the North, 200–201
Intelligence tests, cultural biases in, 192

Jackson, Andrew, 77
Jay, John, 43

Index

Jefferson, Thomas, **57–60**; white superiority views of, 43; and education of Indians, 66; and course of study for his daughter, 71
Jesus of Nazareth, 163
Jews, hostility to, 81

Kansas, common school in, 98–100
Kersey, Harry A., 90f
Kilpatrick, William Heard, 120
Kindergarten, 123p
King, Martin Luther, Jr., 122
King's College, 4
Kozol, Jonathan, **215–220**
Ku Klux Klan, 106, 113–115

Labor organizations, common schools supported by, 63; issue of teachers' joining, 162–167
Land grant colleges, 63, 66
Language, standards for, 55; learning fundamental processes of, 152–153
Leadership, of the teacher, 169–171
Learning, ideal of, 25–27; reality of, 27–30; rote, 125–128; deadening atmosphere for, 129–131
Leisure, worthy use of, 154
Lemon v. Kurtzman, **210–214**
Libarle, Marc, 220f
Lincoln, Abraham, 66
Lindley, Ernest K., 179
Literacy rate, 42, 45
Little Rock, Ark., integration in, 197–199, 216p
Long Shadow of Little Rock, The (Bates), 197
Lord's Prayer, recited in school, 207, 208
Louisiana constitution, 107

Loyalty checks (colonial), 6

McBride, Cornelius, **112–115**
McGuffey readers, 47p, 82–85
McGuffey, William Holmes, 82–85
McLaurin v. Oklahoma State Regents, 196
Madison, James, 209
Mann, Horace, 44, **60–62**
Marqusee, Michael, **220–223**
Massachusetts, first compulsory attendance law in, 46; first common school system in, 60. *See also* Boston
Massachusetts Bay Colony, 3, 4–5, 6, 10, 12–17
Massachusetts Bay General Court, **15–17**
Mather, Cotton, 4, **17–19**, 30
Mather, Increase, 30
Measurement, of school accomplishment, 156–157, 160–162
Memorization, 98, 127, 128
Meyers, James, 198
Michigan Teachers' Institute, **90–93**
Mills, Caleb, 44
Minor v. Board of Education of Cincinnati, **86–88**
Monopoly, 78
Morrill, Justin, 63
Myers, William Starr, **145–148**

National Academy of Sciences, 185
National Association for the Advancement of Colored People (NAACP), 122
National Education Association, **151–154**, 162
Nationalism, education for, 55–57
National period, 42–62

National Society for the Promotion of Industrial Education, 149
National survival, education and, 179–185
Negroes. *See* Blacks
Neighborhood schools, 188, 200–201, 216*p*
New England Primer, 9*p*, **19–22**
New Haven Hopkins Grammar School, 23–25
New Jersey, segregation in, 191
New Jersey College, 4
New York City, House of Refuge in, 74–77; child labor in, 131–133; immigrant education in, 134–136; vocational training in, 148–150
New York state, issue of school prayers in, 204–207
Normal schools, 90
North, *de facto* segregation in, 122, 188, 200; migrations to, 188; educational segregation in, 190–191, 200–201
North Carolina constitution, 107–108
Northwest Ordinance, 44, 65–66

Old Deluder Satan Act, 16, 17
Open-air school, 147
Oregon, challenge to private school attendance in, 202–204
Orphanages, 33, 36–38
Overstreet, Harry A., **162–167**

Parents, advice of, on education, 13–15; responsibility of, 8*p*, 17–19; and educational standards, 181–183; concern of, with grades, 223
Parents and Taxpayers (PAT), 200–201
Parochial schools, legality of, 202; financial aid to, 210–214
Payne, E. George, **190–191**
Peddiwell, J. Abner, 173*f*
Pennsylvania, education supported by workingmen in, 78–80; teaching in common school in, 94–97; and Bible reading in school, 207–210; and aid to parochial schools, 210–214
Philadelphia, Franklin's school in, 49
Philadelphia College, 4
Phillips, Turner, 64*f*
Physical education, 123*p*, 184
Pierce v. Society of Sisters, **202–204**
Plessy v. Ferguson, 106, 194, 195, 196
Pluralism, of American society, 120, 121
Prayer in public schools, 88, 204–207
Prejudice, racial, 190, 192–194. *See also* Racism
Private schools, 145; legality of, 202–204; financing of, 210–214
Process of Education, The (Bruner), 185
Progressive education, 123*p*, 142
Protestant Ethic, 49, 82
Protestantism, colonial, 2, 19; fragmentation of, 42; values of, in schools, 43; and Sunday schools, 63; and sectarianism in schools, 81
Psychological side of education, 142–143
Public schools, founding of, 23; spread of, 42, 43–46; Jefferson's support for, 57–60; established at all levels, 63, 123*p*; and Sunday schools, 64; high schools, 67–71, 120–121, 124–125, 129–131; for females, 47*p*, 72; segre-

gation in, 106–108, 123p, 191; rote learning in, 125–128; deadening routine in, 129–131. See also Common schools. Schools

Punishment, in colonial schools, 8p; tempering of, 18, 19; at House of Refuge, 77

Puritan Ethic, 19–22

Puritans, 3, 5, 10, 33

Quakers, 43

Queen's College, 4

Qoyawayma, Polingaysi, **136–140**

Racism, 101, 121, 123p, 191, 192; institutional, 122

Reading, teaching of, 47p, 98, 128; how a slave learned, 104–105

Reading material, colonial, 6, 8p, 47p

Recitation, 6, 23, 99, 127, 128

Reconstruction period, 45, 109

Redfield, William C., **148–150**

Regimentation, 222

Religion, and colonial education, 2–3, 4, 5, 6, 9p, 10–22; and justification of work, 5; resurgence of, 63; exercises of, in public schools, 81–89, 204–210; freedom of, 89, 208; study of, 209. See also Christianity

Religious schools, legality of, 202–204; financing of, 210–214

Reservations, Indian, 45

Reston, James, 179

Reynolds, June, 201

Rhode Island, and parochial schools, 212

Rhode Island College, 4

Rice, Elizabeth G., **109–112**

Rice, Joseph M., **125–128**

Rickover, Hyman, **179–185**

Riis, Jacob A., **131–133**

Roberts, Chalmers, 179

Roman Catholicism, hostility to, 81, 85; and parochial schools, 203, 210–214

Roosevelt, Theodore, 120, 142

Rote learning, 125–128

Saber-Tooth Curriculum, The (Benjamin) 173–179

Scarsdale, N.Y., 221–223

School board as management, 159, 168

Schools, colonial, 4–5, 6, 8p; dame, 6, 8p; grammar, 6, 8p, 17, 23, 27, 47p, 59, 68; colonial methods of teaching in, 8p, 9p, 23–30; racial segregation in, 43, 106–108, 191; for blacks, 43, 102p, 103p, 110–112, 116, 117; reform movement in, 58–60, 122, 140–167, 215, 216p; for girls, 47p, 71–74; for delinquents, 74–77; dual system of, 101, 106, 107, 108, 122, 188, 195; criticisms of, 121, 122, 124–131, 141, 151, 154, 179, 180, 200, 215–228, 216p; enrollment in, 122, 151, 157; as social institutions, 144; private, 145, 202–204, 210–214; country day, 145–148; bureaucratizing of, 154–162; as factories, 155–157, 158; administrative efficiency in, 155–159; scientific management of, 156–157, 160; to reconstruct America, 168–173; and changing social order, 123p, 173–179; and national survival, 179–185; to serve the future, 185–187; ghetto, 218–220. See also Colleges; Common schools; Public schools

Science teaching, 127–128
Secondary education, redefinition of, 151–154. *See also* High school
Segregation, racial, 43, 45, 121–122, 188, 191; state constitutional provisions for, 106–108, 122; *de facto*, 122, 188, 191, 200; outlawed, 122, 188, 194–197
Segregation, sex, 71
Self-education, 4, 104–106
Self-improvement, Franklin's program for, 51–54
Seligson, Tom, 220f
Seminaries, 68; for girls, 47p, 73–74
"Separate but equal" doctrine, 106, 122, 195
Shepard, Thomas, Jr., **12–15**
Shorter Catechism, 21–22
Slavery, in colonial period, 7, 33, 38–40; opposition to, 43; deprivations of, 101; incompatibility of education and, 101–106; abolition of, 121
Smith-Hughes vocational education bill, 149
Snedden, David, **162–167**
Social change, cities and, 120; schools and, 144–145
Social problems, 141; education as a force for solving, 74, 169–173; curriculum change and, 173–179
Society for Promoting the Manumission of Slaves, 43
Society for the Reformation of Juvenile Delinquents, **74–77**
Sociological side of education, 142–143
South, colonial education in, 33–40; dual system of schools in, 101, 106–108, 122, 188; education for blacks in, during and after Reconstruction, 101–118, 102p, 103p; Yankee teacher in, 109–112; battle for integration in, 197–199, 216p
South Carolina constitution, 108
Spaulding, F. E., 155, **160–162**
Spectator, 34f, 51
Spelling, 99, 104
Spencer, Platt Rogers, 99f
Spivak, Lawrence E., 179, 180, 181, 182, 184
Sputnik I, 179
Standards, educational, 181–183
State-church separation, 81, 202–214
States, regulation of education by, 5; public education required by, 15–17, 44, 65–66, 120–121; teacher training supported by, 90; dual school system established by, 101, 106–108, 122
Steele, Richard, 34f
Stereotypes, 81, 109
Stevens, Thaddeus, 44
Stiles, Henry R., 31f
Stoughton, Thomas, **31–32**
Streit, Peggy, **200–201**
Sunday schools, 63, 64–65
Supreme Court, on school desegregation, 122, 188, 194–197; on church-state separation, 202–214
Sweatt v. Painter, 196

Teachers, colonial, 6, 8p, 23–32, 47p; training for, 90–93; in common schools, 94–97; white, in southern black schools, 102p, 109–115; demands of, 122; in labor movement, 162–167; professional independence of, 166–167; power of, 169–171

Teaching, colonial methods of, 8*p*, 9*p*, 23–30; growth of profession of, 122; discovery approach in, 187
Thompson, Charles, **192–194**
Thorpe, Francis N., 106*f*
Thurston, William, **64–65**
Toole, K. Ross, **223–225**
Transfer of training, 185–186
Turell, Ebenezer, **25–27**
Turell, Jane, 25, 26–27
Tuskegee Institute (Alabama), 103*p*
Tutorial system, 33, 34–36
Tyack, David B., 81

Utilitarianism, 5

Values, colonial, 2, 4, 5, 6, 12–15, 18, 19–22, 33; of national period, 42, 43, 45, 48, 49; Protestant, conservative, 43, 82; held by Franklin, 52–54; in rural common school, 94–97; American, taught to immigrants, 121, 133–136; educational, 158, 161; distorted, 183
Violence, 227
Virginia, appraisal of Negro educational achievement in, 192–194
Vocational education, 45, 63, 148–150, 153

Wald, Lillian, 120
Walker, Edwin A., 198
Washington, Booker T., 103*p*, **115–118**, 122
Washington, George, 33, 43
Webster, Noah, **55–57**
Wheatley, Phillis, 33
Whitefield, George, 7, **36–38**, 42
White superiority view, 43, 191; rejection of, 192–194
Wightman, Joseph, 64*f*
Willard, Emma, **71–74**
William and Mary College, 4
Wilson, Woodrow, 120, 142, 149
Women, education for, 47*p*, 51, 71–74
Woodson, Carter G., 38*f*
Woolman, John, 43
Work, religious justification of, 5; introducing youth to, 149–150
Working Men of Pennsylvania, **77–80**
Writing, 99, 105–106

Yale, founding of, 4
Youth, demands of, 122; criticism of education by, 215, 217*p*, 220–223; and the generation gap, 223–228

Zorach v. Clauson, 207